Enver Hasani | Péter Paczolay | Michael Riegner [eds.]

Constitutional Justice in Southeast Europe

Constitutional Courts in Kosovo, Serbia, Albania and Hungary between Ordinary Judiciaries and the European Court of Human Rights

Nomos giz Deutsche Gesellschaft für Internationale Zusammenarbeit (GIZ) GmbH

On behalf of

BMZ Federal Ministry for Economic Cooperation and Development

Deutsche Gesellschaft für Internationale Zusammenarbeit (GIZ) GmbH
P.O.Box 5180
65726 Eschborn
Germany
www.giz.de

The Deutsche Gesellschaft für Internationale Zusammenarbeit (GIZ) GmbH is implementing the project "Advisory services on legal reform in Kosovo" on behalf of the German Federal Ministry for Economic Cooperation and Development (BMZ).

Die Deutsche Nationalbibliothek verzeichnet diese Publikation in der Deutschen Nationalbibliografie; detaillierte bibliografische Daten sind im Internet über http://dnb.d-nb.de abrufbar.

Die Deutsche Nationalbibliothek lists this publication in the Deutsche Nationalbibliografie; detailed bibliographic data is available in the Internet at http://dnb.d-nb.de.

ISBN 978-3-8329-7701-6

1. Edition 2012

Preface and Acknowledgements

The idea for this book originated at an international conference held in Pristina/Kosovo in November 2010. At that time, the Constitutional Court of Kosovo had just completed its first year of operation and was establishing itself as a strong and independent institution. It was thus looking for inspiration and lessons learned elsewhere, and the German Federal Constitutional Court was often cited in this context. It thus came as natural to the Legal Reform Project of the Gesellschaft für Internationale Zusammenarbeit (GIZ), the development cooperation agency of the German federal government, to support the Constitutional Court of Kosovo in organizing a conference on constitutional justice in a regional comparative perspective.

The conference, held in cooperation with the Justus Liebig University Gießen/Germany, focused on two topics felt to be pressing in Kosovo at the time. These topics soon turned out to be similarly relevant in other jurisdictions and for international legal research. The first issue was the relationship between constitutional courts and domestic supreme courts, which saw some initial irritations in Kosovo after the quashing of a number of last instance judgments, but which is also a recurring and almost timeless theme in many other jurisdictions which adopted the European model of specialized constitutional review. A second pressing issue was the domestic application of the European Convention on Human Rights and the proper domestic role of Strasbourg case law. Both are given a privileged position in the Kosovo Constitution, but equally and increasingly shape constitutional justice in the neighboring countries and all over Europe.

During the conference, it became clear that there was little comparative literature on how the Southeast European constitutional courts played their role as interfaces between domestic judiciaries on the one hand and judicial bodies beyond the nation state on the other. Given the international debate on composite constitutional justice in the European multi-level architecture of fundamental rights protection, the organizers thus decided to develop selected conference papers into academic articles and to publish them in an edited collection addressed to academic audiences in Europe. This involved two rounds of substantive revision of the papers, a full academic peer review over a period of six months, and finally a native speaker and form check. The initial versions of the contributions were drafted in the first half of 2011; they were peer reviewed and revised by the authors in the second half of 2011. The manuscript was completed in January 2012.
GIZ would like to thank, first of all, the authors for their continued commitment to this project. All of them put considerable time and effort into writing and re-

vising their contributions, many of them alongside their challenging full-time occupations as constitutional justices or legal practitioners. GIZ would also like to thank our three editors, Enver Hasani and Péter Paczolay, as well as Michael Riegner, who developed the initial concept for the book and administered the peer review and revision process. We are indebted to everyone who contributed to this project at the Constitutional Court of Kosovo, at the GIZ Legal Reform Project in Kosovo, and at the Chair for Public and Comparative Law of Professor Philipp Dann at the Justus Liebig University in Gießen/Germany. Particular gratitude for their voluntary commitment goes to Matthias Hartwig at the Max Planck Institute for Comparative Public Law and International Law in Heidelberg and to our anonymous peer reviewers. We are grateful to Nomos Verlag for publishing this book. A last but important thank you goes to the many others, too numerous to be named, who supported this book as proof-readers and English language revisers, discussion partners and moral supporters, or in other capacities.

Pristina, January 2012

Volkmar Theobald
Project Leader
GIZ Legal Reform Kosovo

Contents

Abbreviations

ACC	Act on the Constitutional Court of Hungary
CC	Constitutional Court
CoE	Council of Europe
CSP	Comprehensive Proposal for Kosovo Status Settlement ("Ahtisaari-Plan")
ECHR	European Convention for the Protection of Human Rights and Fundamental Freedoms
ECtHR	European Court of Human Rights
EU	European Union
EULEX	European Union Rule of Law Mission in Kosovo
FCC	Federal Constitutional Court of Germany
HRA	UK Human Rights Act 1998
MPs	Members of Parliament

Contributors List

Snezhana Botusharova, Associate Professor of Law, PhD; International Judge at the Constitutional Court of Kosovo; Judge at the European Court of Human Rights from 1998-2008.

Ivan Čukalovič, Judge at the Constitutional Court of Kosovo; Professor of Law, University of Kragujevac, Republic of Serbia.

Vidan Hadzi-Vidanovic, PhD candidate, The University of Nottingham School of Law; associate, Belgrade Centre for Human Rights.

Enver Hasani, President of the Constitutional Court of Kosovo and Professor at the University of Pristina in Kosovo.

Péter Paczolay, Professor of Law; President of the Constitutional Court of Hungary; former Vice-President of the European Commission for Democracy through Law (Venice Commission).

Peter Pavlin, Secretary, Head of the Division for Punitive Law and for the Protection of Human Rights at the Ministry of Justice of the Republic of Slovenia; external expert advisor to the Government of Kosovo.

Michael Riegner, Senior Research Fellow, Justus Liebig University Gießen; Visiting Researcher, Max Planck Institute of Comparative Public Law and International Law, Heidelberg.

Pál Sonnevend, Professor of Law, Eötvös Loránd University Budapest; former constitutional advisor to the President of Hungary László Sólyom.

Xhezair Zaganjori, Professor of Law at the Faculty of Law, Tirana University, and the School of Magistrates; Judge at the Constitutional Court of Albania since 2003.

Constitutional Justice in Southeast Europe between Ordinary Judiciaries and the European Court of Human Rights

*Michael Riegner**

Contents

I. Why compare constitutional justice in Southeast Europe?

Constitutional review originated in the US-American legal tradition and later proliferated in Western Europe in different forms and waves. After the fall of communism, transition states in Central and Eastern Europe adopted the "European" model of concentrated constitutional review.[1] The new specialized constitutional courts played more or less significant roles in the post-communist transformation processes, but most of them were considered "a surprising success".[2] Some even became a motor of political liberalization and the transformation of the state, for instance in Hungary. The institutions also experienced a wave of international scholarly attention in the 1990s and early 2000s.[3] However, that interest seems to have waned after the EU accession of major Central and East European transition states. Some comparatists now even deplore a "painful lack of research"[4] on constitutional justice in the region, and some formerly powerful courts have become heavily embattled institutions, namely in Hungary. Mean-

* Senior Research Fellow, Justus Liebig University Gießen; Visiting Researcher, Max Planck Institute of Comparative Public Law and International Law, Heidelberg; Member of the Schumpeter Research Group "Law and Governance of Development Cooperation".

1 On the history and proliferation of constitutional courts see *Victor Ferreres Comella*, The Rise of Specialized Constitutional Courts, in: Tom Ginsburg/Rosalind Dixon (eds.), Comparative Constitutional Law, 2010, 265. On concentrated or diffuse types of constitutional adjudication, see *Mario Capelletti/William Cohen*, Comparative Constitutional Law, 1979, 84 et seq.

2 *Herman Schwartz*, Surprising Success: The New Eastern European Constitutional Courts, in: Andreas Schedler/Larry Diamond/Marc Plattner (eds.), The Self-Restraining State. Power and Accountability in New Democracies, 1999, 195. For a recent overview, see *Schnutz Rudolf Dürr*, Comparative Overview of European Systems of Constitutional Justice, Vienna Journal on International Constitutional Law 5 (2011), 159, also on the exception of Estonia, which adopted American-style judicial review.

3 From the vast literature see for instance *Georg Brunner*, Development of a Constitutional Judiciary in Eastern Europe, Review of Central and East European Law 18 (1992), 535; *Matthias Hartwig*, The Institutionalization of the Rule of Law: The Establishment of Constitutional Courts in the Eastern European Countries, American University Journal of International Law and Policy 7 (1992), 449; *Marc Verdussen* (ed.), La Justice Constitutionnelle en Europe Centrale, 1997; *Jochen Frowein/Thilo Marauhn* (eds.), Grundfragen der Verfassungsgerichtsbarkeit in Mittel- und Osteuropa, 1998; *Herman Schwartz*, The Struggle for Constitutional Justice in Post-Communist Europe, 2000; *Radoslav Procházka*, Mission Accomplished: On Founding Constitutional Adjudication in Central Europe, 2002; *Wojciech Sadurski* (ed.), Constitutional Justice, East and West. Democratic Legitimacy and Constitutional Courts in Post-Communist Europe in a Comparative Perspective, 2002.

4 *Christian Boulanger*, The "role" and "function" of Constitutional Courts: Reconnecting normative and empirical theorizing in comparative judicial studies, Paper presented at Humboldt-University Berlin conference 22.-24.9.2011, manuscript on file with the author, 2 (with regard to Hungary). But see for later periods *Wojciech Sadurski*, Rights Before Courts. A Study of Constitutional Courts in Postcommunist States of Central and Eastern Europe, 2005, and *infra*, notes 31 and 40.

while, a second wave of constitutional justice has emerged in Southeast Europe, in which constitutional courts play an important but largely unnoticed role.[5]

Consequently, the aim of this book is to offer a comparative analysis of selected Southeast European constitutional courts and their role in the common European legal space. Geographically, the comparison centers on Kosovo, Serbia, Albania and Hungary, each of which represents a different trajectory of constitutional transformation in the region. Thematically, it focuses on the relationship of constitutional courts to the highest ordinary courts on the one hand and to the European Court of Human Rights (ECtHR) on the other. This perspective not only recognizes the immense importance of courts in the wider enterprise of constitutional justice.[6] It also stresses that new constitutional courts have to establish their authority and define their role in two different directions: they must adjust their relationship to the established players in the domestic legal system, including ordinary courts, and they must find their international role within the European multi-level architecture of fundamental rights protection. In this system of intertwined levels of governance, constitutional courts function as important hinges between domestic and international judiciaries and as institutional interfaces between different layers and sources of law. In practice, this leads to dynamic interactions between the three types of courts, shaped not only by cooperation, but also by institutional conflicts. These dynamics of court interaction are not only practically relevant, but also a useful prism for legal research, and thus form the common frame of research for this book.

The questions raised here have rarely been the subject of systematic comparative research specifically focused on the jurisdictions studied in this book. While

5 For some of the rare treatments of the courts studied in this book, see *Otto Luchterhandt/Christian Starck/Albrecht Weber* (eds.), Verfassungsgerichtsbarkeit in Mittel- und Osteuropa, 2006; *Gudrun Haase/Katrin Struger*, Verfassungsgerichtsbarkeit in Europa, 2009; *Constance Grewe/Michael Riegner*, Internationalized Constitutionalism in Ethnically Divided Societies: Bosnia-Herzegovina and Kosovo Compared, in: Armin v. Bogdandy/Rüdiger Wolfrum, (eds.), Max Planck Yearbook of United Nations Law 15 (2011) 1; and *infra*, notes 36 and 37. Comparisons of constitutional justice in Europe often generalize without taking account of Southeast Europe, cf. even the eminent comparatist *Rainer Wahl*, Das Bundesverfassungsgericht im europäischen und internationalen Umfeld, in: Robert van Ooyen/Martin Möllers (eds.), Das Bundesverfassungsgericht im politischen System, 2006, 477, at 482 footnote 36 (noting that individual constitutional complaints "in Europe only exist in Germany, Spain and Portugal", at a time when the courts in Bosnia and Herzegovina, Albania and Serbia already practiced similar proceedings, as discussed below in parts III and IV).

6 The term "constitutional justice" is used in this book to designate the process and system that leads to a constitutionalization of law and politics. It involves multiple actors and sites and encompasses diffuse American-type judicial review. In contrast, "constitutional court" here refers to a specific institution in a system of concentrated judicial review. See *Constance Grewe/Olivier Jouanjan/Eric Maulin/Patrick Wachsmann,* La notion de justice constitutionnelle, 2005; *Wahl* (note 5), 479.

Hungary's constitutional court has received some attention in this regard, comparative research on constitutional justice in Albania and Serbia is generally rare.[7] Kosovo has been the subject of a bourgeoning international law literature[8], but domestic constitutionalism in the newly independent state has met with more limited international interest[9] – despite the fact that its hybrid constitutional court has quickly become an important player in Kosovar politics, causing *inter alia* the successive resignation of the first two presidents of the Republic of Kosovo.[10]

This example is indicative of the potentially significant role constitutional justice can play in the present wave of transition in Southeast Europe. Consequently, comparing these constitutional courts is of interest not only to jurists in the region, but also to comparative lawyers elsewhere in the world. In addition, the comparisons are also relevant for European and international lawyers interested in the domestic reception of the ECHR and in the multi-level architecture of judicial fundamental rights protection in Europe. Finally, the book may also be read by European Union lawyers concerned with the relevance of constitutional

7 *Gábor Halmai*, Who is the Main Protector of Fundamental Rights in Hungary? The Role of the Constitutional Court and the Ordinary Courts, in: Jiri Priban/Pauline Robert/James Young (eds.), Systems of Justice in Transition, 2003, 50; *Pál Sonnevend*, Ungarn, in: Armin v. Bogdandy/Pedro Cruz Villalón/Peter Huber (eds.), Handbuch Ius Publicum Europaeum, vol. II: Offene Staatlichkeit – Wissenschaft vom Verfassungsrecht, 2007, 379. For treatments of constitutional justice in Serbia and Albania, see *Haase/Struger* (note 5); *Wolfgang Stoppel*, Die Verfassungsgerichtsbarkeit in Albanien, in: Luchterhandt/Starck/Weber (note 5), vol. I, 11; *ders*. Albanien vor dem EGMR, Osteuroparecht (2007), 126.

8 See only *Christian Tomuschat* (ed.), Kosovo and the International Community, 2002; *Erika de Wet*, The Governance of Kosovo: Security Council Resolution 1244 and the Establishment and Functioning of Eulex, American Journal of International Law 103 (2009), 83; *Martin Bothe*, Kosovo – So What? The Holding of the International Court of Justice is not the Last Word on Kosovo's Independence, German Law Journal 11 (2010), 837. This book does not engage with the discussions on Kosovo's statehood and status under international law insofar as they do not concern constitutional justice.

9 But see *Joseph Marko*, The New Kosovo Constitution in a Regional Comparative Perspective, Review of Central and East European Law 33 (2008), 437; *Dren Doli/Fisnik Korenica*, What about Kosovo's Constitution: Is there anything special? Discussing the grundnorm, the sovereignty, and the consociational model of democracy, Vienna Journal on International Constitutional Law 5 (2011), 49.

10 Cf. *Michael Riegner*, Die internationalisierte Verfassungsgerichtsbarkeit in Kosovo: Instrument zur Friedenssicherung und Entwicklungsförderung?, Zeitschrift für ausländisches öffentliches Recht und Völkerrecht 71 (2011), 543. According to the *European Commission*, Kosovo 2011 Progress Report, 12.10.2011, SEC (2011) 1207, at 3, 10, the Court "played an important role through the way it exercised its responsibilities" and "has issued a number of key decisions, which made a significant impact".

protections in the Enlargement and the Common Foreign and Security Policy or with supranational guarantees for constitutionalism in existing member states.[11]

The remainder of this introduction explicates the approach and context of the research and summarizes the findings in this book. Part II outlines the thematic, geographical and methodological choices and contexts of our research. Part III summarizes the country studies in this book. Part IV proceeds with a systematic discussion of themes and doctrinal questions which recur in all contributions and jurisdictions. Part V concludes with some tentative thoughts on the future and the legitimacy of constitutional justice in Southeast Europe.

II. Thematic and geographical choices

This book adopts a regional perspective on topics of supra-regional relevance. This concept implies some underlying choices and assumptions, which the following part makes explicit and relates to the research context. They concern thematic focus (1.) and geographical coverage (2.).

1. Comparing the relationship of constitutional justice to the ordinary judiciary and the ECtHR

This book does not purport to compare constitutional justice in general, but focuses on the interplay of constitutional courts with the highest ordinary courts (or "supreme courts"[12]) on the one hand, and with the ECtHR on the other. This interplay raises a number of research questions: How do the respective constitu-

11 *Armin von Bogdandy/Matthias Kottmann/Carlino Antpöhler/Johanna Dickschen/Simon Hentrei/Maja Smrkolj*, Reverse Solange: Protecting the Essence of Fundamental Rights against EU Member States, Common Market Law Review 49 (2012), 489. With regard to EU foreign policy, see *Martina Spernbauer*, EULEX in Kosovo: The Difficult Deployment and Challenging Implementation of the Most Comprehensive Civilian EU Operation to Date, *German Law Journal* 11 (2010), 769; *Robert Muharremi*, The European Union Rule of Law Mission in Kosovo (EULEX) from the Perspective of Kosovo Constitutional Law, Zeitschrift für ausländisches öffentliches Recht und Völkerrecht 70 (2010), 357. On enlargement policy, see *infra*, note 30.

12 In this book, the term "highest ordinary court" or "supreme court" designates the court that renders the last instance judgment on the application of ordinary law. It is not to be confused with the supreme courts in common law jurisdictions, which equally perform constitutional review. Given their unifying function at the top of the ordinary court pyramid, supreme courts are treated here as representatives of all other types and levels of courts in the judicial branch, including specialized administrative courts. Future research would have to differentiate the relationship further, as Serbia for instance has a separate administrative court system, while administrative justice in Kosovo is exercised by a specialized bench within the Supreme Court.

tions regulate the relationship between these three types of courts, and how do courts interpret the applicable legal rules? How do the courts interact in practice – do they cooperate or conflict, and if so, how and why? What effect do the dynamics of court interaction have on domestic constitutionalism in Southeast Europe? And what do they teach us about the multi-level system of constitutional governance in Europe? To address these questions, the individual authors analyze the respective constitutional and legislative framework governing the legal relationship between these three types of courts. They discuss how jurisdictional rules or standards of review are interpreted in practice, refer to case law illustrating the dynamics of court interaction, and offer further contextual analysis and comparisons.

The choice of this thematic focus has two main reasons. Initially, it originated from the practical needs of our authors, whose daily work is significantly shaped by the dynamics of court interaction – work which they perform as presidents of constitutional courts, constitutional justices, or advisors and attorneys in the field of constitutional law. While judicial review of the legislator is undoubtedly a defining feature of constitutional justice, court interactions equally, and at times more directly, shape the experience of legal practitioners. This is also true for those who are, after all, the ultimate beneficiaries of constitutional justice: the citizens. From their perspective, it is not enough for constitutional courts to simply "embody" and "symbolize" the democratic transition and to occasionally strike down a statute in a high profile case brought by an opposition party. Citizens also expect constitutional courts to make a very concrete and appreciable impact on their daily lives, by bringing constitutional protections and European human rights home to their doorstep, or at least to the court next door.[13]

Yet the relationship between the courts is not only important in practice; it also offers a thematic prism for legal research of supra-regional relevance. The dynamics of court interaction studied in this book reflect two general trends in the evolution of constitutional justice in wider Europe: firstly, a shift from the review of legislation to the review of the application of legislation, and secondly the Europeanization of constitutional justice. Both trends have accounted for considerable scholarly literature in constitutional, international and European law, to which this book relates. The first issue, regarding the relationship of constitutional courts to the highest ordinary courts, tunes in with prior comparative research on court interaction and on the constitutionalization of domestic legal

13 This is not to diminish the significance of legislative review, which certainly is important for constitutional justice and remains an important subject for further research, but has already given rise to a considerable general literature, see only *Christine Landfried* (ed.), Constitutional Review of Legislation, 1988; *Sadurski* (note 3).

orders. The characteristic feature of the concentrated, "Kelsenian" model of judicial review is its institutional separation from the traditional judiciary.[14] This separation has required specialized constitutional courts all over Europe to define and redefine their relationship to the ordinary courts.[15] In many jurisdictions, this process was shaped as much by cooperation as by conflict.[16] In particular, the rise of individual access to constitutional courts has created many more situations where constitutional courts review the application of legislation by the ordinary courts. This enables constitutional courts to impose their reading of the constitution on the ordinary judiciary. Over time they have thus accounted for a constitutionalization of many European legal orders and played an important role in the transformation and democratization of post-authoritarian legal systems.[17]

The emergence of judicial mechanisms beyond the nation state has not only transformed the dynamics of court interactions in domestic settings. It has also reproduced these dynamics on a European level, where they also oscillate between cooperation and confrontation.[18] Our second question, regarding the relationship between constitutional courts and the ECtHR, thus relates to discourses about the internationalization of national constitutions in general, and about the transformation of domestic constitutional law through the Strasbourg system in particular.[19] Most constitutions in Southeast Europe have been recently enacted

14 *Hans Kelsen*, Judicial Review of Legislation: A Comparative Study of the Austrian and the American Constitution, Journal of Politics 4 (1942), 183; *Capelletti/William* (note 1), 84 et seq.

15 *Frank Michelman*, The interplay of constitutional and ordinary jurisdiction, in: Tom Ginsburg/Rosalind Dixon (eds.), Comparative Constitutional Law, 2010, 278; *Robert Alexy/Philip Kunig/Werner Heun/Georg Hermes*, Verfassungsrecht und einfaches Recht - Verfassungsgerichtsbarkeit und Fachgerichtsbarkeit, Veröffentlichungen der Vereinigung der Deutschen Staatsrechtslehrer vol. 61, 2002.

16 *Lech Garlicki*, Constitutional courts versus supreme courts, International Journal of Constitutional Law 5 (2007), 44. On the German constitutional court's struggle with the *Bundesgerichtshof*, the highest ordinary court, see *Thomas Henne*, Von 0 auf Lüth in 6 1/2 Jahren: Zu den prägenden Faktoren der Grundsatzentscheidung, in: Id./Arne Riedlinger (eds.), Das Lüth-Urteil in (rechts-)historischer Sicht, 2005, 197.

17 *Gunnar Schuppert/Christian Bumke*, Die Konstitutionalisierung der Rechtsordnung, 2000; *Sascha Kneip*, Constitutional courts as democratic actors and promoters of the rule of law: institutional prerequisites and normative foundations, Zeitschrift für Vergleichende Politikwissenschaft 5 (2011), 131.

18 *Matthias Hartwig*, Much Ado About Human Rights: The Federal Constitutional Court Confronts the European Court of Human Rights, German Law Journal 5 (2005), 869. In EU member states, these dynamics occur also with regard to the European Court of Justice, which is beyond the scope of this book.

19 See only *Dieter Grimm*, The Constitution in the Process of Denationalization, Constellations 12 (2005), 447; *Jochen Frowein*, The Transformation of Constitutional Law through the European Convention on Human Rights, Israel Law Review 41 (2008), 489; *Armin v. Bogdandy/Pedro Cruz Villalón/Peter Huber* (eds.), Handbuch Ius Publicum Europaeum, vol. II: Offene Staatlichkeit – Wissenschaft vom Verfassungsrecht, 2007.

or reformed, and one may be curious how drafters have dealt with questions of open statehood in light of West European experiences. At the same time, not only laws, but also constitutions in the region are increasingly measured against the common European constitutional standards embodied in the ECHR – and at times fail the test.[20]

Finally, constitutional courts in Southeast Europe are equally building blocks of the multi-level architecture of fundamental rights protection in Europe. Not only are they important gatekeepers for the caseload of the ECtHR and enforcers of its decisions. They also take part in the ongoing judicial dialogues that influence European fundamental rights jurisprudence.[21] To capture these complex vertical and horizontal processes of mutual influence and integration, the relationship between domestic and European courts has been conceptualized as *Verfassungsgerichtsverbund*, or "composite constitutional justice".[22] This composite architecture raises, on the one hand, practical questions concerning *inter alia* the implementation of ECtHR judgments by domestic courts and the *erga omnes* effect of Strasbourg case law on the interpretation of domestic fundamental rights[23] – issues constitutional justice in Southeast Europe also deals with intensely, and at times innovatively. On the other hand, the multi-level interactions raise questions regarding the very nature of constitutional justice in Europe. Many scholars now see the Convention system as a prime example of constitutionalization beyond the nation state, characterized by the hierarchization of different layers of

20 ECtHR, *Sejdić and Finci v. Bosnia and Herzegovina*, Application Nos. 27996/06 and 34836/06, Grand Chamber Judgment of 22 December 2009, holding that the Dayton Constitution of Bosnia and Herzegovina violates the passive right to vote and the principle of non-discrimination. For case comments, see *Marko Milanovic*, AJIL 104 (2010), 636; *Samo Bardutzky*, The Strasbourg Court on the Dayton Constitution: Judgment in the case of Sejdić and Finci v. Bosnia and Herzegovina, European Constitutional Law Review 6 (2010), 309. For an application to Kosovo, see *Riegner/Grewe* (note 5), 30 et seq. The new Hungarian Basic Law adopted in 2011 will also have to stand the test of the ECtHR, see below part II.2.

21 *Eirik Bjorge*, National supreme courts and the development of ECHR rights, International Journal of Constitutional Law 9 (2011), 5, at 9 et seq., points out that most of the 119,300 applications pending before the ECtHR originate in transition states, and illustrates how domestic constitutional adjudication influences doctrinal construction in Convention jurisprudence.

22 *Andreas Voßkuhle*, Der europäische Verfassungsgerichtsverbund, Neue Zeitschrift für Verwaltungsrecht (2010), 1; *Stefan Oeter*, Rechtsprechungskonkurrenz zwischen nationalen Verfassungsgerichten, Europäischem Gerichtshof und Europäischem Gerichtshof für Menschenrechte, Veröffentlichungen der Vereinigung der Deutschen Staatsrechtslehrertagung vol. 66, 2006, 361.

23 For a comparative overview, see *Giusepppe Martinico/Oreste Pollicino* (eds.), The National Judicial Treatment of the ECHR and EU Laws, 2010; *Peter Huber*, Vergleich, in: Bogdandy/Villalón/Huber (note 19), 403. On the example of Germany, see *Hartwig* (note 18).

law and adjudication.[24] Others rather interpret it as a form of legal pluralism, marked by intertwined heterarchical layers and horizontal processes of mutual cross-fertilization and contestation.[25] In any event, a better understanding of these processes certainly requires more "work into the spread, shape and intensity of the links between domestic and international layers of law in different parts of the globe".[26] This book contributes such work on the constitutionalizing dynamics of court interaction in one part of the globe – Southeast Europe.

2. Mapping the constitutional geography of Southeast Europe

Southeast Europe is not a clearly defined geographical area or homogenous legal space. This raises methodological questions regarding the selection and comparability of the legal orders selected for study in this book. This section thus explicates reasons why Kosovo, Serbia, Albania and Hungary lend themselves to comparison. On the one hand, such a comparison has some common ground because, firstly, all four legal orders emerged from a communist system and, secondly, all four are now part of a common European legal space. On the other hand, the selection is informed by a logic of difference, as the four selected states have reached different stages of domestic transformation and European integration, and each of them typifies a different development path of constitutional justice in Southeast Europe.

The first common ground and reason for comparison is that all four legal orders share the experience and challenges of the triple transition from communism to political democracy, to rule of law, and to market economy.[27] The second is that all four selected legal orders are arguably part of an emerging common European legal space. This space is wider than the EU and smaller than the Council of Europe membership. It is defined firstly by a serious commitment to the effective implementation of Council of Europe standards, namely the ECHR, and secondly by a legal sensitivity to the EU's constitutional values and the *acquis*

24 *Alec Stone Sweet*, Sur la consitutionnalisation de la convention européenne des droits de l'homme, Revue trimestrielle de droits de l'homme (2009), 923; *Frank Hoffmeister*, Die Europäische Menschenrechtskonvention als Grundrechtsverfassung und ihre Bedeutung in Deutschland, Der Staat 40 (2001), 349.

25 *Nico Krisch*, Beyond Constitutionalism, 2010, namely 109 et seq.; *Bogdandy et al.* (note 11).

26 *Krisch* (note 25), 11.

27 On the legal challenges involved, see *Christian Boulanger* (ed.), Recht in der Transformation. Rechts- und Verfassungswandel in Mittel- und Osteuropa, 2002.

communautaire.[28] It is submitted here that the countries studied in this book display such a commitment to Strasbourg standards: either as members of the Council of Europe, as in the case of Hungary, Serbia and Albania, or by autonomously subjecting themselves to these standards as a matter of domestic constitutional law, as in the case of Kosovo.[29] With regard to the EU, Hungary is already a member, and Albania, Serbia and Kosovo are officially considered "potential candidate countries" subject to stabilization and association instruments. Moreover, their legislative and adjudicative practice gravitates towards the *acquis communautaire* and the Copenhagen accession criteria with substantial EU support.[30] As a result, membership in the common European legal space accounts for a modicum of normative convergence that facilitates comparison.

Beyond these commonalities, however, the four selected legal orders represent different groups of countries on different trajectories of constitutional transformation. Firstly, Hungary fulfills the function of the most dissimilar case in our comparison, as it differs from Kosovo, Serbia and Albania in two important respects: its domestically driven constitutional transformation started in 1989, and it has been a member of the EU since 2004. It thus represents the first wave of post-communist legal transition in Europe and the legal orders transformed by the Eastern enlargement of the EU. Of all attempts at constitutional justice in this first wave, the Hungarian constitutional court, established in 1989, has become one of boldest and most influential in the region, "and perhaps in the world".[31] It

28 *Constance Grewe*, Definition und Begrenzung des europäischen Verfassungsrechts: Überlegungen zur Existenz eines europäischen Rechtsraumes, Paper presented at UFA Doctoriales Berlin 23-25 June 2011, manuscript on file with author. She includes all countries studied in this book. The concept serves essentially a heuristic function in legal research, but has also been used to justify judicial approximation to European constitutional standards, cf. Supreme Court of Estonia, Constitutional Chamber, judgment No. III-4/A-5/94 (1994).

29 The inclusion of Kosovo may prompt counter-arguments, given its ineffective court system, its serious problems with the enforcement of law and order in Serb-populated Northern Mitrovica, and its general reputation for lawlessness and inter-ethnic conflict, cf. *International Crisis Group*, The Rule of Law in Independent Kosovo, Europe Report No. 204, 19 May 2010; *Anita McKinna*, Kosovo: The International Community's European Project, European Review 20 (2012), 10. Yet, the Kosovo Constitution is a generally useful framework for the constitutionalization and Europeanization of the legal order, and the constitutional court makes active use of that framework, see parts III and IV below.

30 EU approximation is beyond the scope of this book, but a prominent issue in all states studied here, see *Rudi Kocjančič*, Stabilisierungs- und Assoziierungsprozess auf dem Gebiet des ehemaligen Jugoslawien, Zeitschrift fuer ausländisches öffentliches Recht und Völkerrecht, 66 (2006), 435. See also the yearly European Commission Progress Reports on the potential candidate countries, e.g. *supra*, note 10. More critically *Tina Freyburg/Solveig Richter*, National Identity Matters. The Limited Impact of EU Political Conditionality in the Western Balkans, Journal of European Public Policy 17 (2010), 263.

31 *Herman Schwartz*, Eastern Europe's Constitutional Courts, Journal of Democracy 9 (1998), 100, at 104. See also *Kim Scheppele*, The New Hungarian Constitutional Court,

has also been regarded as a model for other constitutional courts in the region, which initially motivated the inclusion of Hungary into our comparison. In contrast, Kosovo, Serbia and Albania are part of a second and later wave of post-communist constitutional transformation in Europe, as they took their most recent steps towards full liberal constitutionalism only in 1998, 2006 and 2008 respectively.[32] Their transformation also involved the (re)establishment or strengthening of constitutional courts. These courts represent a second wave of constitutional justice, distinct from the one that swept across Central and Eastern Europe just after 1989.[33] This book places its – selective – focus specifically on the courts embodying that second wave. In doing so, it consciously sets aside other Southeast European jurisdictions, namely in former Yugoslavia, which are further down their path of transition.

Although this second wave shares important characteristics, it is by no means internally homogenous. Rather, Kosovo, Serbia and Albania represent three distinct trajectories of constitutional transformation in that second wave. To begin with, constitutionalism in Albania, unlike in Kosovo and Serbia, did not emerge from a disintegrating federal superstructure, and constitutional justice had no precursors in communist times. Albania established its first ever constitutional court as early as 1992, but the institution gained in importance only incrementally, notably after the enactment of the new constitution in 1998 and with the pro-

East European Constitutional Review 8 (1999), 81; *Laszlo Sólyom/Georg Brunner* (eds.), Constitutional Judiciary in a New Democracy. The Hungarian Constitutional Court, 2000; *András Sajó*, Educating the Executive: The Hungarian Constitutional Court's Role in the Transition Process, in: Joachim Hesse/Gunnar Schuppert/Katharina Harms (eds.), Verfassungsrecht und Verfassungspolitik in Umbruchsituation, 2000, 229; *Gábor Halmai*, The Transformation of Hungarian Constitutional Law from 1985 to 2005, in: *András Jakab/Peter Takács/Allan Tatham* (eds.), The Transformation of the Hungarian Legal Order 1985–2005, 2007; *Péter Paczolay* (ed.), Twenty years of the Hungarian Constitutional Court, 2009; and *infra*, note 40.

32 These dates mark the enactment of the newest constitutions in the respective jurisdiction and are of course only one possible, formal indicator among others, but are nevertheless important for constitutional change. In Serbia, for instance, the change could also be pinned down to the 2003 Constitutional Charter of Serbia and Montenegro with the attached Charter on Human and Minority Rights. On the courts, see respectively *Stoppel* (note 7); *Čukalovič*, in this volume; *Michael Riegner*, The two faces of the internationalized *pouvoir constituant*: Independence and constitution-making under external influence in Kosovo, Göttingen Journal of International Law 2 (2010), 1035.

33 Comparative literature offers different narratives on "waves" of constitutional justice in Europe and the world. See only *Haase/Struger* (note 5), who identify three waves after WW II, with 1989 being the third. *Michael Fromont*, La justice constitutionnelle dans le monde, 1996, 17 et seq., mentions three "generations" of constitutional courts, with the German court leading the second. In this book, the "second" wave refers only to the proliferation and increased role of constitutional review in Southeast Europe.

spect of EU accession.[34] In contrast, Serbia and Kosovo were part of the Socialist Federal Republic of Yugoslavia (SFRY) and already had their constitutional courts in communist times. But the successors of these courts had to reinvent themselves in the context of new democratic polities, whose constitutional identity was recalibrated and renegotiated intensely – and at times violently.[35]

Beyond their common constitutional history, Kosovo and Serbia however represent two distinct configurations of constitutional justice. The first configuration took shape in the post-conflict context of internationalized constitution-making and international efforts at state- and nation-building. This type is represented here by Kosovo, but equally comprises the much-studied case of Bosnia and Herzegovina.[36] Both constitutional courts, (re)established in 2009 and 1997 respectively, started out as hybrid institutions with an internationalized composition, and they operate in the peculiar context of multi-ethnic consociational democracies, intensely influenced and supervised by the international community.[37] This is not the case in the second type, represented here by Serbia. Here constitutional transformations were less influenced by civil war and less driven by international presences, but rather impeded during the 1990s by the ethno-nationalist Milošević regime.

Serbia's constitutional court developed more incrementally after the fall of communism, was less internationalized than in Bosnia and Kosovo and had to forge different domestic alliances to establish its authority. It nevertheless paved the way for the fall of the Milošević regime when it found ballot irregularities in the 2000 election and ordered a new vote. The court's development trajectory thus differed in many ways from the paths taken in those former Yugoslav re-

34 In 1998, *Schwartz* (note 31), at 112, still counted the Albanian court among the ones that "largely failed". On the difficult progress, see *Stoppel* (note 7), and the contribution of *Xhezair Zaganjori*, in this volume.

35 *Tibor Várady*, Minorities, Majorities, Law, and Ethnicity: Reflections of the Yugoslav Case, Human Rights Quarterly 19 (1997), 9; *Elmar Pichl*, Kosovo in den jugoslawischen Verfassungssystemen: 1974 bis 1998, in: Joseph Marko (ed.), Gordischer Knoten Kosovo/a, 2000, 75; *Haase/Struger* (note 5), 102, 196-225.

36 On constitutional justice in Bosnia and Herzegovina, see *Joseph Marko*, Five Years of Constitutional Jurisprudence in Bosnia and Herzegovina: A First Balance, European Diversity and Autonomy Papers 7/2004; *Dragica Banovic*, Die Verfassungsgerichtsbarkeit in Bosnien und Herzegowina, 2009. Constitutionalism and thus the cases before the constitutional court in Bosnia and Herzegovina differ from Kosovo however in that the former is a strongly federalized state, whereas the latter is nominally a unitary state.

37 *Grewe/Riegner* (note 5), 39 et seq.; *Steven Hill/Paul Linden-Retek*, Supervised Independence and Post-Conflict Sovereignty: The Dynamics of Hybridity in Kosovo's New Constitutional Court, Yale Journal of International Law 36 (2010), 26; *Visar Morina*, The Newly Established Constitutional Court in Post-Status Kosovo: Selected Institutional and Procedural Concerns, Review of Central and East European Law 35 (2010), 129; *Dren Doli/Fisnik Korenica*, Kosovar Constitutional Court's Jurisdiction: Searching for Strengths and Weaknesses, German Law Journal 11 (2010), 803.

publics that seceded and liberalized earlier, such as Slovenia and Croatia. In other respects, it may however be modestly representative of some other post-Tito courts that are also part of the second wave of constitutional justice, namely in newly independent Montenegro, whose constitutional court was substantially reformed by the new Constitution of 2007, and possibly in Macedonia.[38]

This mapping of Southeast Europe's constitutional geography has a number of consequences for the comparison of court interaction. On the one hand, it stresses the truism that comparative constitutional law is a highly context-dependent undertaking, and that any such comparison should ideally account for the entire legal context as well as a host of extra-legal factors.[39] Thus this book does not postulate easily transferable "lessons learned" based on a simplistic functionalist logic. On the other hand, the mapping shows some convergence namely towards European standards and thus helps identify subjects for comparisons as well as some of the relevant contextual factors. Against this background, context-sensitive comparisons between newer courts and more established "models" are useful in the sense that they may illustrate possible scenarios and determinants for the long-term development of constitutional justice in transition.

One such scenario is evidenced by the "model" court in Hungary, which however looks more ambivalent twenty years down the road. As much as the Hungarian justices, and namely their first president László Sólyom, initially set a model for many other courts in the region, as much have the constitutional reforms enacted by the Hungarian parliament in 2010 and 2011 cast doubts on this success story. The parliamentary supermajority curtailed the court's competence *ratione materiae*, did away with *actio popularis* review of legislation and changed the rules on composition and appointment.[40] According to its makers, the new Basic Law concludes the transition period and restores true democracy[41],

38 On these other former Yugoslav courts see e.g. *Haase/Struger* (note 5), 196 et seq. The Former Yugoslav Republic of Macedonia is more difficult to classify and seems to be between the waves and types identified here. On its internationally-brokered, multi-ethnic constitutional arrangements, see *Joseph Marko*, The Referendum on Decentralization in Macedonia 2004: A Litmus Test for Macedonia's Interethnic Relations, European Yearbook of Minority Issues 4 (2004-2005), 695. By only including the Serbian court here, the book does not address the particular role of the constitutional courts in other former republics in the processes of secession and independence vis-à-vis the former Yugoslavia, which Serbia dominated and struggled to keep together.

39 *Günther Frankenberg*, Critical Comparisons: Re-thinking Comparative Law, Harvard Journal of International Law 26 (1985), 411; *Rainer Wahl*, Verfassungsvergleichung als Kulturvergleichung, in: Festschrift Helmut Quaritsch, 2000, 163.

40 For overviews of the reforms, see the contributions of *Sonnevend* and *Paczolay*, in this volume, and *Kriszta Kovács/Gábor Attila Tóth*, Hungary's Constitutional Transformation, European Constitutional Law Review 7 (2011), 183.

41 Cf. the preamble of the new Basic Law, and below part V.2.

whereas critics fear an "authoritarian slide"[42] and consider, in particular, the reforms to the constitutional court as "a serious step back".[43] So far, the court has kept performing its function and struck down important pieces of unconstitutional legislation, notably parts of the heavily criticized media law. But the backlash certainly recalls the voices of early sceptics of constitutional courts in the region, who were concerned early on about the weak democratic legitimacy of the courts or about their limited role as a successful pre-EU-accession "public relations asset".[44]

These competing narratives of success and failure in Hungary may prompt a turn to less ambivalent models, and the German Federal Constitutional Court (FCC) is often mentioned in that respect. Hence, a few final words seem warranted about the potential role model of the *Bundesverfassungsgericht* in Karlsruhe, given also that this book is printed by a German publisher and made possible by the German development agency *Gesellschaft für Internationale Zusammenarbeit* (GIZ). The FCC is generally considered not only as a successful historical example of constitutional justice, but also discussed as an export model for constitutional democracies all over the world.[45] This view is echoed in the present book, namely by the president of the Kosovar Constitutional Court and in the contribution on the Constitutional Court of Serbia, furnishing examples of constitutional "migration" from Germany to Southeast Europe.[46] More generally, the reception of German law and the active promotion of the *Rechtsstaat* abroad

42 *Kim Scheppele*, Hungary's Constitutional Revolution, New York Times, 19 December 2011.

43 *Kovács/Tóth* (note 40), 202; *European Commission for Democracy through Law* („Venice Commission"), Opinion on the new Constitution of Hungary, CDL-AD(2011)016, para. 93 et seq.

44 *Procházka* (note 3), 268. Critical also *Wojciech Sadurski*, Legitimacy and Reasons of Constitutional Review After Communism, in: Id. (note 3), 163; *Stephen Holmes*, Back to the Drawing Board, East European Constitutional Review 2 (1993), 21; *Renata Utiz*, The Rule of Law in Post-Communist Constitutional Jurispridence. Concerned Notes on a Fancy Decoration, in: Gianluigi Palambella/Neil Walker (eds.), Relocating the Rule of Law, 2009, 71;

45 *Klaus v. Beyme*, Modell für neue Demokratien? Die Vorbildrolle des Bundesverfassungsgerichts, in: Robert v. Ooyen/Martin Möllers (eds.), Das Bundesverfassungsgericht im politischen System, 2006, 519; *Juliane Kokott*, From Reception and Transplantation to Convergence of Constitutional Models in the Age of Globalization – with Special References to the German Basic Law, in: Christian Starck (ed.), Constitutionalism, Universalism and Democracy, 1999, 71. A recent empirical study found that the worldwide appeal of the German Basic Law peaked in the 1990s but decreased since then: *David Law/Mila Versteeg*, The Declining Influence of the United States Constitution, New York University Law Review 87 (2012), 762. For overviews of the Court in general, see Special Issue: Fifty Years of the German Federal Constitutional Court, German Law Journal 2 (2001), available at www.germanlawjournal.com.

46 *Hasani*, in this volume, parts I and III.2; *Čukalovič*, in this volume, part II.2.a). See generally, *Sujit Choudhry* (ed.), The Migration of Constitutional Ideas, 2006.

currently arouse more scholarly interest and feature prominently on the agenda of German development practitioners and foreign policy-makers.[47] It is in this context that GIZ supports the consolidation of constitutional justice in Kosovo and promotes legal reform throughout Southeast European transition states, alongside many other resourceful donors such as the EU and USAID.[48] Comparative constitutional law can usefully accompany these practical efforts, which can in turn inform legal research and education.[49] In that sense, the present book is also the result of such a cooperation between research and practice.

III. An overview of the contributions to this book

The book is organized by country chapters that generally cover one aspect of inter-court relationships in one jurisdiction, sometimes complemented by comparative side-glances. This section briefly summarizes the contributions.

1. Kosovo

Enver Hasani, President of the Constitutional Court of Kosovo, opens the debate with his contribution on "Constitutionalism in Kosovo and the Relationship between Constitutional Justice and the Supreme Court". Hasani firstly offers his reading of Western constitutionalism and firmly anchors the Constitution of the Republic of Kosovo enacted in 2008 in that tradition. Inspired by the German Basic Law, the Constitution is the first to effectively enshrine the rule of law, limitations of power, human rights and multi-ethnic democracy in Kosovo's le-

47 Cf. *Michael Riegner/Thomas Wischmeyer*, Rechtliche Zusammenarbeit mit Transformations- und Entwicklungsländern als Gegenstand öffentlich-rechtlicher Forschung, Der Staat 50 (2011), 436, with further references. On the efforts to promote German law abroad, see only *Dirk Mirow/Stefan Hülshörster*, Rechtstransfer und Rechtstransformation im Focus der Justizaußenpolitik, Deutsche Richterzeitung (2011), 383.

48 See generally *Bundesministerium für wirtschaftliche Zusammenarbeit und Entwicklung*, Recht und Justiz in der deutschen Entwicklungszusammenarbeit, 2002. On the influence of US-American lawyers on constitutional drafting in Kosovo, see *John Tunheim*, Rule of Law and the Kosovo Constitution, Minnesota Journal of International Law 18 (2009), 371. On EULEX, see *supra*, note 11.

49 On interactions between research and practice, see *Philipp Dann*, Verfassungsberatung in Afrika als Grenzgang zwischen Entwicklungszusammenarbeit und rechtswissenschaftlicher Forschung, in: Gabriele Britz (ed.), Freiheit und Risiko der Forschung, 2012, 95; *Riegner/Wischmeyer* (note 47). For a proposal on how to train lawyers for the international and interdisciplinary challenges of legal reform and cooperation, see *Michael Riegner/Philipp Dann*, „Recht und Entwicklung" als Gegenstand der Juristenausbildung: Konturen und Didaktik eines intra- und interdisziplinär vernetzten Studienfachs, Verfassung und Recht in Übersee 41 (2008), 309.

gal system. This commitment is embodied by the new specialized Constitutional Court, again modeled on the German *Bundesverfassungsgericht.* According to Hasani, the Constitutional Court's broad list of competences outlines a clear theoretical division of labor with the Supreme Court of Kosovo. In practice, the Constitutional Court has quashed numerous Supreme Court decisions already in its first year of operation, as is illustrated by the subsequent discussion of the case law. Hasani concludes however that the relationship of the two institutions has remained within the limits of the law, and that occasional "soft collisions" are "sometimes a price worth paying" in the struggle for constitutionalism.

In the next contribution, *Snezhana Botusharova,* international judge at the Constitutional Court of Kosovo and formerly Bulgarian justice at the ECtHR, addresses the relationship between "The Constitutional Court of Kosovo and the European Court of Human Rights". She first outlines the international origins and context of constitutional justice in Kosovo, which also shape its relationship with the ECtHR: following international demands, the constitution accords direct effect in domestic law to the (unratified) ECHR and makes ECtHR case law binding on all public authorities. Botusharova subsequently shows how this framework affects the relationship between citizens, the state and constitutional justice and discusses case law illustrating the intense reliance on Convention jurisprudence by the Court. She concludes that Strasbourg has greatly helped her court to contribute to the development of the rule of law, democracy and constitutionalism in Kosovo.

In the last piece on Kosovo, *Peter Pavlin,* secretary at the Slovenian Ministry of Justice, pulls the threads together and analyzes a crossroads where all three types of courts meet, namely the effective protection of the right to trial within reasonable time (Art. 6 read in conjunction with Art. 13 ECHR) in Kosovo. ECtHR case law, incorporated into the Kosovo Constitution, requires the existence of legislation on an effective remedy against delays of justice, but despite heavy backlogs in its courts Kosovo has yet failed to enact such a mechanism. Pavlin thus compares compensatory and acceleratory solutions already in place in Austria, the Czech Republic, Slovenia, Italy and Croatia, and concludes that in the meantime, the Constitutional Court must remedy delays by accepting individual constitutional complaints, thus making the Court the said hinge between the ECtHR requirements and domestic courts.

2. Serbia

Ivan Čukalovič, professor of law at Kragujevac University in Serbia and judge at the Constitutional Court of Kosovo, analyzes "The Relationship between the

Constitutional Court and the Supreme Cassation Court of Serbia". The 2006 Constitution brought an "expansion of the Constitutional Court's jurisdiction", indicating "the acceptance of political pluralism in the Serbian political system". Inspired by German and Austrian models, the Court has broad competences, including individual "constitutional appeals" against last instance judgments. The Supreme Cassation Court is thus an object of constitutional review, but also plays an active role in that it can initiate abstract norm control and appoints five of the 15 constitutional justices. Consequently, *Čukalovič* also identifies a peculiar personal dimension in the relationship of the two courts, alongside the jurisdictional and procedural one. Despite some jurisdictional overlap, he finds little case law indicating either cooperation or confrontation and concludes that at least the new constitutional framework for both courts has brought the Serbian legal system closer to other European models.

Vidan Hadzi-Vidanovic, associate at the Belgrade Centre for Human Rights and researcher at Nottingham University, provides a more critical account of "The European Convention on Human Rights in the Serbian and English Constitutional Orders: A Comparative Analysis". Such a contrast study is tempting, because at first sight the constitutional framework seems to be much more Convention-friendly in monist Serbia than in dualist England. But in practice the opposite is the case, and Serbian judges and lawyers seem generally reluctant to rely on the Convention in practice, and the Constitutional Court only slowly increases its use of ECtHR case law. To explain this, Hadzi-Vidanovic then conducts an empirical analysis of legal context and extra-legal determinants, but concludes that the most important factor "is the courage of one generation of English senior judges to refuse to side too often with ministers and other governmental officials, and the lack of such courage among their Serbian colleagues."

3. Albania

Xhezair Zaganjori, judge at the Constitutional Court of Albania, delivers a comprehensive analysis of the relationship between constitutional justice and the high court in Albania, in which he also discusses the significant influence of the ECHR and the ECtHR. The 1998 Constitution regulates the different tasks of the constitutional and ordinary courts quite clearly in theory, but in practice namely individual constitutional complaints have given rise to collisions. The main source of conflict is the Constitutional Court's "due process control" of ordinary court proceedings, which the Court largely equates to the standards of the – domestically applicable – ECHR. Zaganjori offers a comprehensive survey of the case law of both courts, and concludes that although the Constitutional Court met with some resistance against its own rulings and ECtHR judgments, generally the decisions and standards of constitutional justice have been accepted and reflected in the practice of the ordinary judiciary.

4. Hungary and beyond

The two contributions on constitutional justice in Hungary look back at 20 years of past practice under the 1989 Constitution, but also forward to the new Basic Law and the potential changes that come with its entry into force on 1 January 2012. The comparisons between the old and new Constitution paint a differentiated picture, promising progress in some respects and giving rise to concern in others. *Pál Sonnevend*, professor at Eötvös Loránd University Budapest and former constitutional advisor to the President of Hungary László Sólyom, discusses the "The Position of the European Convention on Human Rights in the Hungarian Legal Order". He finds that under the 1989 Constitution, the ECHR formally enjoyed an important position in domestic law, but that its primacy was hard to enforce in the specific case before the Constitutional Court. Moreover, past constitutional justices were hesitant to regard Strasbourg standards as binding guidance for the interpretation of the fundamental rights enshrined in the Constitution. This situation may change for the better with the new Basic Law, which makes the precedence of international treaties over conflicting national statutes an explicit constitutional rule.

Péter Paczolay, President of the Constitutional Court of Hungary, concludes the book on a more ambivalent note in his contribution entitled "Constitutional Justice between Courts, Citizens and Politics: Lessons Learned from the Transition Experience in Hungary and Beyond". He offers a survey of the constitutional court's evolution in its first two decades, in which it quickly gained unexpected importance, sustained by the procedural framework namely for *actio popularis* review of legislation. The relationship to the ordinary judiciary was "a sensitive issue" and characterized by the limited standard of review in constitutional complaints. This situation changes with the new Basic Law, which introduces the constitutional complaint with full review competence for the court. Paczolay situates the constitutional reform in two wider contexts. Firstly, in terms of geographical scope, the introduction of the constitutional complaint reflects a general trend in constitutional adjudication within Council of Europe states, namely, the rise of individual access to constitutional courts, which leads to a shift from the review of the legislator to a review of the judiciary. Secondly, in his conclusion Paczolay addresses the wider political context of the entire constitutional reforms in Hungary. After a discussion of changes to constitutional justice enacted in 2010 and 2011, he situates the developments in the discourse on law and politics, concluding that courts "cannot distract themselves from the processes of the larger political environment in which they have to act, survive, and fulfil their proper task. Public reaction to the court decision must not be a decisive factor; nevertheless it is difficult to completely ignore it."

IV. Recurring themes and doctrinal questions

The following section takes a systematic and comparative look at the findings of the individual contributions and situates them in the broader research context. It first addresses the relationship of constitutional courts to the domestic judiciary (1.), and then turns to their interaction with the ECtHR (2.).

1. The relationship of constitutional courts to the ordinary judiciary: The constitutionalizing dynamics of conflict and cooperation

The findings from country studies can be structured according to two broad categories: firstly, empirical findings on the actual patterns of interaction and its socio-legal determinants (a), and secondly legal analysis of the applicable rules, namely on jurisdiction and standards of review (b). Both inform some generalizing conclusions (c).

a) Empirical observations: Patterns and determinants of conflict and cooperation

The comparison highlights different patterns and determinants of court interaction and constitutionalization in Southeast Europe. It generally confirms the thesis that some measure of conflict is systemic in constitutionalized legal systems with concentrated judicial review, as the entrenchment of specialized constitutional courts has led to some resistance from ordinary courts all over Southeast Europe.[50] This resistance typically takes the form of non-execution of constitutional court judgments, which occurs with moderate frequency. But in some cases it goes so far that the ECtHR does not consider constitutional complaints as an effective remedy (which must be exhausted before applying to Strasbourg), as is

50 On systemic tensions, see *Garlicki* (note 16), 63.

the case in Albania.[51] In other legal orders, ordinary courts seem more cooperative, as Enver Hasani finds for instance for Kosovo. Again in others, direct collisions are mitigated by the procedural framework and take different forms, as in Hungary.

The reasons for patterns of conflict and cooperation are complex, and this book can only shed three spotlights on some contextual factors and legal determinants. The first highlights the historical and sociological context. Historically, constitutional courts were latecomers in all four legal systems studied in this book, and in Southeast Europe generally. Where they pre-existed under communist regimes, as in former Yugoslavia, they had a different function, and ordinary courts typically kept applying ordinary law. After regime change, many jurisdictions created the new constitutional courts as visible instruments of change, institutionally separated from the traditional judiciary and easy to staff with judges with different social backgrounds and value systems.[52] This set-up may explain some of the initial tensions between the courts, but does not account for divergences and continued tensions in the long run.[53] Hence, if conflicts occur these days, they must also be seen in the context of the wider transformation of constitutional adjudication, as identified by Péter Paczolay and as evidenced by other contributions to this book:[54] namely, the rise of individual access to constitutional courts. In practice, this rise leads to a shift from constitutional review of the legislator to review of the ordinary courts, as constitutional justices are confronted much more frequently with the (mis)application of legislation in last instance judgments.

51 *Zaganjori*, in this volume, part II.4. See generally *Dürr* (note 1), 170 et seq. on the effective remedy question, and also on the problem of excessively lengthy proceedings in this context, discussed with a different impetus by *Pavlin*, in this volume. On the question of execution, see *Venice Commission*, Decisions of constitutional courts and equivalent bodies and their execution, 17.5.2001, CDL-INF (2001).

52 *András Sajó*, Contemporary Problems of the Judiciary in Hungary, in: International Centre for Comparative Law and Politics, The Social Role of the Legal Profession, 1993. But see *Sadurski* (note 44), 8, who points out that by no means all ordinary judges had been politicized, and not all constitutional justices had been politically inactive.

53 In Kosovo, most judges are professors, many of them educated abroad. The Albanian court also features a fair share of academics, whereas the new appointment modality in Serbia now brings fewer professors and more ordinary judges to the bench. If and when elite change in the ordinary judiciary progresses with educational and recruitment reforms, as implemented step by step for instance in Albania, social background becomes less of a dividing line.

54 *Paczolay*, in this volume, part III; *Kovács/Tóth* (note 40), 201. Kosovo, Serbia and Albania already have the individual constitutional complaint, whereas Hungary introduced it with the new Basic Law. The trend is also evident in statistics: for instance, out of 285 cases brought before the Constitutional Court of Kosovo by June 2011, 170 or 59.6 per cent concerned review of supreme court decisions, *Hasani*, in this volume, part IV.2.

However, whether the rise of individual access actually leads to tensions in a given legal order, and to what extent these tensions are systemic, depends on the exact specifications of the procedural framework. In this respect, it is telling to compare in particular the abstract *actio popularis* procedure that made the Hungarian court with the German-type constitutional complaint operated in other jurisdictions such as Kosovo and Albania: the quasi-petition system gave the Hungarian justices broad competences to review legislation, but in principle no power to quash ordinary court rulings. This opposed the court head-on to parliament and government and located conflicts in this inter-branch relationship. Where individual constitutional court complaints against last instance judgments are more prominent, constitutional courts often get into intra-branch struggles with the ordinary judiciary, as indicated in the case studies on Kosovo and Albania.[55] Similar patterns can be observed in the Czech Republic and in the early days of the German constitutional court, which in the first decade of its existence confronted the ordinary courts much more than parliament or government.[56] In sum, this aspect illustrates that besides all sensitivity for contextual factors, the importance of legal rules and their judicial construction should not be underestimated either.

b) Doctrinal reconstructions: Individual complaints and standards of review

The legal relationship between constitutional and ordinary courts can be systematically reconstructed according to two analytical categories that emerge from the country studies. The first category comprises jurisdictional rules regarding competences and types of proceedings of the constitutional court. The second concerns the substantive standards of review, which determine the intensity of constitutional control of ordinary courts.[57] As regards jurisdiction, the compari-

55 *Boulanger* (note 4), 16. On the *actio popularis* procedure in Hungary, see *Kovács/Tóth* (note 40), 185; *Halmai* (note 7), 56 et seq. The constitutional courts in Kosovo, Albania and Serbia do review legislation, but the Court in Kosovo for instance did not render a single final judgment in any norm control proceeding in its first 1 ½ years of operation, whereas there were hundreds of applications for review of Supreme Court judgments, and dozens of them were quashed.

56 *Garlicki* (note 16), 44 et seq.; *Boulanger* (note 4), 16. The Hungarian Constitutional Court developed other techniques of control directed at the ordinary courts, see below part IV.1.b).

57 Other aspects relevant in practice and raised in the contributions, but not dealt with here in detail, include *inter alia* procedural questions as discussed by *Pavlin*, in this volume, part III.1 (exhaustion of legal remedies), and *Zaganjori*, in this volume, parts II.4, III.6,

son illustrates that the dynamics of court interaction in Southeast Europe depend significantly on whether constitutional courts are competent to hear constitutional complaints against the application of the law by ordinary courts. This is the case in Kosovo, Albania and Serbia, but also elsewhere in the region.[58] These courts interpret the applicable rules as "full" constitutional complaint, which entitles them to constitutional review of last instance judgments. Consequently, constitutional complaints are the defining moments in these constitutional courts' practical relationship with the ordinary judiciary, much more than the occasional ordinary court references for incidental norm control. It is the individual complaint that definitely subordinates the ordinary judiciary to the constitutional court and enables the latter to impose its reading of the constitution on the former. Constitutional complaints are thus the procedural valve that constructs constitutional justice as a hinge between ordinary law and constitutional law. Or in other words: Constitutional complaints are the procedural motor driving the constitutionalization of ordinary law.

In contrast, the Constitutional Court in Hungary has been less characterized by its competence for constitutional complaints because the 1989 Constitution did not allow the Court to review last instance judgments unless the underlying legislation on which the judgment was based was unconstitutional. The Constitutional Court developed some other techniques to control ordinary courts, but attempts to interpret the constitutional complaint more generously were largely fended off by the Supreme Court.[59] Whether this normative choice is "better" remains open to discussion, but a few tentative conclusions emerge from the material in this book: the Hungarian model of limited constitutional complaints has the distinct advantage that it entails a clear functional separation between constitutional justice and ordinary courts. It thus bears less potential for direct jurisdictional conflicts, and may also help control the caseload arising from violations of ordinary law at the constitutional court. On the other hand, this approach bars constitutional judges from remedying a great number of – at times obvious – violations of the constitution in individual cases, and fails to bring constitutional

(enforcement procedure), and personal linkages, as are prominent in Serbia, see *Čukalovič*, in this volume, part IV.3.

58 Art. 113 of the Constitution of Kosovo, Art. 169 in Serbia, Art. 131 in Albania. Constitutional review of last instance judgments is also practiced in Bosnia and Herzegovina, cf. *Grewe/Riegner* (note 5), 45 et seq. In Serbia and Bosnia and Herzegovina, the constitutional complaint is however limited in a different respect, namely in that the courts refuse to review the legislation underlying the challenged last instance judgments and limit review to the application of the law.

59 *Paczolay*, in this volume, part II.3; *Garlicki* (note 16), 61 et seq; *Halmai* (note 7), 58 et seq.

justice home to the citizens' doorsteps.[60] In practice, the balance seems to tip in favor of the full constitutional complaint, as exemplified by the new Hungarian Basic Law.

In light of this trend, the delimitation of competences between constitutional courts remains an issue also for comparative research. From that perspective, constitutional lawyers, including our authors, seem to converge in the formula that constitutional courts only apply constitutional law and that they may not become a court of last (third, fourth) instance.[61] Yet this mantra hardly resolves the doctrinal predicament of how to determine *in abstracto* under which circumstances a misapplication of ordinary law is also a violation of constitutional standards, and when it is not. This problem cannot be solved by procedural means, but is intrinsically linked to the standards of review applied by the constitutional courts. For it is these standards that determine the extent and intensity to which ordinary court judgments are materially subject to constitutional review, and thus the pervasiveness of constitutional law.

The standards of review fall into two categories: firstly, procedural guarantees of fair trial and due process along the lines of Articles 6 and 13 ECHR. These guarantees account for the bulk of the cases in Kosovo and Albania, and their interpretation in constitutional jurisprudence largely seems to follow the ECtHR's case law. A second and trickier standard of review concerns the violation of non-procedural fundamental rights by ordinary courts, such as the right to property or freedom of speech. The enforcement of such rights in ordinary court proceedings has constitutionalized civil, criminal and administrative law in many other legal orders, and has given rise to doctrines of conform interpretation of ordinary law or to conceptions of the constitution as an "objective order of values" permeating the entire legal system.[62] As regards the Southeast European courts studied here, no clear trend emerges from the case law cited in the contributions. The Constitutional Court of Kosovo, drawing from ECtHR jurisprudence, may be understood to have accorded some sort of indirect horizontal effect to the right to property in a case involving the misapplication of contract

60 On advantages and disadvantages, see *Dürr* (note 1), 168 et seq.; *Georg Brunner*, Structure and Proceedings of the Hungarian Constitutional Judiciary, in: Id./Sólyom (note 31), 84.

61 *Hasani*, in this volume, part IV.2; *Čukalovič*, in this volume, part IV.2. Cf. the so-called "Heck"-formula used to define the reach of constitutional review in Germany, cited in *Hans-Jürgen Papier*, Das Verhältnis des Bundesverfassungsgerichts zu den Fachgerichtsbarkeiten, Deutsches Verwaltungsblatt (2009), 473, at 478.

62 *Garlicki* (note 16), 44 et seq. On these concepts in German constitutional law, see e.g. *David Currie*, The Constitution of the Federal Republic of Germany, 1994, 184 et seq; *Matthias Kumm*, Who is Afraid of the Total Constitution? Constitutional Rights as Principles and the Constitutionalization of Private Law, German Law Journal 7 (2006), 341.

law.[63] However, more research is needed to determine whether this is indicative of a general trend towards a doctrine of conform interpretation or horizontal effect and respective theories of fundamental rights.

c) Generalizations: Constitutionalizations and Europeanizations

If the material in this book permits any generalizations, then two tentative conclusions, subject to further research, emerge. Generally speaking, our research confirms the general thesis that constitutional courts contribute to the constitutionalization of legal systems by imposing their reading of the constitution on the ordinary courts. Yet the resulting dynamics of court interaction evidence two different forms of constitutionalization. These forms are in turn linked to the rule of law conception underlying and informing the constitutional court's interpretation of the applicable constitutional norms.[64] On the one hand, the prominence of fair trial and due process in the case law in Albania and Kosovo evidences a formal, or "thin" rule of law at work. This conception focuses mainly on the enforcement of the principle of legality and procedural fairness, leading to a formal constitutionalization of legal process. On the other hand, the courts follow "thicker" conceptions on other occasions, based on the enforcement of substantive fundamental rights and constitutional values in all areas of law and also in horizontal situations. This leads to a much more pervasive constitutionalization of the legal order.

As indicated by the studies on Kosovo and Albania, both forms can lead to collisions with ordinary courts, while only the latter is more likely to lead to conflict with the legislature.[65] In sum, intra-branch struggles between courts may be a price worth paying for bringing rights home to the citizens, but the intensity of

63 Constitutional Court of Kosovo, *Imer Ibrahimi and 48 other former employees of the Kosovo Energy Corporation vs. 49 Individual Judgments of the Supreme Court of the Republic of Kosovo,* KI 40/ 09, judgment of 23 June 2010, available at: http://www.gjk-ks.org. See *Botusharova*, in this volume, part IV.2.c); *Hasani*, in this volume, part IV.3 on the KEK-case, and part II.3. for a positioning of Kosovo between individualized and more social conceptions of fundamental rights. Whether the KEK-case is actually one of horizontal effect is not entirely clear as the respondent was a public company subject to privatization.

64 See only *Paul Craig*, Formal and Substantive Conceptions of the Rule of Law: An Analytical Framework, Public Law 1997, 467; *Rainer Grote*, Rule of Law, Rechtsstaat und „Etat de Droit", in: Christian Starck (ed.), Constitutionalism, Universalism and Democracy, 1999, 269.

65 There are obviously exceptions: as illustrated in the contribution by *Pavlin*, in this volume, the formal guarantee of an effective remedy against delays of justice can create legislative duties. On conflicts with the legislature and the "counter-majoritarian difficulty" see below part V.

these struggles depends as much on good legal drafting at the outset as on the cooperative spirit of the judges at later stages. The more determinate the applicable constitutional rules are, the more likely are the conflicts between the courts to remain constrained and rationalized by legal argument. This may sound like a rather trivial result of the comparison, but is by no means self-understood in legislative practice.[66]

A second conclusion concerns the multi-level nature of constitutional adjudication, which also affects the domestic court interactions. A recurring theme in the contributions is that the relationship between constitutional and ordinary courts can no longer be considered in isolation from the international standards emanating notably from the ECtHR. These standards often provide a "neutral" normative frame of reference for the adjudicative practice of both courts and redefine the procedural and substantive dimensions of their interaction. Convention standards also account for some convergence of the domestic jurisprudence in Southeast Europe, namely in terms of procedural guarantees, and thus partly harmonize patterns of domestic constitutionalization. However, the reception of Strasbourg standards occurs in different legal frameworks and intensities, which results in different forms of Europeanization of the constitutionalizing dynamics of court interaction.

2. Constitutional justice and the European Court of Human Rights: Incorporation, implementation and multi-level constitutional justice

The relationship between constitutional courts and the ECtHR can be analyzed from at least two distinct but interconnected perspectives. The first focuses on the application and reception of the ECHR and Strasbourg jurisprudence in domestic constitutional orders, while the second is concerned with the place of domestic courts in the multi-level architecture of constitutional adjudication in Europe. The focus of the research in this book is mainly on domestic reception, which the individual authors approach primarily from a doctrinal perspective on applicable law (a). These findings are qualified by some empirical findings (b) and complemented here by reflections on the multi-level architecture of constitutional review in Southeast Europe (c).

66 The Constitutional Court of Bosnia and Herzegovina, for instance, has long suffered from its ill-defined competences, whereas Kosovo's constitutional text provides a much more determinate basis for legal argument, see *Grewe/Riegner* (note 5), 44 et seq.

a) Doctrinal reconstructions: ECHR applicability, hierarchy, and effect of case law in domestic law

As the domestic application of the ECHR is in principle not regulated by the Convention itself, it falls to constitutional law to define the relationship between national courts and the ECtHR.[67] Unlike many older West European constitutional texts, the new or recently reformed constitutions of Southeast Europe explicitly regulate many of the relevant questions and thus construct explicit "interface norms" between constitutionalism within and beyond the nation state.[68] In this, they are often inspired by the interpretative work of more established constitutional courts, but also find innovative and more far-reaching textual solutions. The constitutions studied in this book are innovative in that they often explicitly single out the ECHR, and sometimes even ECtHR case law, to regulate its domestic status and interpretation separately from "ordinary" international law. In terms of the substance of this regulation, our authors largely confirm earlier scholarship which found that constitutional texts in the region are generally friendly towards the ECHR, sometimes even more friendly than those in Western Europe.[69]

More specifically, the relationship between constitutional courts and the ECtHR raises at least three distinct, but interrelated questions: namely, the Convention's applicability in domestic law, its hierarchical position, and the domestic effect of ECtHR decisions. Regarding applicability, the studied Southeast European constitutions all provide for the domestic application of the ECHR, as do most other Council of Europe members. Individuals can thus invoke Convention rights directly in domestic court proceedings. This also applies to Kosovo, which has not ratified the ECHR due to its still disputed international status, but whose constitution autonomously incorporates the Convention into domestic law.[70] As

67 The new pilot procedure operated by the ECtHR qualifies this situation, as it aims specifically at obliging domestic parliaments to legislate on systemic problems. This also affects the relationship between courts, as illustrated for instance by the Strasbourg requirement for legislation on an effective remedy against delays of justice, as discussed by *Pavlin*, in this volume.

68 On the importance of interface norms, see *Krisch* (note 25), 285 et seq.

69 *Pál Sonnevend*, International Human Rights Standards and the Constitutional Jurisprudence of Transition States in Central and Eastern Europe, ASIL Proceedings 96 (2002), 397.

70 Article 22 Constitution of Kosovo incorporates and gives direct effect to unratified human rights instruments, including the EHCR. For a discussion, see the contributions of *Botusharova* und *Pavlin*, in this volume, and *Visar Morina/Fisnik Korenica/Dren Doli*, The relationship between international law and national law in the case of Kosovo: A constitutional perspective, International Journal of Constitutional Law 9 (2011), 274. In the other states, the ECHR is applicable by transformation of the international treaty:

regards the hierarchical rank of the Convention in domestic law, all studied legal orders stipulate that the Convention enjoys supremacy at least over ordinary domestic legislation.[71] This is mostly understood as placing the ECHR at a "mezzanine" level between the constitution and ordinary law, as is the case in many longstanding Council of Europe members.[72] However, some authors argue that the applicable provisions should be construed to the effect that the Convention ranks on the same level as the constitution, a situation also found in a few established West European member states.[73]

The hierarchy issue is not a merely theoretical question, but is relevant for the third aspect of the relationship between the courts, namely the effect of ECtHR decisions in domestic law. As regards individual Strasbourg decisions directly addressed to Southeast European states, constitutional courts generally enforce these decisions, but at times meet the resistance of ordinary courts.[74] Beyond individual decisions, however, Southeast European constitutions and constitutional courts take different positions when it comes to the *erga omnes* effect of ECtHR case law. In most legal orders, including the ones in Kosovo and Serbia, the constitutional courts are obliged to follow the interpretation of the ECtHR when ap-

Arts. 16 para. 2, 18 para. 2 in Serbia; Art. 5 in Albania; Art. 5 of the 1989 Hungarian Constitution.

71 In Kosovo (Article 22), Serbia (Article 194 para. 4 and 5) and Albania (Article 116, 122 para. 2), this derives from the Constitutional text, whereas in Hungary it could only be based on the Constitutional Court Act until recently. Whether the entry into force of the new Basic Law will change this, will depend on the interpretation of the new Basic Law, see *Sonnvened*, in this volume, part IV.

72 *Marko* (note 9), 448; *Grewe/Riegner* (note 5), 51 et seq. Similar solutions are found in Switzerland, Belgium and Spain, while a formally different solution is adopted e.g. in Germany, where the Convention enjoys the rank of an ordinary statute, but influences the interpretation of constitutional fundamental rights provisions, see *Frank Hoffmeister*, Germany: Status of European Convention on Human Rights in Domestic Law, International Journal of Constitutional Law 4 (2006), 722.

73 *Botusharova*, in this volume, part II.2; *Zaganjori*, in this volume, part. II.3, based on Art. 17 para. 2 of the Constitution of Albania. This also corresponds to the position of the Constitutional Court of Bosnia and Herzegovina, cf. *Grewe/Riegner* (note 5), 49 et seq. For similar solutions in the Netherlands and Austria, see e.g. *Peter Van Dijk/Fried van Hoof/Arjen van Rijn/Leo Zwaak* (eds.), Theory and Practice of the European Convention on Human Rights, 4th. ed., 2006, 27.

74 They do so by quashing last instance judgments, by remanding them back to the ordinary courts for reassessment, or by ordering the re-opening of proceedings, if need be in analogous application of existing legislative provisions, see *Zaganjori*, in this volume, part II.6; *Hadzi-Vidanovic*, in this volume, part IV.2; *Sonnevend*, in this volume, part II.2. More skeptical for other states in the region: *Dia Anganostou/Yonko Grozev*, Human Rights Litigation and Restrictive State Implementation of Strasbourg Court Judgments: The Case of Ethnic Minorities from Southeast Europe, European Public Law 16 (2010), 401.

plying the Convention itself in domestic law.[75] Beyond this, the picture is mixed: the Court in Hungary has so far refused to interpret domestic fundamental rights in light of Convention jurisprudence. Some other constitutions explicitly accord Convention case law a far-reaching interpretive function *erga omnes*: Article 53 of the Kosovo Constitution stipulates that all fundamental rights, including the domestic catalogue of rights enshrined in the Constitution, "must be interpreted consistent with" ECtHR case law. The Albanian Constitutional Court has adopted a similar practice. This technique of Convention-conform constitutional interpretation seems to be inspired by, but goes even beyond, the approach in other Council of Europe members such as Germany, where courts are required to "take into account" Convention jurisprudence when interpreting domestic fundamental rights catalogues.[76] In sum, the countries represented in this book display a clear normative commitment to Council of Europe standards, which differs in intensity but puts all constitutional orders in close connection and interaction with the common European legal space.

b) Empirical observations: The complexities of implementation

Beyond the law on the books, however, the practical implementation of Strasbourg standards is another matter. In the actual practice of the constitutional courts, different patterns of Convention use emerge. Most of the courts at least invoke the Convention fairly regularly, and also refer to Strasbourg case law to an increasing extent. This qualifies some earlier research, which found reference to international instruments and case law still to be the exception in the region.[77] Yet, it remains true that even where such reference is made, it usually does not determine the matter alone, and some courts are more enthusiastic than others in effectively bringing the Convention to live in their respective legal orders.

At one end of the spectrum, the Constitutional Court of Kosovo seems to make the most of the Convention-friendly framework. It uses Strasbourg standards as a constant normative orientation, interestingly not only in substantive rights interpretation, but also when assessing the admissibility of individual constitutional complaints before the Constitutional Court. As a result, the non-

75 Art. 53 Constitution of Kosovo; Art. 18 para. 3 in Serbia. In Hungary and Albania, this is a matter of constitutional interpretation, see *Sonnevend*, in this volume, part III.2, and *Zaganjori*, in this volume, *passim*, on this and the following.

76 On the situation in Germany, see *Hartwig* (note 18). Cf. also Article 10 para. 2 of the Constitution of Spain; UK Human Rights Act 1998, Sec. 2; Article 20 of Romanian Constitution, which is interpreted to carry an obligation to follow ECtHR case law, cf. *Sonnevend* (note 69).

77 *Sonnevend* (note 69), with regard to the whole of Eastern and Central Europe.

member state Kosovo paradoxically presently boasts one of the most enthusiastic constitutional courts in Southeast Europe when it comes to the *erga omnes* use of Convention jurisprudence. Among the states already members of the Council of Europe, the practice in Albania also seems to be shaped by rather intense Convention use, namely when it comes to due process control of ordinary court proceedings. Elsewhere, the appeal of European standards is less pronounced, and courts are more hesitant in their reception. In Hungary, the Constitutional Court does not regard Strasbourg case law as an orientation for the interpretation of the Constitution, and recent ECtHR rulings against Hungary had only a "minor impact" on legal practice.[78] In Serbia, a closer empirical look reveals an even more mixed picture: if the surveys cited in the contribution by Hadzi-Vidanovic are a valid indicator for popular attitudes, then there still is a widespread perception that human rights, and the courts tasked with their implementation, are rather instruments of the smart and the powerful than a source of legal protection for ordinary citizens. In light of these attitudes, Convention-friendly black letter law remains insufficient and will not ensure implementation on the ground unless legal education, legal attitudes and political mentalities change. This is recognized by all contributors to this book, who, while clearly desiring their states to be part of the European constitutional project, do note the difficulties in keeping human rights and fundamental liberties alive in the "in the hearts and minds of men and women".[79]

The conclusion that emerges is that generally favourable textual frameworks should not belie the fact that in practice, constitutional courts in Southeast Europe still position themselves at different places on the spectrum between open statehood and national sovereignty, between new national and post-national constitutionalism.[80] This emphasizes the importance of legal culture and contextual factors, as identified in the earlier mapping exercise. The presence of international judges in hybrid courts may increase the capacity and sensitivity of the institution in terms of Convention use, and the Court in Kosovo initially benefitted from intense international supervision. In addition, in ethnically divided societies European standards may also be a convenient neutral point of reference in the absence of a strong common political identity. Where more homogenous and nationally oriented political identities exist in the context of less internationalized constitutionalism, the use of European standards depends more on the continuing

78 *Kovács/Tóth* (note 40), 202.

79 Judge Learned Hand, Spirit of Liberty speech, 1944, quoted after Schwartz (note 31). On the problems of implementation, see *Hasani*, in this volume, part II.1; *Botusharova*, in this volume, part III.1; *Hadzi-Vidanovic*, in this volume, part IV; *Anganostou/Grozev* (note 74), and *supra*, note 29.

80 On "post-national" constitutionalism, see *Krisch* (note 25), 27 et seq.

appeal of the EU integration perspective, as seen in Albania on the one hand and Hungary on the other, with Serbia probably being somewhere in between the two. In sum, Hadzi-Vidanovic aptly sums up the lessons learned when he concludes that "formalities of law are not sufficient barriers to or safeguards for [human rights] implementation in the domestic legal systems. No provision can prevent their advance if there is a sincere adherence to the idea of human rights, just as no provision can guarantee their sensible protection if human rights are seen as alien ideology."[81]

c) Southeast Europe's constitutional courts in the multi-level architecture of European fundamental rights protection

A last aspect concerns the place of domestic constitutional courts in the European multi-level architecture of fundamental rights protection and composite constitutional justice. Most of our authors see the Convention and its domestic application essentially as an instrument to approximate Southeast European legal orders to the European legal space. Most constitutional courts increasingly share this perception. In this view, the relationship between domestic constitutional courts and the ECtHR is essentially one of reception, in which domestic courts function as conduits channelling international constitutional values and standards into domestic systems.[82] As long as this does not involve contestation on the part of domestic courts, this would point towards the thesis of multi-level constitutionalization of the Convention system rather than legal pluralism. On the one hand, such a constitutionalization would subject constitutional courts to Strasbourg's standards. On the other hand, reliance on Strasbourg standards may increase constitutional court authority in domestic settings where European values have strong popular appeal. Where such domestic appeal is lacking, European courts may at least complement domestic checks and balances, even though they certainly cannot replace them altogether.

Besides the reception of European standards, domestic constitutional courts, including the ones from Southeast Europe, have however more active roles to play in the European multi-level system of composite constitutional justice. Domestic constitutional courts all over Europe are implicated in transnational judicial dialogues, horizontally among national institutions, but also with regard to the European courts. The latter dialogue is not purely vertical, but draws on con-

81 *Hadzi-Vidanovic*, in this volume, part V.

82 *Nancy Maveety/Anke Grosskopf*, "Constrained" Constitutional Courts as Conduits for Democratic Consolidation, Law and Society Review 38 (2004), 463.

tributions from both levels. And Southeast Europe is not silent in that dialogue: courts equally decide on issues of general relevance, such as the wearing of headscarves in school, or access to justice against measures implementing targeted UN Security Council sanctions.[83] Conversely, when applying the margin of appreciation doctrine or interpreting Convention rights, the ECtHR looks closely for common ground in domestic constitutional jurisprudence, not only in Western Europe.[84] Finally, many domestic constitutional courts practice a reasonably context-sensitive form of reception. This does not mean selective reception at will, but rather describes a legitimate reaction if, and only if, Strasbourg case law is in itself inconsistent, or if horizontal and multi-polar rights collisions require a wider margin of appreciation for the complex balancing of several Convention rights.[85] For specifically in the latter cases, the reconciliation of competing fundamental rights claims remains the primary responsibility of democratically elected legislatures, and the multi-level system of constitutional adjudication must still be squared with basic tenets of democratic governance.[86] The aspect of democratic legitimacy brings us to some concluding remarks regarding the – closely linked – issues of the future and the legitimacy of constitutional justice in transition.

V. The future and legitimacy of constitutional justice in Southeast Europe

The research in this book indicates that a second wave of constitutional justice is sweeping across Southeast Europe. At the same time, the first wave has met a breakwater in Hungary, with an open outcome. For a conclusion, this raises questions regarding the future of constitutional justice in the region (1.), which is intrinsically linked to its legitimacy (2.).

83 Cf. *Botusharova*, in this volume, part IV.2.a), for the treatment of the headscarf in the Kosovo Constitutional Court's case law. Cf. *Zaganjori*, in this volume, part III.3.b), for the handling of targeted sanctions in a case of the Albanian Constitutional Court that involved an applicant equally implicated in the Kadi-cases before the European Court of Justice (cf. *Kadi and Al Barakaat International Foundation v. Council and Commission,* C-402/05 P and C-415/05 P, 3 September 2008).

84 *Bjorge* (note 21), 10 et seq.

85 On the problems with the domestic reception of international human rights law, see *Sonnevend* (note 69), 398. On balancing problems and multi-polar rights collisions, see *Wahl* (note 5), 490. On the discussion about conditions of a potential departure from Convention jurisprudence, see *Hadzi-Vidanovic*, in this volume, III.2; *Bjorge* (note 21), 14 et seq.

86 On the primary role of the legislator in the resolution of rights collisions, see *Christoph Möllers*, Gewaltengliederung. Legitimation und Dogmatik im nationalen und internationalen Rechtsvergleich, 2005, 60ff., 156.

1. Scenarios and determinants for the evolution of constitutional justice

From the perspective of the second wave, it seems tempting to look at the "models" in Hungary and Germany to compare longer-term developments and identify some determinants for success and failure in the respective circumstances. The two courts evidence two different scenarios: in Germany, after an early period of prudent yet sustained self-assertion, the *Bundesverfassungsgericht* has acquired an almost unchallenged authority now lasting decades. In Hungary, the Sólyom court became a powerful institution and a motor of transformation in its first decade, but after its second could not sustain its authority against a hostile parliamentary supermajority. This may only be a temporary backlash, but the German court never experienced a comparable set-back.[87]

Explaining these divergences is complex, but one may draw some indication from earlier comparative research which has identified some general determinants of constitutional court success and failure in terms of its authority. They include, *inter alia*, the overall political context and general ease of the transition, political culture and party systems, other available checks and balances within the political system, public support from domestic allies and its interplay with international audiences.[88] Other factors cited are the institutional design of the court, convincingly argued impartial decisions, adept leadership by eminent justices and a politically prudent judicial strategy.[89]

These factors have different explanatory force in different contexts, and are certainly not a ready-made recipe for the second wave of constitutional justice in Southeast Europe. Yet with the benefit of hindsight, they go some way to explaining different trajectories in Germany and Hungary.[90] In post-war Germany, the fledgling court could draw on the democratic Weimar tradition and established its authority in a period of rapid economic recovery under the watchful

87 For a detailed comparison of the development trajectories of the two courts and their determinants, see *Boulanger* (note 4), 12 et seq. For a recent critical account of the German Constitutional Court's development and jurisprudence, see *Markus Jestaedt/Oliver Lepsius/Christoph Möllers*, Das entgrenzte Gericht, 2011.

88 *Martin Shapiro*, Some Conditions for the Success of Constitutional Courts: Lessons from the US Experience, in: Sadurski (note 3), 37; *Schwartz* (note 31), 111 et seq.; *Ethan Klingsberg*, Judicial review and Hungary's transition from communism to democracy, 1992, 137.

89 *Manfred Baldus*, Frühe Machtkämpfe - Zu den historischen Gründen der Autorität des Bundesverfassungsgerichts, in: Thomas Henne/Arne Riedlinger (eds.), Das „Lüth"-Urteil in (rechts)historischer Sicht, 2005, 237; *Schwartz* (note 31), 113; *Brunner* (note 60), 81.

90 On the following, *Boulanger* (note 4), 13 et seq; *Kovács/Tóth* (note 40), 185 et seq.; *Richard Häußler*, Der Konflikt zwischen Bundesverfassungsgericht und politischer Führung. Ein Beitrag zu Geschichte und Rechtsstellung des Bundesverfassungsgerichts, 1994.

eyes of democratic occupying powers, soon complemented by strong domestic allies within the strong horizontal and vertical separation of powers in the federal and bicameral system of government. In contrast, the Hungarian Court, emerging from decades of authoritarianism in 1989, was drawn into the hefty political struggles that went with the difficult transition towards market economy and that resurged with the severe financial crisis starting in 2008. After EU accession, it lost the attention of many international audiences and ended up being the only counterweight against parliamentary majorities in the strongly centralized and unicameral system of government. Some observers add that successful constitutional courts, such as the one in Germany, took time to build up institutional authority and first aligned weaker players such as ordinary courts before they intensely confronted political majorities. Looking at Hungary with the benefit of hindsight, the Sólyom court may thus have wanted too much too fast.[91]

2. The legitimacy of constitutional justice in transition

Many of the considerations about the future of constitutional justice go back to one overarching normative question: namely, the institutional legitimacy constitutional courts enjoy within the respective democratic system of separation of powers.[92] This legitimacy, both in its sociological and normative dimension, is intrinsically linked to the democratic theory preferred by the relevant actors and audiences. Constitutional courts may enjoy sufficient functional legitimacy if they manage to appear as innocent guardians of the constitutional text, as neutral arbiters sustaining the separation of powers and federalism, or as institutional remedy for the representational deficits of electoral democracy.[93] Yet their legitimacy looks more precarious if emphasis is placed on the counter-majoritarian difficulties of their decisions, on judicial "activism" based on subjective preferences of unaccountable judges, or on the (self-)incapacitation of the political sys-

91 *Boulanger* (note 4), 19. Judging with hindsight is however easier than it is for judges to walk the fine line between *Hadzi-Vidanovic's* call for "courage [...] to refuse to side too often with ministers and other governmental officials" (in this volume, part I) and *Paczolay's* realization that judges "cannot distract themselves from the processes of the larger political environment in which they have to act, survive, and fulfil their proper task" (in this volume, part IV.2). See also *Shapiro* (note 88) for the US-Supreme Court that amassed political capital even for more than 100 years before it really struck.

92 Legitimacy issues were beyond the intended scope of research in the contributions, but feature implicitly as legal-theoretical reflections on the nature of constitutional justice, as distinct from the judicial branch, in the separation of powers doctrine, see *Hasani*, in this volume, part IV.1; *Čukalovič*, in this volume, part II.2.

93 *Oliver Lembcke*, Hüter der Verfassung, 2007; *John Hart Ely*, Democracy and Distrust, 1980; *Shapiro* (note 88); *Kelsen* (note 14).

tem displacing the responsibility to make difficult policy choices.[94] This legitimacy controversy is prominent in the common law world and also present in continental European discourse, but in Germany it never led to serious political challenges to the Constitutional Court's authority.

The classical legitimacy debate is mirrored in the discussions about the democratic credentials of constitutional courts in post-communist Europe. On the one hand, constitutional courts were introduced to promote democratic consolidation in the first place: they should sustain newly democratic procedures, help establish a system of representative institutions and political parties, and protect individual rights important for democratic deliberation.[95] Some even considered constitutional courts as "more democratic than parliaments" in the special circumstances of "transitional justice".[96] On the other hand, skeptics criticized that the politically unaccountable constitutional courts interfered with economic policy making better left to the other branches, and deplored that the courts practiced a form of judicial paternalism detrimental to the development of democratic culture in the long run.[97]

There is surprisingly little empirical evidence to support either claim, also with regard to Southeast Europe.[98] Studies of the German "model" attest the court a positive influence on democratization in post-war Germany, and democratic criticisms of constitutional justice were never as strong as elsewhere.[99] In Hungary, the Court drew criticism namely for its "activism" in economic and

94 *Robert Dahl*, Democracy and its Critics, 1989, 187 et seq.; *Karsten Fricke*, Zur Kritik der Staats- und Verfassungsgerichtsbarkeit, 1995; *Mark Tushnet*, Taking the Constitution away from the Court, 1999; *Ran Hirschl*, Towards Juristocracy, 2004; *Jeremy Waldron*, The Core of the Case Against Judicial Review, Yale Law Journal 115 (2006), 1346.

95 *Brun-Otto Bryde*, Die Rolle der Verfassungsgerichtsbarkeit in Umbruchsituationen, in: Joachim Hesse/Gunnar Folke Schuppert/Katharina Harms (eds.), Verfassungsrecht und Verfassungspolitik in Umbruchsituationen, 1999, 197.

96 *Kim Scheppele*, Democracy by Judiciary (Or Why Courts Can Sometimes Be More Democratic than Parliaments), in: Adam Czarnota/Martin Krygier/Wojciech Sadurski (eds.), Rethinking the Rule of Law after Communism, 2005, 26; *Ruti Teitel*, Transitional Justice, 2000, 191 et seq.

97 *Wojciech Sadurski*, Constitutional Courts, Individual Rights, and the Problem of Judicial Activism in Postcommunist Central Europe, in: Jiri Priban/Pauline Robert/James Young (eds.), Systems of Justice in Transition, 2003, 1. For the further criticisms, see *supra*, note 44.

98 Critics who argue that constitutional courts have a detrimental effect on democracy do not provide supporting empirical evidence, but neither do those who claim the opposite, cf. *Boulanger* (note 4), 2. See generally *Lee Epstein/Jack Knight/Olga Shvetsova*, The Role of Constitutional Courts in the Establishment and Maintenance of Democratic Systems of Government, Law and Society Review 35 (2001), 117.

99 *Kneip* (note 17); *Brun-Otto Bryde*, Der Beitrag des Bundesverfassungsgerichts zur Demokratisierung der Bundesrepublik, in: Robert van Ooyen/Martin Möllers (eds.), Das Bundesverfassungsgericht im politischen System, 2006, 321.

social policy, and one of the main arguments brought forward to justify the curtailment of its powers was democratic self-determination:[100] whereas early transition needed an activist court to purge the legal order, so the argument ran, it was now time to revert to true democracy, privileging the will of the parliament and the people over the will of unelected judges.[101]

While such a view is sometimes echoed in democratic theory, it does reflect a very specific and narrow understanding of majoritarian democracy. This understanding not only ignores classical justifications of constitutional review based the protection of fundamental rights against the tyranny of the majority. It also disregards the democracy-enabling and -enhancing function of constitutional justice. Even advocates of majoritarian democracy recognize the need for independent checks and balances to sustain the separation of powers, preserve the democratic process and protect free public deliberation.[102] These arguments hardly depend on the stage of transition or regional specificities. Other justifications seem even more valid under the circumstances of present-day Southeast Europe. We know by now that electoral democracy alone hardly guarantees equal political representation of all societal interests. Constitutional courts make marginalized voices heard in a political process that would otherwise not listen.[103] This is true in every democracy, but becomes particularly relevant in periods of democratic consolidation where the political party system and other channels of democratic feedback may still be deficient. Such initial deficits are not unlikely in a young democracy like Kosovo or in Serbia which embraced political pluralism only recently.[104]

The same argument goes even further in ethnically diverse societies where political mobilization runs along ethnic lines, as is the case in Kosovo, but also with regard to minorities in Serbia, Hungary and other states in the region. In such circumstances, unchecked majority rule may not only permanently disen-

100 See only *András Sajó*, How the Rule of Law Killed Hungarian Welfare Reform, East European Constitutional Review 5 (1996), 31.

101 Cf. *Boulanger* (note 4). See for instance the statement by the Hungarian Minister of Justice, *Tibor Navracsics*, in an interview of 5 November 2011, quoted at www.origo.hu (retrieved 29 January 2012).

102 On post-communist Europe, see *Sarah Wright Sheive*, Central and Eastern European constitutional courts and the anti-majoritarian objection to judicial review, Law and Policy in International Business (1995), 1201. On legitimizing reasons for constitutional justice in general, see *Möllers* (note 86); *Shapiro* (note 88); *Bryde* (note 99).

103 *Carlos Nino*, The Constitution of Deliberative Democracy, 1996; *Ely* (note 93).

104 *Thorsten Gromes*, Demokratisierung trotz fehlender Voraussetzungen? Bosnien und Herzegowina, Kosovo und Makedonien im Vergleich, Zeitschrift für Vergleichende Politikwissenschaft (2012), forthcoming. *McKinna* (note 29); *Aaron Presnall*, Which Way the Wind Blows. Democracy Promotion and International Actors in Serbia, Democratization 16 (2009), 661.

franchise minorities, but may eventually lead to the disintegration of the society or even the entire state. In light of this danger, many of the new constitutions in ethnically diverse Southeast Europe establish mechanisms of consociation and affirmative action to ensure minority participation in state and society. These arrangements are regarded as an integral part and defining feature of their very democratic identity.[105] If democracy is defined in this way precisely by this inclusive nature, and if constitutional courts protect precisely these integrative arrangements, then constitutional review does not diminish, but enables democratic self-determination.

If understood and practiced in this way, constitutional justice may not exactly be more democratic than parliaments – but constitutional courts can arguably be the most democratic of the three types of courts studied in this book. Only they carry the uniquely legitimate authority generated by their democracy-enabling function within the nation state. Hence, they are also important hinges for the transmission of legitimacy in the dynamics of court interaction. After all, the multi-level judicial architecture of Europe is not only a system of adjudication, but also a system of mutual legitimation in which courts collectively develop and legitimize the standards they will eventually enforce and be subjected to.[106]

In these processes of mutual influence and legitimation, comparative constitutional law has an important double role to play. Firstly, inquiries into constitutional justice beyond familiar geographies can unearth new contributions to the common European legal space and thus deepen the understanding of multi-level constitutionalism in Europe. And secondly, conducting such research may demonstrate and mobilize European commitment to and support for legitimate forms of constitutional justice in democratic transition states – in Southeast Europe and beyond.[107]

105 Namely in Kosovo and Bosnia Herzegovina, cf. *Grewe/Riegner* (note 5); *Doli/Korenica* (note 9). On Macedonia, *Marko* (note 38). Generally, *Sujit Choudhry* (ed.), Constitutional Design for Divided Societies, 2008.

106 *Bjorge* (note 21), 31; *Wahl* (note 5), 492; *Krisch* (note 25).

107 See the appeal by *Kovács/Tóth* (note 40), 203: "The future of the Hungarian constitutionalism, however, depends [also on the] commitment of European societies."

Constitutionalism in Kosovo and the Relationship between Constitutional Justice and the Supreme Court

*Enver Hasani**

Contents

I. Introduction

Constitutional Courts in the former communist countries have been instruments of change following the collapse of communism. Their establishment and operation proved to be very useful in promoting the rule of law and constitutionalism. Their establishment, however, also proved to be a source of tension between them and the ordinary courts of higher instance. In some cases, it was the legal and constitutional framework that stood behind this tension, but in most cases it was the very legal culture and the local histories that accounted for that tension. Kosovo and its Constitutional Court, the youngest in Europe, are not an exception to this. This paper thus discusses the relationship between the Constitutional Court of Kosovo and the Supreme Court of Kosovo. The discussion is based on cases from both Courts as well as on the constitutional and legal frameworks regulating this relationship. As will be seen, this relationship has still been less tense than elsewhere, despite the large number of judgments of the Supreme Court quashed by the Constitutional Court.

In order to achieve the main goal of the paper, we devote considerable attention to the history and practice of constitutionalism and its relevance for Kosovo in part II of this paper. We hope that we thereby can assist in establishing a firm position for Kosovo among the newly established constitutional democracies of Europe. The main reason for this approach is the fact that the Constitution of Kosovo is modeled upon the Western continental constitutional and legal tradition, first and foremost the tradition of post-1945 Germany based on the *Grundgesetz*, the Basic Law, promulgated on 23 May 1949. Part III then describes the development and current features of constitutional justice in Kosovo. Against this background, part IV discusses the relationship between the Constitutional Court and the Supreme Court of Kosovo, notably in light of the case law. We do not wish to come to any final conclusions on the matter in this paper, but rather aim at the promotion of a debate as to the nature of the relationship of the two courts.

II. Constitutionalism and its relevance for Kosovo

The idea of judicial review is part and parcel of the struggle for constitutionalism, albeit the latter is older than the former. While its beginnings stretch as far back as the Middle Ages[1], the first implementation of judicial review seems to

* President of the Constitutional Court of Kosovo and Professor at the University of Pristina in Kosovo.

1 For a thorough theoretical analysis and the history of the phenomenon of constitutionalism, see *Nannerl O. Keohane*, Claude de Syessel and Sixteenth Century Constitutional-

have happened only in 1803 in the United States of America in the famous case *Marbury v. Madison.* This was a product of the advent of modernity and the belief that "enlightenment", "reason" and the belief in progress were not the domain or reserve of literature and art, but also of other fields of human life and work, such as the judiciary. Seen from this perspective, judicial review is an elite type of institution, while constitutionalism belongs to a middle class as an instrument of the struggle to oppose rulers since medieval times.[2] This does not mean, however, that in particular cases the emergence of a judicial review and constitutionalism are conditioned by the passing of a given society through Enlightenment and the existence of a middle class as such. Kosovo, as part of former Yugoslavia, belonged to that area of Europe which was not at the core of the enlightenment movement and lacked a middle class by the time it established its own Constitutional Court in 2009, following the collapse of the Milosevic-led Serbian regime in Kosovo in June 1999.

In addition to this difference between constitutionalism and judicial review in terms of the latter's appearance on the historical stage, there is one more difference between these two phenomena reflecting deeper and more profound features. That difference is related to the very nature and the function of constitutionalism and judicial review. As to the former, judicial review is an institution whose main function is judicial implementation of the constitution, while constitutionalism is an ideal whose fulfillment requires normative judgments relating to three of its main characteristics: rule of law; limitations of power; and, human rights and fundamental freedoms. These three characteristics contained in the concept of constitutionalism render it an ideal whose real meaning is determined by normative and value judgments of a society in a given time and space. Thus, judicial review is a mechanism designed to protect the constitution and its text with or without the context of constitutionalism as an ideal of the liberal West, because normative contents and value judgments regarding the scope and form of constitutionalism in a society depend upon the mindset of a given time and space.

Kosovo and former Yugoslav territories are a case in point in this regard. While Kosovo had its constitutional court since the mid-seventies of the last century, designed to protect the text of the 1974 communist Constitution, the liberal ideal of constitutionalism as a set of normative and value judgments on matters

ism in France, in: J. Roland Penoch/John W. Chapman (eds.), Constitutionalism, 1979, 47-83; *Bruno Aguilera*, Law as Limit to Power – The Origins of the Rule of Law in the European Legal Tradition, in: Susana Galera (ed.), Judicial Review. A Comparative Analysis Inside the European Legal System, 2010, 15-35.

2 Cf. more on this in *Norman Dorsen/Michael Rosenfeld/Andras Sajo/Susanne Baer* (eds.), Comparative Constitutionalism: Cases and Materials, 2003, 1-98 at 14.

regarding the rule of law, separation of powers, limits on the exercise of political powers and respect for human rights were entirely absent from it and were confined to the academic world only. To evaluate as to how far this has changed today, we will first address the aforementioned three core values underlying constitutionalism, before turning to constitutional justice in Kosovo today.

1. Rule of law

Rule of law throughout history has had different meanings in various legal traditions. This is seen from the very notion that is used to denote the American "rule of law" concept and distinguish it from the German "Rechtsstaat" and the French "État de droit".[3] However, the concept under discussion has, despite its different meanings in various legal cultures, some minimal content.[4] In its "thin" version, rule of law requires a fair and honest rule through general prospective norms which enjoy substantial legal predictability requiring them to be published in advance so that the public is aware of their existence, clear separations between the legislative, executive and judicial powers and, finally, wide support for the proposition that no one is above the law. Some authors include only the principle of legality and the independence of the judiciary and see it as a situation not necessarily dependent on the prevalence of the liberal ideology of constitutionalism.[5] This, however, is not sufficient for a constitutional democracy to exist; it has more requirements and is more demanding than that alone. In its "thicker" version, rule of law has to do with legitimacy of the rule. In order to be legitimate, rule of law has to include the components of democratic accountability, procedural fairness and a substantive support for liberal values (such are the values of justice and the independence of judiciary, equality, freedom, protection of minorities, and so on).[6]

3 Cf. *Pietro Costa/Danilo Zolo* (eds.), The Rule of Law. History, Theory and Criticism, 2010, 153-319.

4 Some authors define these as "thin" and "thick" meanings of the rule of law. Cf. *Jane Stromseth/David Wippman/Rosa Brooks*, Can Might Make Rights? Building the Rule of Law After Military Interventions, 2006, 56-84, at 70-71.

5 *Jan-Eric Lane*, Constitutions and Political Theory, 2011, 90-112.

6 Cf. more on this in *Vicki C. Jackson*, Constitutional Engagement in a Transitional Era, 2010, 1-102, 254-285, especially at 259-261, where the author discusses the role of international community in legitimizing of domestic constitutions as far as the rule of law in its "thicker" sense, as discussed in this paper, is concerned. As for the judiciary, there is a fundamental consensus among Western democracies that in any event the judiciary should be impartial and independent from, in particular, government interference. Cf. *Aalt Willem Heringa/Philip Kiiver*, Constitutions Compared. An Introduction to Comparative Constitutional Law, 2009, 21-23, 145-170.

Both versions of the rule of law have been enshrined in the Constitution of the Republic of Kosovo and, not without good reason, they are foreseen in Chapter I (Basic Provisions). Throughout this Chapter, the rule of law is mentioned twice (Art. 3 and 7), which is to be understood in its both meanings as stated above. This mentioning of the concept of the rule of law is done in the context of the type and form of the public authority in Kosovo, equality before the law, the separation of powers, the independence of the judiciary and, in the context of other constitutional values of western liberal democracies.

Outside these two above-noted traditional meanings of the rule of law, there is a third meaning which has been created by scholars following the collapse of communism: the rule of law in transition. As such, this concept differs from the traditional meanings discussed above. As Ruti Teitel, the founder of this concept put it: "[I]n societies in transition law is caught between the past and the future, between the backward-looking and forward-looking, between retrospective and prospective".[7] This further means that in these transitional societies, a conception of justice emerges that is contextualized and partial: it is constituted by and constitutive of the transition.[8] In other words, in this case we face a unique challenge to the rule of law, especially its component of legal certainty and security. This is so because in transitional justice, constitutional and other general norms are new and are supposed to undo past wrongs, that is, the new legal infrastructure represents a legal response to the past. There are different legal responses to the past but they all have in common their goal of rebalancing the values of justice in times of transition. This different approach can be seen not only from the experiences in Europe, but also beyond e.g. in Argentina, Chile and Uruguay, where past state actions were reconceptualized and were not allowed to serve as a shield for gross violations of human rights of the past regimes. In a similar manner, Turkey with respect to the tragic events with its Armenian population recently had to approach the issue from a transitional justice perspective setting aside its own constitutional limitations. Turkey definitely recognizes that there was in the past massive violence committed against other non-Turkish nationalities living within Turkey.[9]

As for Kosovo, its Constitution clearly breaks with the past, but without any of its provisions foreseeing grounds for engagement in transitional-type of justice, excluding two provisions of the Ahtisaari Plan dealing with restitution of

7 *Ruti Teitel*, Transitional Rule of Law, in: Adam Czarnota/Martin Krygier/Wojciech Sadurski (eds.), Rethinking the Rule of Law After Communism, 2005, 279-294, at 279.

8 *Ibid.* 280.

9 Cf. more in *Ruti Teitel*, Transitional Justice and the Transformation of Constitutionalism, in: Tom Ginsburg/Rosalind Dixon (eds.), Comparative Constitutional Law, 2011, 57-76.

property.[10] Namely, Art. 1 (13) of Annex XII of the Ahtisaari Plan foresees a duty of Kosovo to enact a law on restitution, which has not been done yet. This provision is in furtherance of Art. 8 (5) of the General Provisions of the same document. This non-enactment by Kosovo of the Law on Restitution is a result of the specificities of transition taking place in Kosovo based on the Ahtisaari Plan, whereby the international community has been enjoying a huge leverage to influence the process of transition.[11]

The most universally accepted and general feature of all three meanings under discussion is that the key to implementing the rule of law is an independent judiciary. Without an independent judiciary there can be no discussion about the rule of law in all of its meanings mentioned above.[12] This can be seen more clearly in countries of transition, including Kosovo. In almost all countries of the former Communist bloc, creating an independent judiciary has been a huge challenge. Inefficacy of the regular courts in these countries as a result of corruption and other bad practices proved to be a serious obstacle to the rule of law. It is for this reason that newly established constitutional courts in these countries have had to bear on their shoulders the brunt of transition.[13] Kosovo is not an exception. The latest Progress Report on Kosovo by the European Commission bears witness to this. It makes very clear that the independence of the judiciary in Kosovo is far from being what it should be and that a radical change is required in order for the judiciary of Kosovo to become an instrument of change and the very basis of the rule of law.[14]

10 The current Constitution of the Republic of Kosovo was adopted on 9 April 2008 and entered into force on 15 June 2008. It was based on the so-called Ahtisaari-Plan, which stands for the "Comprehensive Proposal for the Kosovo Status Settlement" of 2 February 2007. This document was meant to replace Resolution 1244 of the UN Security Council of 10 June 1999, establishing a UN Mission in Kosovo, known as UNMIK. Only Kosovar Albanians accepted the Ahtisaari-Plan, and the declaration of independence of Kosovo of 17 February 2008 is based on it. The Serbian side rejected it. This document is named after former President of Finland, Martti Ahtisaari, who led the peace talks that aimed at bringing an end to the undecided political status of Kosovo then still pending. For the international context of the Kosovo Constitution in general, and the Ahtisaari-Plan in particular, see the contribution of *Snezhana Botusharova*, in this volume.

11 Other former Communist countries, as opposed to the case of Kosovo, foresaw in their constitutions a clear legal basis for whole-sale restitution and other actions designed to remedy past wrongs, such as lustration measures. These measures were aimed at transitional justice, restoring the lost rights and liberties. However, they proved to be detrimental to the rule of law in these societies while in the phase of transition. Cf. more in *Csongor Kuti*, Post-Communist Restitution and the Rule of Law, 2009.

12 Cf. more in *Tom Bingham*, The Rule of Law, 2010, 171-174.

13 Cf. the eloquent study of this issue in *Herman Schwartz*, The Struggle for Constitutional Justice in Post-Communist Europe, 2002.

14 *European Commission*, Kosovo 2011 Progress Report, 12.10.2011, SEC (2011) 1207.

2. Limitations of power

Limitations on power, as the second characteristic of the ideal of constitutionalism, start with the so-called "mixed government". This was a first step in limiting the powers of the King in 17th century England. It was called "mixed government" because it was a mixture of a rule by the King, the Lords and the Commons, representing a mechanical division of powers but at the same time representing the decline of the English concept of the supreme and absolute parliamentary rule.[15] This form of the balance of powers emerged as a result of the reaction *ab intra* to the social forces leading, as a consequence, to a *de facto* limitation of the power in England at that time. As such, it represents the beginnings of the practice of the separation of powers to emerge later on in the United States of America. The limitations on power in the "mixed government" stem as much from the balance of forces within the government as from any specific constitutional provision.[16]

The forms of limited government are as diverse as the paths to limiting crude power: sometimes the power is limited via a constitution, sometimes through a *de facto* balance of powers. The limited government based on both constitution and the separation/division of powers as a mode of controlling and balancing power can also be termed constitutional government. However, constitutional government is more than this. It rests not only on the balanced powers based on a constitution: constitutional government is a form of limited government in which the constitution, together with the law and the other offices that are prescribed by it, provide the limits on, and approval of, every exercise of power. Thereby it is impossible for any officer to transgress the constitution without ceasing to hold power legitimately and potentially being removed from office.

Hobbes, Locke, Montesquieu, and their many followers developed theories of constitutional government, versions of which are now widely accepted as being

15 Cf. more on this in *M. J. C. Ville*, Constitutionalism and the Separation of Powers, 1998, 1-23; *Jeffrey Goldsworthy*, The Sovereignty of Parliament. History and Philosophy, 1999, 124-135.

16 In fact, it is worth noting that even the most savage and brutal systems, such as those led by Stalin and Hitler, or other despotic systems from ancient worlds, cannot be absolute because life itself and social forces around it create limits on every power, no matter how harsh it might be. What is discussed here has to do with the limits on power placed consciously by human action in their political dealings. It is in this sense that the term "limited government" is used, that is, as any form of government in which sovereign power is limited by law, constitution or instruments presenting checks and balances to its exercise. Cf. more on this, the eloquent study in three volumes by *S. E. Finer*, The History of Government Vol. I to III, 1999, especially Vol. I, 72-94, where the author develops a typology of power constraints based on how these constraints are made throughout human history.

both a true representation of political liberty, and the preferred way of exercising political power. This governmental power expresses not the will of those who wield it, but the rights of the citizens whom they govern. In other words, constitutional government requires that in addition to the separation/division of powers and the rule of law, the exercise of power is done through office. Fundamental to all these things is the citizen's ability to judicially challenge *ultra vires* acts of public authorities, together with procedural rules and guarantees that make legitimate powers discernible.[17]

Almost all modern states have written constitutions regulating the exercise of all power, and the Kosovo Constitution enshrines a formal separation of powers along the lines of a parliamentary democracy, reinforced by additional features of consociational democracy and minority protection. This distinguishes Kosovo's and most Western constitutions from other systems of government not based on a constitutionally formalized separation of powers, which is thus not constitutional government. Moreover, it is the field of human rights which is the key test for detecting as to whether constitutional government is being properly exercised or whether it is just a farce, a cover up for the illegitimate exercise of political power.

3. Human rights and fundamental freedoms

The third feature of constitutionalism is human rights and fundamental freedoms, which represent the very crux of the human struggle for constitutionalism. At the beginning, the idea and practice of human rights developed within national systems of sovereign states, starting with the famous Magna Charta (1215), the revolutionary documents of the USA and France, the eloquent American Declaration of Independence (4 July 1776) and the French Declaration of the Rights of Men and the Citizen (26 August 1789). Constitutional developments within states regarding the role and importance of human rights and fundamental freedoms were of two kinds: the first is a liberal approach as embraced by the United States which puts an emphasis on individual liberty vis-à-vis public authorities so that the latter is supposed to have as little say as possible in the life of the individual citizens, while the second one is a Western European one. It focuses, in addition to the vertical promotion and protection of human rights, on horizontal protection and promotion vis-à-vis other individuals qua neighbors and on their relationships that emerge as a result of living together.

17 Cf. more on this in *Friedrich A. Hayek*, The Constitution of Liberty, 1978.

Kosovo represents a combination of both, which is due to its tragic historical past where gross violations of human rights were a common practice. Thus, the Constitution of Kosovo contains two chapters regarding human rights. One is the second chapter (Arts. 21-56) containing general provisions on human rights. The second is chapter three that deals with the rights of Kosovo ethnic communities (Arts. 57-62). The second chapter is a classical approach to the issue of human rights and their protection as against public authorities, while the third chapter is meant to protect non-majority communities living in Kosovo, both at the vertical as well as at the horizontal level.[18]

In addition to these characteristics within national systems, there is another difference stemming from international political developments existing during the Cold War and afterwards. Those were the differences between the former communist world and the rest of the Western liberal world that were sanctioned in the Final Helsinki Act in 1975. This Act is interesting in that it posed a fundamental problem for the philosophy of human rights: are all rights really freedoms in the sense of being limitations on the acts of others? Or, are some rights also duties requiring the active provision of something not available without human efforts? The first list of rights, proposed by nations of the Western countries, followed the pattern of freedom – i.e., it consisted in a set of limitations on what the state might do to the citizens (e.g. arrest them arbitrarily, imprison them without trial, punish them for expression of personal views, etc.). The states of the former communist countries, followed by Third World countries, insisted that certain other rights should be added – notably the right to work (as well as other social and economic rights), which requires the state and other agencies to actively provide opportunities, and not merely to permit things to happen in the sense liberal democracies of the West fought for. This international rhetoric has continued since the adoption of the Universal Declaration on Human Rights (1948), both Pacts on Human Rights of 1966 and became reflected in all Constitutions of both sides of the East-West divide. In fact, the battle for human rights and fundamental freedoms during the Cold War was just another reflection of the prevailing spirit of constitutionalism in former communist and Third World countries counteracted by the liberal West.

Although the Cold War ended and communism collapsed, the liberal conception of universal application of human rights still faces dilemmas and problems that it encountered throughout most of the previous century. Transition to democracy of the former communist countries did not progress without serious

18 On additional human rights protection by incorporation of the European Convention of Human Rights into the Kosovo Constitution, see the contribution of *Snezhana Botusharova*, in this volume.

problems and the vacuum it left behind was filled with other nationalistic ideologies and practices equally hostile to human rights and their promotion. It should be noted, however, that almost all former communist countries accepted and fully inserted into their Constitutions the basic concept of human rights and freedoms, including viable mechanisms for their implementation modeled upon Western liberal standards. Specific chapters of these constitutions foresaw the basic provisions on human rights and fundamental freedoms and democracy and the rule of law. In the transition to democracy all of these constitutional provisions proved to be of the utmost importance. There is one human right, however, which seems to have commanded a universal reception when understood, and to have precipitated the transition from tyranny to constitutional government when upheld – the right to due process and to judicial independence which it requires.

III. Historical context and current features of constitutional justice in Kosovo

1. Historical developments and context

The Constitutional Court of Kosovo is the last institution of its kind established in Europe. By this I mean the Constitutional Court of the Republic of Kosovo. Kosovo had its own Constitutional Court during communist times from 1972 to 1989, when it was abolished by Milosevic and his regime alongside with the autonomy of Kosovo in general.[19] This means that in theory and from an historical point of view, constitutional justice of Kosovo falls in the second generation of this kind of justice established after the end of the Second World War. This type of justice, as we know it, makes a distinction between judicial and constitutional review. This system of review is also known as the Kelsenian model because it is based on a separate Constitutional Court dispensing constitutional justice and is separate from the ordinary judicial system composed of ordinary courts. Of course, the system invented by the Austrian lawyer *Hans Kelsen* has undergone substantial changes ever since it was proposed by him after World War I, both in form and in its very content. What remains the same, however, is the fact that constitutional justice is exercised by a separate court which is not part of the or-

19 Cf. more on constitutional developments in the former Yugoslavia since 1963 in *Jovan Gjorgjeviq,* E Drejta Kushtetuese, (Constitutional Law), Prishtine 1972, 75-114; *Dimitrije Kulic*, Ustavno Sudstvo u Svetu (Constitutional Justice in the World), Leskovac 1972, 157-190; *Miroslav Cerar*, Slovenia's Constitutional Court within the Separation of Power, in: Wojciech Sadurski (ed.), Constitutional Justice, East and West. Democratic Legitimacy and Constitutional Courts in Post-Communist Europe in a Comparative Perspective, 2002, 213-245 at 213, footnote 2.

dinary system. The central idea of Kelsenian constitutional justice is that the Constitutional Courts act more as a legislative institution than as a court.[20] Between 1918 and 1939, only Czechoslovakia (February 1920) and Austria (October 1920) had such institutions, and their work was very weak.[21]

It was only after World War II that constitutional justice took the lead and became a widespread phenomenon among Europeans: Constitutional Courts as proper deliberative institutions were established in Germany, Italy, and Austria. Afterwards they spread though Europe, Latin America and elsewhere. In the cases of Germany, Italy and Austria their primary goal was not only to help these countries detach themselves from their bitter past but also to re-model them alongside liberal democratic standards of constitutional democracy based on the rule of law, democracy and respect for human and minority rights. This trend that started after World War II spread rapidly after 1989 and the collapse of communism and the end of the Cold War.[22] It can be now freely said that the Kelsenian or European model of constitutional justice, that is, a model of separate courts dealing with constitutional justice, is the dominant model in the world no matter what large differences exist in the political systems of different States. Kosovo is no exception to this, as can be seen from the discussion below.

2. Constitutional justice under the 2008 Constitution

Established in January 2009, with its own Law No. 03/L - 121 on the Constitutional Court[23], the Constitutional Court of the Republic of Kosovo has a jurisdiction that is wider in scope than any other in the region of the Balkans: modeled upon the German Constitutional Court it has a jurisdiction almost over every aspect of the actions of public authority. The only competence that is not provided for is the bringing of an *actio popularis*. Beyond that, Article 113 of the Consti-

20 *Hans Kelsen*, Judicial Review of Legislation: A Comparative Study of the Austrian and the American Constitution, The Journal of Politics 4 (1942), 183-200.

21 In Czechoslovakia, for example, during its existence from 1920 to 1939, it reviewed only two laws. Cf. *Wojciech Sadurski*, Rights Before Courts in Post-Communist States of Central and Eastern Europe, 2005, 1-26.

22 See *Taylor Cole*, Three Constitutional Courts: A Comparison, The American Political Science Review 53 (1959), 963-984; *Christopher F. Zurn*, Deliberative Democracy and Its Institutions of Judicial Review, 2007, 253-341; *John Ferejohn/Pasquale Pasquino*, Constitutional Courts as Deliberative Institutions: Towards an Institutional Theory of Constitutional Justice, in: Wojciech Sadurski (ed.), Constitutional Justice, East and West, 2002, 21-36.

23 The Law was approved by the Assembly, dated 16 December 2008, and promulgated by the Decree of the President of the Republic of Kosovo, No. DL-070-2008, dated 30 December 2008.

tution gives the Constitutional Court jurisdiction, *inter alia,* over all sorts of abstract review of the constitutionality of legislation and other legal texts, *ex ante* and *ex post*[24], incidental/concrete control of constitutionality based on the action of any regular Court in Kosovo[25], conflict of jurisdiction among and between central authorities[26], protection in general of the rights of municipalities vis-à-vis central authorities[27], constitutional violations by the head of state[28], review of the constitutionality of a decision declaring a state of emergency and the proposed referendum[29], the validity of the parliamentary elections[30], and notably jurisdiction over individual constitutional complaints after exhaustion of other remedies.[31]

IV. The relationship between the Constitutional Court and the Supreme Court of Kosovo

Concrete or incidental constitutional review and the constitutional review undertaken by the Court based on an individual complaint are the two meeting points between the Supreme Court and the Constitutional Court.[32] The Constitutional Court reviews, based on its jurisdiction concerning individual complaints, many types of decisions issued by any public authority in Kosovo, including those of the Supreme Court. The relationship between these two Courts of Kosovo so far has been within the legal framework regulating their respective jurisdictions. No "war of the courts" has emerged in Kosovo, as it did for example in Italy in 1965

24 Art 113 para. 5 and 6 of the Constitution.
25 Art. 113 para. 8 of the Constitution. In some countries, such as Italy, Poland and Bulgaria, to mention a few of them, the Court can be activated only by highest instances of the regular courts.
26 Art 113 para. 3. point 1 of the Constitution.
27 Art 113 para. 4 of the Constitution.
28 Art 113 para. 6 of the Constitution.
29 Art 113 para. 3. point 2 and.3 of the Constitution.
30 Art 113 para. 3. point 5 of the Constitution.
31 Art 113 para. 7 of the Constitution.
32 So far, there has been only one case pending before the Constitutional Court of Kosovo which was initiated by the Supreme Court, that is, "The Request of the Supreme Court of Kosovo for the Review of Constitutionality of the Law No. 03/L- 139 on Expropriation, Arts. 35, 36, 37 and 38 of the Law", dated 17 January, 2011. The Request has to do with the constitutionality of the right to appeal decisions of the Supreme Court as is foreseen in the above-mentioned Articles of the Law No. 032/L-139 on Expropriation. The Supreme Court of Kosovo is the final judicial authority in Kosovo, yet this Law talks about the appeal against the decisions of the Supreme Court in much the same way as the regular appeals that can be exercised against the decisions of other regular courts of lower instance existing in the Kosovo legal system.

lasting until very recently[33], despite the fact that at the time of writing the Constitutional Court of Kosovo had quashed more than one hundred judgments of the Supreme Court of Kosovo. In addition, because of the professional and dedicated work of the Judges of both Courts, it seems that the clear legal framework of Kosovo, within which the two courts have been operating, leaves little room for misunderstanding between these two institutions.

1. The role and the position of the Supreme Court in the legal system of Kosovo

In the legal system of Kosovo there is a sharp and clear-cut division of labor between the Constitutional Court and the Supreme Court. The latter has, as its main task, to apply and implement the law in line with constitutional requirements, while the former has the duty to give a final interpretation of the provisions of the Constitution. This division of labor is reflected in the Constitution and other laws regulating the work of these two institutions. In fact, the form of the government in Kosovo, as foreseen by the Constitution, makes it clear that Kosovo "is a democratic Republic based on the principle of separation of powers and the checks and balances among them."[34] Art. 4 para. 5 of the Constitution stipulates that the "judicial power is unique and independent and is exercised by courts". In line with the general standard of the Kelsenian/European model, the Constitutional Court is not part of the judiciary but entirely separate from it and from any

33 This expression was used in the context of the relationship between the Italian Constitutional Court and the Court of Cassation, to describe this relationship, and later on to describe the same relationship within the Czech legal system. However, this relationship has been a general feature of the work of almost all constitutional and supreme courts of the former Communist societies. In these societies, Supreme and other High Courts declined to obey most of the time rulings of the Constitutional Courts or were overtly reluctant to follow the texts of their constitutions sticking to the application and interpretation of the ordinary laws instead. Cf. *Giancarlo Rolla/Tania Grappi*, Between Politics and the Law: The Development of Constitutional Review in Italy, in Wojciech Sadurski (ed.), Constitutional Justice, East and West, 2002, 143-149; *Roberto Bin/Giovanni Pirtruzzella*, Diritto Costituzionale, 2010, 424-479; *Roberto Scarcglia*, L' organizzazione giudizaria, in: Lucio Pegoraro/Antonio Reposo/Angelo Rinella/Roberto Scarciglia/Mauro Volpi (eds.), Diritto Costituzionale e Pubblico, 2005, 369-379; *Lucio Pegoraro*, Le garanzie costituzionali, in: Lucio Pegoraro/Antonio Reposo/Angelo Rinella/Roberto Scarciglia/ Mauro Volpi (eds.), Diritto Costituzionale e Pubblico, 416-484; *Gustavo Zagrebelsky*, La giustizia costituzionale, 1989, 73-98, 481-524; *Jiri Priban*, Judicial Power vs. Democratic Representation: The Culture of Constitutionalism and Human Rights in the Czech Legal System, in: Wojciech Sadurski (ed.), Constitutional Justice, East and West, 2002, 373-394; *Jean-Pierre Massias*, Droit Constitutional des Etats d'Europe de l'Est, 1999, 14-140, 421-563; *Schwartz* (note 13) 236-238.

34 Art. 4 of the Constitution, "Form of Government and Separation of Powers".

other power. Its duty is, as an independent organ of the Constitution, to protect constitutionality and make final interpretations of the Constitution. These general provisions are further operationalised in Chapter VII of the Constitution.[35]

The Constitution of Kosovo specifies the role of the Supreme Court in the same manner as other countries of Europe do in their constitutions: "The Supreme Court of Kosovo is the highest judicial authority"[36], while "its organization, function and jurisdiction, as well as that of other courts of general jurisdiction is regulated by law".[37] As far as the legal side of work of the Supreme Court is concerned, there are three laws regulating it. The law applicable during the first few years of the Kosovo Republic is the Law on Regular Courts of 1990.[38] This law has been applied since 1999 and based on the United Nations Mission in Kosovo (UNMIK) Regulation No. 1999/24 on the Law Applicable in Kosovo of 12 December 1999 (as amended by UNMIK Regulation No. 2000/59 of 2 October 2000), and remains in force to this date.[39] The second Law on Courts, passed by the Assembly of the Republic of Kosovo on 22 July 2010, shall enter into force on 1 January 2013.[40] Until then, the jurisdiction of the regular courts, including the Supreme Court of Kosovo, is regulated jointly by the previous two legal acts. According to them, the Supreme Court of Kosovo is competent and has jurisdiction, *grosso modo*, over similar issues as in other countries, such as:

- to decide on cases brought before it via extraordinary legal remedies;
- to decide on appeals against the decisions of the lower Courts;
- to decide on cases regarding the competence conflicts between lower courts;
- to judicially review administrative acts; and

35 Justice System: Art. 102 - 107 of the Constitution.

36 Art. 103 para. 2 of the Constitution.

37 Art. 103 para. 1 of the Constitution.

38 "Ligji për Gjykatat e Rregullta" ("Law on Regular Courts"), Gazeta Zyrtare e Krahinës Socialiste Autonome të Kosovës (Official Gazette of the Socialist Autonomous Province of Kosovo) Nr. 14, 17 April 1990.

39 According to these two UNMIK legislative acts, the law applicable in Kosovo after 10 June 1999 (end of the war in Kosovo), shall be the regulations promulgated by the Special Representative of the UN Secretary General and subsidiary instruments issued thereunder and the law in force in the territory of Kosovo on 22 March 1989. In case of a conflict, the regulations of UNMIK and subsidiary instruments issued thereunder shall take precedence. If a subject matter or situation is not covered by these laws in force in the territory of Kosovo on 22 March 1989 but is covered by another law in force in Kosovo after 22 March 1989 which is not discriminatory and which complies with "international human rights standards", such laws shall apply.

40 Law No. 03/L-199 on Courts of the Republic of Kosovo (22 July 2010). In Art. 43 ("entry into force"), this Law provides that as far as jurisdiction and the competence of the regular courts of Kosovo is concerned, it shall enter into force on 1 January 2013. For other provisions, its entry into force was 1 January 2011.

- to enact and pronounce common and general positions that aim at a unified and identical application of the law within the whole territory of Kosovo.[41]

2. The scope and extent of constitutional review of Supreme Court judgments

Out of 285 referrals brought before the Constitutional Court by June 2011, 170 or 59.64 per cent of them concern review of the Supreme Court decisions. Among them, 65 referrals belong to the so-called category of the "KEK Cases" to be discussed further below. Despite this large number of decisions of the Supreme Court reviewed by the Constitutional Court, there has not been any serious tension in the relationship between the two institutions. This tension has been common, on the other hand, in the dealings between higher courts and the Constitutional Courts in other European countries. In my view, there are two reasons for this state of affairs in Kosovo.

Firstly, out of this number of referrals, most of them have not been allowed, i.e. the Constitutional Court has not found any violation and has generally been in agreement with the findings of the Supreme Court, both as far as the facts and the law were concerned. The Constitutional Court has repeatedly stated that it is not a court of appeal, or a court of fourth instance in relation to the decisions taken by ordinary courts, including the Supreme Court. The Constitutional Court has further reiterated that it is the ordinary courts which are tasked with the duty of interpreting and applying the pertinent rules of both procedural and material law. So, the Court has not manifested any tendency to overstep its own jurisdiction, that is, it has been satisfied with the evaluation of "adjudicative facts" and law (both material and procedural) under which those facts are subsumed by ordinary courts, including the Supreme Court.

The second reason has to do with the fact that out of these cases relating to the judicial review of the decisions of the Supreme Court, the Constitutional Court has found violations of the constitutional rights of the applicants only in three of its judgments. In these cases, the Court has emphasised the above-noted general principle of subsidiarity, i.e. the principle that the Constitutional Court has a jurisdiction to enquire as to whether the ordinary court proceedings, including those conducted before the Supreme Court, correctly implement the rights protected by the Constitution of Kosovo. This means that the Constitutional Court

41 Art. 15 of the Kosovo Law on Courts of 1990 in connection with Art. 22 of the Law No. 03/L-199 on Courts of the Republic of Kosovo.

has no jurisdiction to substitute its factual findings or finding on ordinary law for those of the ordinary courts, including the Supreme Court.

3. Illustrations from the case law of the Constitutional Court

The cases in which the above-noted approach is reflected conspicuously and shall be the primary object of the discussion to follow are: "KEK Case I, KEK Case II, III, IV and KEK CASE V"[42], and the "PAK Case".[43] In the "KEK Cases", the Court dealt with the issue of alleged violation of the right to property (Art. 46 of the Constitution of Kosovo and Art. 1 of Protocol 1 to the European Convention on Human Rights (ECHR)) and the violation of the right to fair and impartial trial (Art. 31 of the Constitution of the Republic of Kosovo and Art. 6 of the ECHR). As regards the right to property, the Court found violation of Art. 46 of the Constitution (Protection of Property) and Art. 1 of Protocol 1 to the ECHR as interpreted in conjunction with Art. 53 of the Constitution of Kosovo.[44] The issue at stake was the unilateral termination of the Agreement for Temporary Compensation of Salary for Termination of Employment Contract by KEK (Kosovo Energy Corporation), which it had concluded with each of the individual applicants (former workers of the KEK). Article 1 of this Agreement provided that pursuant to Article 18 of the Law on Pension and Invalidity Insurance in Kosovo[45] and based on the evaluation of the invalidity Commission, each of the Applicants was entitled to interim compensation by KEK for the early termination of their employment contracts. This compensation was to be paid until the establishment and functioning of the Kosovo Fund on Pension Invalidity Insur-

42 Constitutional Court of Kosovo, Imer Ibrahimi and 48 other former employees of the Kosovo Energy Corporation vs. 49 Individual Judgments of the Supreme Court of the Republic of Kosovo, KI 40/ 09,, judgment of 23 June 2010, available at: http://www.gjk-ks.org/repository/docs/ki_40_09_ang_vendimi_meritor.pdf. Here we have over 115 Referrals of the Constitutional Court, but they are joined and then divided through a Pilot Judgment into three groups since they relate to a quite similar factual and legal background and situation. For this reason they appear in the records of the Court as "KEK I, II, and III".

43 Constitutional Court of Kosovo, Kosovo Privatization Agency vs. the Special Chamber of the Supreme Court of Kosovo, Application no. KI No. 25/10, judgment of 31 March 2011..PAK stands for the "Kosovo Privatization Agency".

44 Art. 53 of the Constitution: "Human Rights and Fundamental Freedoms guaranteed by the Constitution shall be interpreted consistent with the court decisions of the European Court of Human Rights". The ECHR is directly applicable in Kosovo by virtue of Art. 22 of the Constitution. See on the role of the ECHR and ECtHR case law under the Kosovo Constitution the contribution of *Snezhana Botusharova*, in this volume.

45 Official Gazette of the Socialist Autonomous Province of Kosovo No. 26/83, 26/86 and 11/88.

ance. The establishment and functioning of the Kosovo Fund on Pension Invalidity Insurance was the crux of the issue, for, as the Court noted, only if this rescinding condition was met, KEK could cease payments. The fulfillment of this condition was to be evaluated according to the Law on Contract and Torts (Law on Obligations).[46] Yet the Supreme Court of Kosovo did not take into account this condition when deciding this case.

Due to this, the Constitutional Court considered that the Applicants, when signing the Agreements with KEK, had a legitimate contractual expectation that they would be entitled to the monthly payment until the Pension and Invalidity Insurance Fund was established. Such legitimate expectation, as the Court noted, was a property right, guaranteed by Art. 1 of Protocol 1 to the ECHR. Its nature was concrete and not a mere hope, and it was based on a legal obligation or a legal act, i.e. the individual agreement with KEK. The unilateral cancellation of the Agreements by KEK, prior to the rescinding condition having been met, breached the Applicants' pecuniary interests which were recognized under the applicable law of Kosovo and which were subject to the protection of Art. 1 of the Protocol I to the ECtHR and Art. 46 of the Constitution.

In addition to the violation of the right to property, the Court found the Applicants' claims in relation to the violation of their right to a fair trial justified. The Court first described at length the jurisprudence of the European Court on Human Rights based on Art. 6 of the ECHR and compared it with the provision of Art. 31 of the Constitution of Kosovo.[47] Then the Court went on to say that the Supreme Court did not take into account the Applicants' argument, i.e. the fulfillment of the rescinding condition of Article 3 of the Agreements, despite the explicit reference to this before every other judicial instance. The Supreme Court, instead, viewed this as an undisputed fact, meaning that the Respondent Party (KEK) fulfilled the obligation towards the Applicants by paying salary compensation for specified periods in time, i.e. until the establishment and functioning of the Invalidity and Pension Insurance Fund in Kosovo effective from 1 January 2004.[48] In the view of the Constitutional Court, the Supreme Court, by neglecting the assessment of this point altogether, even though it was specific, pertinent and important, fell short of its obligation under Art. 6 para. 1 ECHR and Article 31 of the Constitution.

The PAK case involved the Privatization Agency of Kosovo (PAK) established under Kosovo law and concerned a different issue. Although it dealt with

46 Official Gazette of the Socialist Federal Republic of Yugoslavia No. 29/1978 and amended in 39/1985, 45/1989, 57/1989.

47 "1. Everyone shall be guaranteed equal protection of rights in the proceedings before courts, other state authorities and holders of public powers".

48 Cf. paragraphs 26 and 71 of the Judgment.

the violation of the right to free and fair trial under Article 6 of the ECHR in conjunction with Article 31 of the Constitution, in its *obiter dicta* the Court came to more general legal conclusions that are worth noting here in greater detail. First, as far as free and fair trial is concerned, the Court stated that the Special Chamber of the Supreme Court of Kosovo violated Art. 31 paras. 1 and 2 of the Constitution in connection with Article 6 of the ECHR, because it had requested UNMIK to provide a clarification as to the interpretation of the applicable law. This violated fair trial, because UNMIK was itself party to the dispute pending before the Special Chamber of the Supreme Court of Kosovo. Also, this clarification was not communicated to the Applicant, i.e. PAK, in order to allow it to express its opinion about it, but it was instead used by the Special Chamber in the wording of the Decision ASC-09-089 of 4 February 2010, reviewed by the Constitutional Court.

In line with the above, the Constitutional Court of Kosovo considered that one of the aspects of fair trial is that a party must be entitled to effectively participate in the court proceedings, something denied to PAK by the Special Chamber of the Supreme Court. This Chamber treated the PAK as a *de facto* entity but not having any legal standing before it, as provided for by the applicable law of Kosovo. By not recognizing the law regulating the legal standing of PAK, the Special Chamber violated provisions of the Ahtisaari Plan[49], see Annex IV (Article 1.1: Justice System). Article 1.1. of Annex IV of this Document clearly provides that the Supreme Court shall ensure the uniform application of the law by deciding on appeals brought before it in accordance with law. In fact, the uniform application of the law is one the key functions of each and every high court in modern constitutional democracies.

Second, the Constitutional Court elaborated and considered the approach taken by the Special Chamber. As noted, the Chamber did not recognize as valid and applicable Law No. 03/L-067 on the Privatization Agency of Kosovo, meaning that PAK was effectively denied any legal standing before the Special Chamber. In fact, the Court stated, in paragraph 53 of the Judgment, that the Chamber simply ignored the existence of Kosovo as an independent State and the legislation emanating from its Assembly. In this connection, in paragraph 54, the Court referred to the Advisory Opinion of the International Court of Justice of 22 July 2010, according to which the adoption of the declaration of independence of Kosovo 17 February 2008 did not violate general international law, Se-

49 Cf. more on this in *Ray Murphy*, UN Peacekeeping in Lebanon, Somalia and Kosovo, 2007; *Mauro Mazza*, L' ordinamento costituzionale del Kosovo, 2008.

curity Council Resolution 1244 (1999)[50] or the Constitutional Framework for the Self-Government in Kosovo.[51] The Constitutional Court thus declared invalid the judgment of the Special Chamber of the Supreme Court of Kosovo, on the basis that it violated Art. 31 and 102 of the Constitution and Art. 6 para. 1 of the EHCR.

4. Conclusions from the case law

Here I discuss only the trends of constitutional review of the decisions of the Supreme Court of Kosovo under the jurisdiction foreseen in Art. 113 para. 7 of the Constitution.[52] This means that we have left aside other aspects of constitutional review as provided for in other parts of Art. 113 concerning the jurisdiction of the Constitutional Court of Kosovo. The first general trend that we can see from the above discussion is that most of the referrals submitted to the Constitutional Court are declared as inadmissible. In a first report on the work of the Constitutional Court of Kosovo on this matter, Jean Marc Lacourciere criticized the fact that since its establishment the Court declared 85 per cent of the cases submitted to it inadmissible.[53] Second, in its review of the decisions of the Supreme Court of Kosovo, the Constitutional Court has made it clear throughout that it is not a court of appeal or a court of fourth instance, meaning that it has no original jurisdiction and that it reviews only the aspects regarding the constitutional credibility and integrity of the proceedings conducted before the Supreme Court and

50 Resolution 1244 of the UN Security Council of 10 June 1999 was enacted after the end of the 78 days of the NATO-led air campaign against the Federal Republic of Yugoslavia (Serbia and Montenegro) aimed at preventing further killings and ethnic cleansing of the Kosovo Albanian majority population. The Resolution foresaw that there was to be a political process in the near future in order to finally settle the political status of the then province of Kosovo. Until such process was complete, the establishment of an UN-led administration took place on the ground. It was meant to be of a transitional character and was named as UNMIK.

51 "Constitutional Framework for Provisional Self-Government in Kosovo", promulgated as UNMIK Regulation No. 9/2001 on 15 May 2001.

52 "Individuals are authorized to refer violations by public authorities of their individual rights and freedoms guaranteed by the Constitution, but only after exhaustion of all legal remedies provided for by law". Art. 113 para. 7 of the Constitution.

53 Cf. *Jean Marc Lacourciere*, Report on the Jurisprudence of the Constitutional Court of Kosovo on Human Rights and Minority Rights (Kosovo Law Center: Pristina, 2011), 91-131, at 112. This trend of inadmissible referrals is present in the work of other constitutional courts of former Communist countries in Europe. Cf. *Ferejohn/Pasquino* (note 22), 21-36; *Sergio Bartole*, Conclusions: Legitimacy of Constitutional Courts: Between Policy Making and Legal Science, in: Wojciech Sadurski (ed.), Constitutional Justice East and West, 2002), 409-432; *Schwartz* (note 13), 22-48, 226-248; *Massias* (note 33), 421-563.

the other regular courts of Kosovo. Lastly, the grounds used by the Constitutional Court in the process of reviewing and invalidating the decisions of the Supreme Court have to do mainly with the failure of the Supreme Court to preserve the overall credibility and integrity of the proceedings before it leading to the violation of the constitutional right for a fair and impartial trial as foreseen in Art. 31 of the Constitution in conjunction with Art. 6 of the ECHR.

V. General conclusion

The battle for constitutionalism is the battle for human dignity. It has been, as such, a feature of human history in its struggle for freedom and liberty from oppressive government. As an ideal and a system of beliefs, constitutionalism is filled with concepts, such as limited government, separation/division of powers, human rights and the rule of law. Through revolutions or in the fight between ideologies of the liberal West and the totalitarian and communist East, constitutional democracy has shaped itself and become what it is today. The key concept on this path to the rule of constitutional democracy has been and remains judicial independence, without which no meaningful rule of law society can exist.

In its rulings the Constitutional Court has made it clear that it has no intention of serving as a Court of fourth instance. In addition to this, the Court has stated on several occasions that it intends to respect the principle of subsidiarity, that is, that it intends to preserve and review only as far as the integrity of the proceedings before the Supreme Court is concerned. This means that the Constitutional Court respects the "adjudicative facts" as subsumed by the Supreme Court and the legal (both material and procedural) provisions applied to them. Only when the Supreme Court has violated constitutional rights with its rulings shall the Constitutional Court quash such rulings, and it will give detailed reasons for this. As far as the legal effects of the decisions of the Constitutional Court are concerned, it is worth noting that they are obligatory for all public authorities, not only regarding the operative part of the judgments of the Constitutional Court but also as far as their legal recommendations in the reasoning are concerned.

Without any doubt it can be said that thus far the relationship between the Supreme and Constitutional Courts has been within the limits of law and the Constitution, a normal and correct relationship based on professionalism and without any serious tension between the two institutions. The Constitutional Court of Kosovo did not have to rely on any additional doctrine, such as that of the "living law" in the case of the Italian legal system[54], to push ahead its own doctrine in its relationship with the Supreme Court of Kosovo. This was due to the fact that Kosovo's legal framework is clear and it provides a sufficient answer as to the manner in which the relations between the two institutions should be conducted. Whilst the Constitutional Court protects constitutionality in Kosovo, the Supreme Court takes care of legality of the work of the regular courts in Kosovo. Only when the latter fails to execute this task leading to violations of the Constitution of Kosovo, the Constitutional Court enters the scene and then only as a remedial institution of the last instance only on matters of constitutional law.

The very soft collision with the Supreme Court of Kosovo that happened, as elsewhere in former communist Europe, should not necessarily be seen as a "bad" thing in itself for two reasons. First, it means that where there is tension between two courts, it is the ordinary judiciary that is failing to implement the new constitution to its fullest extent. Secondly, too smooth a relationship with the Supreme Court might mean that aspirations expressed in the new Constitution were not being given a concrete and operational meaning. Institutional collisions, as *Victor Ferreres Comella* rightly put it, are sometimes a price worth paying.[55]

54 *Giancarlo Rolla/Tania Groppi*, Between Politics and the Law: The Development of Constitutional Review in Italy, in: Wojciech Sadurski (ed.), Constitutional Justice, East and West, 2002, 143-159 at 149.

55 *Victor Ferreres Comella*, The Rise of Specialized Constitutional Courts, in: Tom Ginsburg/Rosalind Dixon (eds.), Comparative Constitutional Law, 2010, 265-277.

The Constitutional Court of Kosovo and the European Court of Human Rights

*Snezhana Botusharova**

Contents

I. Introduction

The European Convention for the Protection of Human Rights and Fundamental Freedoms (ECHR) and its Protocols are considered the most powerful and effective international instruments for protection of human rights and fundamental freedoms. They are "the foundation of justice and peace in the world"[1] and are a common European and international heritage. In addition to the catalogue of civil and political rights and freedoms, the Convention introduces a mechanism for their enforcement through the European Court of Human Rights (ECtHR), thus establishing and promoting consolidated human rights standards through the Court's case law. The ECtHR itself calls the Convention "a constitutional instrument" of European public law.[2]

Kosovo is not a member of the Council of Europe. Nevertheless, the 2008 Constitution of the Republic of Kosovo[3] has adopted the ECHR and its Protocols as one of the international agreements and instruments in the sphere of fundamental rights and freedoms which are directly applicable in domestic law, as provided for by Article 22 of the Constitution. In addition, Article 53 stipulates that the rights and freedoms guaranteed in the Kosovo Constitution are to be interpreted consistent with the court decisions of the ECtHR. Finally, Article 112 para. 1 defines the Constitutional Court as the final authority for the interpretation of the Constitution.

These constitutional provisions raise important questions related to Kosovo constitutional law and to the scope of jurisdiction and interpretive powers of the Kosovo Constitutional Court. Three main questions will be addressed in this paper, namely: a) the position of the ECHR within the legal system of the Republic of Kosovo, and how can its legal effects be characterized (Part II); b) the institutional and procedural dimensions of the incorporation of the ECHR into the Kosovo constitutional system (Part III); c) the role of the ECHR and Strasbourg case law in the Constitutional Court's jurisprudence (Part IV).

* Associate Professor of Law, PhD; International Judge at the Constitutional Court of Kosovo; Judge at the European Court of Human Rights from 1998-2008.

1 Preamble, Convention for the Protection of Human Rights and Fundamental Freedoms.

2 ECtHR, *Loizidou vs. Turkey*, Preliminary Objections, Application no. 15318/89, judgment of 23 March 1995, para. 75/2/. See also for example *Alec Stone Sweet/Jud Mathews*, Proportionality Balancing and Global Constitutionalism, Columbia Journal of Transnational Law 47 (2008), 73, at 146-160.

3 The Constitution of the Republic of Kosovo, available at: http://www.kushtetutakosoves.info/repository/docs/Constitution.of.the.Republic.of.Kosovo.pdf (all web links in this article last updated December 2011).

II. The position of the ECHR in the legal system of Kosovo

There are two basic approaches to the status of international treaty law in the national legal system: monism or dualism.[4] As far as the ECHR is concerned, each state has discretion to decide on its domestic legal status.[5] Kosovo accords a privileged position to the ECHR in its domestic law. This position is defined not only by the Constitution of the Republic of Kosovo which entered into force on 15 June 2008, but by two further documents: the Comprehensive Proposal for the Kosovo Status Settlement of 26 March 2007, proposed by the United Nations Special Envoy for Kosovo, also known as the *Ahtisaari*-Plan[6], and the Kosovo Declaration of Independence, proclaimed on 17 February 2008.[7] The latter two documents will be addressed first, because they provide the historic and international normative framework for the domestic rules on the ECHR.

1. International origins and context

The ECHR was introduced for the first time to the Kosovo legal system through the Constitutional Framework for Provisional Self-Government in Kosovo, en-

4 See for example *Peter van Dijk/Fried van Hoof/Arjen van Rijn/Leo Zwaak*, Theory and Practice of the European Convention on Human Rights, 4th ed., 2006, 27 et seq; *Victor Ferreres Comella*, Constitutional Courts and Democratic Values. A European Perspective, 2009, 139 et seq; *D.J. Harris/Michael O'Boyle/Colin Warbrick*, Law of the European Convention on Human Rights, 2nd ed. 2009, 23-25; *Frank Hoffmeister*, Germany: Status of European Convention on Human Rights in domestic law, International Journal of Constitutional Law 4 (2006), 722–731; *André Alen/Michel Melchior*, The relations between the Constitutional Courts and the other national courts, including the interference in this area of the action of the European courts, General report at the Conference of European Constitutional Courts, XIIth Congress, Brussels, Egmont Palace, 14-16 May 2002, 48 et seq., available at: http://www.confcoconsteu.org/reports/rep-xii/General-report-EN.pdf.

5 Consequently, the domestic status of the Convention varies in member states. For instance, the German Constitutional Court confirmed in its decision of 14 October 2004, 2 BvR 1481/04 (*Görgülü*) that the ECHR enjoys the status of a federal statute according to Article 59 para. 2 of the Basic Law. With this, Germany may be grouped with Belgium, Finland, Italy, Liechtenstein, Lithuania, San Marino, Hungary, Denmark, Sweden, Iceland, and the United Kingdom. Other Council of Europe states, such as Bulgaria, Estonia, France, Greece, the Netherlands, Luxembourg, Poland, Portugal, Russia, Slovenia, Spain, Cyprus, Latvia, Malta, Norway, Romania, the Czech Republic, Slovakia, and most recently Turkey, opted to accord the Convention a rank higher than that of federal statutes but lower than that of their respective constitutions. See *Hoffmeister* (note 4), 727.

6 U.N. Doc. S/2007/168/Add. 1, 26 March 2007, available at http://www.unosek.org/unosek/en/statusproposal.html.

7 Available at: http://www.assembly-kosova.org/?cid=2,128,1635.

acted by the United Nations Mission in Kosovo (UNMIK) in 2001.[8] The next step was the *Ahtisaari*-Plan, which required the adoption of the ECHR system in Kosovo in Article 2 para. 1. It calls upon Kosovo authorities to "take all necessary measures towards ratifying the European Convention for the Protection of Human Rights and Fundamental Freedoms and its Protocols". Furthermore, the same article stipulates that "Kosovo shall promote, protect and respect the highest level of internationally recognized human rights and fundamental freedoms, including those rights and freedoms set forth in the Universal Declaration on Human Rights, the International Covenant on Civil and Political Rights, and the European Convention for the Protection of Human Rights and Fundamental Freedoms and its Protocols". This provision should be read in conjunction with Article 2 para. 1 of Annex I of the Comprehensive Proposal, which lists the international instruments to be incorporated into the Constitution of Kosovo. Even though the *Ahtisaari*-Plan was not endorsed by the Security Council or by an international treaty, it drew particular attention to the human rights dimension of the new state and provided guarantees for them in the new polity.

The Plan became legally binding on Kosovo with the new state's Declaration of Independence, which contains a unilateral commitment of Kosovo to abide by that plan. The Declaration "accept[ed] fully the obligations for Kosovo contained in the *Ahtisaari* Plan", expressed "commitment to respect the human rights and fundamental freedoms of all our citizens, particularly as defined by the European Convention on Human Rights" and included the following provision: "Kosovo shall be legally bound to comply with the […] obligations […] under the *Ahtisaari*-Plan".[9] Constitution makers were thus politically and legally obliged to make provision for the respect of the Plan and for the incorporation of the ECHR in the constitutional text. Moreover, the Plan already envisaged a Constitutional Court to enforce substantive guarantees.

Both requirements regarding the ECHR and the Constitutional Court were subsequently met in the Kosovo Constitution, which entered into force in June 2008. The *Ahtisaari*- Plan itself was incorporated into the Constitution through Article 143 of the Constitution.[10] This has raised the question of the hierarchy between the Plan and the constitutional text itself.

8 Constitutional Framework for Provisional Self-Government in Kosovo, Chapter 3, 3.2, UNMIK, available at: http://www.assembly-kosova.org/common/docs/ FrameworkPocket_ENG_Dec2002.pdf.

9 Kosovo Declaration of Independence, paras. 4, 5 and 12.

10 Article 143 [Comprehensive Proposal for the Kosovo Status Settlement]
Notwithstanding any provision of this Constitution:
1. All authorities in the Republic of Kosovo shall abide by all of the Republic of Kosovo's obligations under the Comprehensive Proposal for the Kosovo Status Settlement dated 26 March 2007. They shall take all necessary actions for their implementation.

The majority of academic authors and legal practitioners consider that the *Ahtisaari*-Plan takes precedence over the Constitution itself and over other legal acts in Kosovo.[11] Others argue that from a domestic legal perspective the Constitution adopted the Plan's political authorization for a conditionally independent state mechanism. Thus, some of these authors consider that since the Plan is enforced through the Constitution of Kosovo, the Constitution cannot be subordinated to the plan. They therefore conclude that the Constitution sits atop the hierarchy of Kosovo's legal system.[12] This sits uneasily with the words of the Constitution itself as Article 143 of the Constitution recognizes the legal supremacy of the *Ahtisaari*-Plan. Further, it seems contradictory if the same authors conclude that Kosovo's Constitution and the *Ahtisaari* Plan are of the same rank and represent two apexes in Kosovo's constitutional order. Instead, the superiority of the *Ahtisaari* Plan and its legally binding nature derives from two sources.[13] The first is the Kosovo Declaration of Independence, which contains a unilateral commitment of the State to abide by that Plan. This implies an obligation under international law to respect the powers of the International Civilian Representative (ICR), who is supreme vis-à-vis the Constitution and organs established by it. The second source is found in Articles 146 and 147 of the Constitution, which confirms the ICR's powers and require Kosovo institutions to give effect to the ICR's decisions. The normative supremacy of the *Ahtisaari* Plan

2. The provisions of the Comprehensive Proposal for the Kosovo Status Settlement dated 26 March 2007 shall take precedence over all other legal provisions in Kosovo.
3. The Constitution, laws and other legal acts of the Republic of Kosovo shall be interpreted in compliance with the Comprehensive Proposal for the Kosovo Status Settlement dated 26 March 2007. If there are inconsistencies between the provisions of this Constitution, laws or other legal acts of the Republic of Kosovo and the provisions of the said Settlement, the latter shall prevail.

11 See in this sense: *Steven Hill/Paul Linden-Retek*, Supervised Independence and Post-Conflict Sovereignty: the Dynamics of Hybridity in Kosovo's New Constitutional Court, Yale Journal of International Law Online 36 (2010), 33 et seq; *Robert Muharremi*, The European Union Rule of Law Mission in Kosovo(EULEX) from the Perspective of Kosovo Constitutional Law, ZaöRV/Heidelberg Journal of International Law 70 (2010), 363; *Michael Riegner*, The two faces of the internationalized pouvoir constituant: Independence and constitution-making under external influence in Kosovo, Goettingen Journal of International Law 2 (2010) 3, 1035-1062; *Visar Morina/Fisnik Korenica/Dren Doli*, The relationship between international law and national law in the case of Kosovo: A constitutional perspective, International Journal of Constitutional Law 9 (2011), 274, 278.

12 In that direction, *Dren Doli/Fisnik Korenica*, What about Kosovo's Constitution: Is there anything special? Discussing the grundnorm, the sovereignty, and the consociational model of democracy, Vienna Journal on International Constitutional Law 5 (2011), 49, at 52, 57, available at: www.icl-journal.com.

13 See for example *Constance Grewe/Michael Riegner*, Internationalized Constitutionalism in Ethnically Divided Societies: Bosnia-Herzegovina and Kosovo Compared, Max Planck Yearbook of United Nations Law (15) 2011, 1, at 59 et seq.

over the Constitution is thus evidenced, and complemented, by this enforcement mechanism.

Moreover, in practice the Constitutional Court of Kosovo gives priority to the *Ahtisaari* Plan and enforces its provisions in its case law. One of the benchmark decisions is the case entitled "Kosovo Privatization Agency vs. the Decision of the Special Chamber of the Supreme Court of Kosovo".[14] Through this Judgment the Constitutional Court confirmed the importance and the priority of the *Ahtisaari* Plan. The Court found a violation of Article 31 [Right to Fair and Impartial Trial] of the Constitution and Article 6 (Right to Fair Trial) of the ECHR as the Special Chamber of the Supreme Court proved not to be an impartial tribunal. The Court applied the criteria and standards of the ECtHR jurisprudence to the Special Chamber of the Supreme Court, in that the Chamber must be an impartial and independent tribunal and as such must apply the law in force in the State and obey that law only. The Special Chamber had not accepted the Law on the Privatization Agency of Kosovo, Law No.03/L-067, as applicable law in the State and had treated the Law only as valid and binding in internal rules of organization within the privatization process.[15]

Moreover, the *Ahtisaari* Plan, the provisions of which take precedence over all legal provisions in Kosovo, clearly provides, in Annex IV [Justice System], Article 1 para.1 that "The Supreme Court shall ensure the uniform application of the law by deciding on appeals brought in accordance with the law". The Special Chamber, as part of the Supreme Court, is, therefore, obliged to abide by this provision.[16] In these circumstances, the Court held that the Special Chamber of the Supreme Court by its decision clearly did not "ensure the uniform application of the law", as envisaged by the Comprehensive Proposal, nor did it act in conformity with its duties under the above Article 102 of the Constitution, since it did not apply Law 03/L-067. Instead, it considered it not as a Law duly adopted by the Assembly of Kosovo but merely as "valid and binding internal rules of organization for the Privatization Agency of Kosovo, which it characterized as a factual entity, instead of an independent public body possessing full legal standing, as laid down in Law No. 03/L-067".[17] The Constitutional Court, therefore,

14 Constitutional Court of the Republic of Kosovo, *Referral of the Kosovo Privatization Agency for Constitutional Review of the Decision of the Special Chamber of the Supreme Court of Kosovo*, case no. ASC-09-089, judgment of 4 February 2010 and, case no. KI 25/10, judgment of 31 March 2011, available at: http://www.gjk-ks.org/repository/docs/ki_25_10_ag_ang.pdf.

15 *Ibid.*, para 47.

16 *Ibid.*, para 57.

17 *Ibid.*, para 60. For a discussion of the same case from the perspective of interactions between the Constitutional and Supreme Court of Kosovo, see the contribution of *Enver Hasani*, in this volume.

annulled the Judgment of the Special Chamber and remanded it for reconsideration in line with the Constitutional Court's Judgment.

2. The status of the ECHR under the 2008 Constitution

The ECHR can become domestically relevant in different ways. For example, the wording of many fundamental rights provisions in the 2008 Kosovo Constitution follows the ECHR text. Generally speaking, human rights and fundamental freedoms guaranteed by the Kosovo Constitution are consistent with the norms of the ECHR. They are required to be applied in Kosovo and they prepare the state of Kosovo for accession to European international organizations. However, here another aspect of the ECHR's impact will be focused upon, namely the direct application of the Convention itself in domestic law. The Kosovo Constitution regulates the domestic status of international law in two different manners. On the one hand, Article 19 covers the domestic applicability of international law generally and stipulates that ratified international agreements and legally binding norms of international law have superiority over the laws of Kosovo. On the other hand, Article 22 enumerates a number of international human rights instruments and makes them directly applicable even without ratification.

Consequently, some Kosovo constitutional law scholars argue that the Constitution of Kosovo provides for a monist model of the relationship between international law and national law, because it incorporates treaties – and, to a certain extent, also customary international law – into the domestic legal order.[18] The Kosovo Constitutional Court, without having explicitly pronounced on this issue, applied the monist approach as seen in the case of "Cemailj Kurtisi and the Municipal Assembly of Prizren".[19]

Turning to the status of the ECHR in particular, the most important provision in this regard is Article 22.[20] Its list of directly applicable international instru-

18 *Morina/Korenica/Doli* (note 11).

19 Constitutional Court of the Republic of Kosovo, *Cemailj Kurtisi vs. The Municipal Assembly of Prizren*, case no. KO 01/09, judgment of 18 March 2010, para. 40. For a more detailed discussion of this case, see *Grewe/Riegner* (note 13), 23 et seq.

20 Article 22 reads: "Human rights and fundamental freedoms guaranteed by the following international agreements and instruments are guaranteed by this Constitution, are directly applicable in the Republic of Kosovo and, in the case of conflict, have priority over provisions of laws and other acts of public institutions:
(1) Universal Declaration of Human Rights;
(2) European Convention for the Protection of Human Rights and Fundamental Freedoms and its Protocols;
(3) International Covenant on Civil and Political Rights and its Protocols;
(4) Council of Europe Framework Convention for the Protection of National Minorities;

ments includes the ECHR and all its Protocols, which are thus part of the domestic constitutional order without ratification. While this is undisputed, there are different views on the hierarchical rank of the ECHR under the Kosovo Constitution. Article 22 itself stipulates that in the case of conflict, the ECHR and its protocols have priority over provisions in laws and other acts of public institutions. They thus have clear priority over legislative acts, regulations, acts of the government, ministers, and other public bodies. This is understood by some commentators as placing the ECHR in a mezzanine position between ordinary law and the Constitution.[21] In any event, the Convention takes precedence over conflicting national legislation and all Kosovo state organs must be aware of the ECHR and other international instruments and apply them in their daily practice. In terms of theoretical hierarchy, the *Ahtisaari* Plan seems to call for a reading that places the ECHR at least on the same level as the other constitutional norms. One can thus argue that the ECHR is on the same level as the other constitutional provisions, but not placed above the Constitution itself. Another argument in favor of this reading is Article 53 on the domestic effect of Strasbourg case law, which will be discussed now.

3. The effect of Strasbourg case law within the legal system of Kosovo

The ECHR differs from all the other international instruments enumerated in Article 22 in that it disposes of a judicial enforcement mechanism, namely ECtHR, which provides clear standards for interpretation. Council of Europe Members have discretion with regard to the *erga omnes* domestic effect of Strasbourg case law, and they have adopted a variety of approaches in this regard. The Kosovo Constitution contains an explicit rule on the domestic status of ECtHR case law, which emphasizes the privileged status of the ECHR compared to other international instruments. Article 53 stipulates that "[h]uman rights and fundamental freedoms guaranteed by this Constitution shall be interpreted consistent with the court decisions of the European Court of Human Rights". The legal effect of this provision is clear in most cases and is to be developed further in practice. But it seems that the Constitution looks at the ECtHR case law not only as a minimum

(5) Convention on the Elimination of All Forms of Racial Discrimination;
(6) Convention on the Elimination of All Forms of Discrimination Against Women;
(7) Convention on the Rights of the Child;
(8) Convention against Torture and Other Cruel, Inhumane or Degrading Treatment or Punishment."

21 See *Joseph Marko*, The New Kosovo Constitution in a Regional Comparative Perspective, Review of Central and East European Law 33 (2008) 437, 447; *Grewe/Riegner* (note 13), 51.

standard but more as a binding authority for constitutional interpretation by all institutions in the state. Therefore, the ECtHR's case law is a mandatory recourse for all interpretations as far as human rights are concerned. But at the same time, it also entitles and legitimizes the Constitutional Court, in particular, to rely on the case law and provide effective protection, notably when a question is posed to it by the ordinary courts, or in an individual constitutional referral.

Three aspects of the binding effect of Strasbourg case law should be taken into consideration. First, as is the case within the Council of Europe, states can provide a wider scope of human rights catalogues and even better protection of human rights than the minimum standards the ECtHR requires. Secondly, the case law of the ECtHR does in principle not have *erga omnes* effect. But if a situation is similar or comparable and a standard is universally relevant, then the standards determined by the ECtHR in a particular case against one state should raise the level of human rights protection in other states, including Kosovo by virtue of its own Constitution. Lastly, Article 53 does not mean that a judgment of the ECtHR has immediate legislative effect in the Republic of Kosovo, as might be argued. This also applies to the "soft law" of the Council of Europe and its bodies[22], which nevertheless has an important guiding and inspiring role for promoting democracy and rule of law. The Strasbourg case law is a source of knowledge, standards and help for the interpretation of the different rights of the Convention and of the Constitution of Kosovo. It is for the law-makers, the judiciary, legal practitioners and the Constitutional Court to jointly develop effective compliance with the constitutional requirements in the sphere of human rights. In practice, the Constitutional Court of Kosovo applies the Convention and its case law and has not found any problems so far regarding the scope of Article 53. The standards of review applied by the Court are the same as those applied by the ECtHR with respect to the Convention. This harmonizes the Constitution with recent European human rights law developments and contributes to the further Europeanization of Kosovo constitutional law.

In sum, the combined normative effect of the constitutional provisions analyzed so far goes beyond the protections provided by a number of other European democracies. These arrangements can be viewed as a means to fill a gap in the protection of human rights, as Kosovo is not, thus far, a member of the Council of Europe. The burden is on the Constitutional Court to bridge that gap, and therefore it substantially relies on the ECtHR jurisprudence to do so, in substitution for the recourse that citizens of other European countries have to claim their rights in Strasbourg. More generally, the Kosovo Constitution evidences the

22 For a different view that attributes binding effect also to official Council of Europe restatements of the ECtHR case law, see the contribution of *Peter Pavlin*, in this volume.

global trend that human rights in international law and fundamental rights in constitutional law influence each other more and more, and interweave on many levels and in many layers. This can be understood as a process of mutual backup and multi-layered justification, which also reinforces the legitimacy and effectiveness of human rights protection in Kosovo.[23]

III. The institutional and procedural dimensions of the ECHR in Kosovo constitutional law

The incorporation of ECHR standards into domestic law also has institutional and procedural consequences. Notably, it affects the position of and the relationship between three main actors: individuals, other state organs, and the Constitutional Court.

1. The individual

The individual has a dual constitutional position. On the one hand, he or she is subjected to and bound by the Constitution. Article 16 on the supremacy of the Constitution stipulates that "[e]very person and entity in the Republic of Kosovo is subject to the provisions of the Constitution." Article 21 para. 3 holds that "[e]veryone must respect the human rights and fundamental freedoms of others". On the other hand, individuals, as well as legal persons, are entitled to have their human rights and fundamental freedoms respected by everyone and protected by the state of Kosovo (Art. 21 paras. 2 and 3). This entitlement is institutionally and procedurally safeguarded by the right to enforce protection in the Constitutional Court. Namely, Art. 113 para. 7 on the Constitutional Court's jurisdiction stipulates that "[i]ndividuals are authorized to refer violations by public authorities of their individual rights and freedoms guaranteed by the Constitution, but only after exhaustion of all legal remedies provided by law".

The individual referral procedure before the Constitutional Court is the direct institutional and procedural link between citizens and the Convention. In their submissions to the Court, they may rely on the Convention and Strasbourg case law. In fact, reliance on the ECHR and accompanying case law should not be limited to the Constitutional Court. Individuals can invoke its standards in ordinary court proceedings, based on the general provision of Article 21 para. 3 and Article 53. All public authorities, including the ordinary courts, are bound to ap-

23 On these general trends see *Gráinne de Búrca/Oliver Gerstenberg*, The Denationalization of Constitutional Law, Harvard International Law Journal 47 (2006), 243, at 258.

ply the ECHR and relevant case law, so there should be possibilities of enforcing the Convention and its jurisprudence in ordinary court procedures, all the more so because there are no procedural obstacles. Transposed to a national level this might, for the time being, be demanding and practically difficult in many cases. It goes without saying that such a mechanism, if it is to be applied effectively in practice, presupposes a complex of legislative, judicial, jurisdictional, educative, and other measures. In fact, individuals may even be obliged to raise constitutional and conventional rights in ordinary courts. Strasbourg standards require the alleged violation of human rights to be explicitly raised during ordinary court proceedings as one of the requirements for the application to be considered admissible. This practice of the ECtHR needs to be evaluated carefully by the Constitutional Court and ordinary courts as the case law evolves.

2. State organs

As far as the state is concerned, it may be considered in two different capacities regarding the ECHR. First, as a bearer of the positive obligation under Article 1 of the ECHR, namely, as having the obligation to respect human rights and to "secure to everyone within [its] jurisdiction the rights and freedoms defined in Section I of the Convention", and to protect and guarantee these rights under Article 21 para. 2 of the Constitution. This entails the obligation of the state to adopt practical and legal, legislative, administrative and judicial measures aiming at guaranteeing the effective protection of the recognized rights and freedoms. These obligations require substantive measures, i.e. measures meant for the protection of the substantive human rights, but also procedural measures, i.e. an effective mechanism of protection.[24]

Secondly, the State may through its public authorities, commit violations of individual rights and freedoms guaranteed by the Constitution, including the ECHR. The final authority to decide upon such violations is the Constitutional Court (Article 112 para. 1), but this is only effective when the issue is referred to it by individuals pursuant to Article113 para. 7. In a situation where the Constitutional Court finds a violation, it is the duty of the state to repair the damage either by following the measure/s suggested by the Court, or by other effective

24 *Francoise Tulkens*, The European Court of Human Rights is Fifty: Recent Trends in the Court's Jurisdiction, Constitutional Law Review Georgia 3 (2010), 3, available at: http://constcourt.ge/files/J-En.pdf. See the contribution of *Peter Pavlin*, in this volume, for the practically relevant example of the right to trial within a reasonable time, whose effective protection requires practical, organizational as well as legislative measures.

means within its own discretion. One should distinguish these different circumstances when violations of individual rights occur.

3. The role of the Constitutional Court

Hence, the Constitutional Court plays a key role in the enforcement of constitutional and Convention standards. The Court, established in 2009, is the newest of its kind in Europe. Although the existence of constitutional courts is not an entirely new phenomenon in Kosovo, the new Constitutional Court differs considerably in terms of its enhanced powers and internationalized nature.[25] The Court has a hybrid form, both by its composition, which includes international and national members, and by its functional mandate to apply domestic and international law as a mechanism to administer justice in a post-conflict context, to strengthen local institutions and to universalize the international values the Constitution promotes.[26]

The strength of the Constitutional Court stems from its well defined competences. Article 112 emphasizes that the Court is the final authority for the interpretation of the Constitution and the compliance of laws within the Constitution. This is qualified by Article 53: Also the Constitutional Court is bound by Strasbourg case law to the extent that this provision applies – but the constitutional interpretation of the meaning and scope of Article 53 itself is again within the exclusive competence of the judges of the Constitutional Court. The main competences of the Court are enumerated in Article 113, which lists different authorized parties and types of proceedings. These include questions of compatibility of a variety of legal acts with the Constitution, disputes among central state organs and between central and municipal authorities, references by ordinary courts and individual complaints against acts of public authorities. The competences further include the possibilities for several variants of abstract control, initiated by central or local institutions, representatives of communities. The central state authorities may also raise constitutional questions and ask for interpretation

25 On the historical development and current features of constitutional justice in Kosovo, see the contribution of *Enver Hasani*, in this volume; *Grewe/Riegner* (note 13), 39.

26 *Hill/Linden-Retek* (note 11); *Fisnik Korenica/Dren Doli*, Constitutional Rigidity in Kosovo: Significance, Outcomes, and Rationale, Pace International Law Review 2 (2011), 1; *Grewe/Riegner* (note 13); *Dren Doli/Fisnik Korenica*, Kosovar Constitutional Court's Jurisdiction: Searching for Strengths and Weaknesses, German Law Journal 11 (2010), 803.

of constitutional provisions.[27] These competences have generated an important amount of case law.[28]

IV. The impact of ECtHR case law on the jurisprudence of the Kosovo Constitutional Court

The Constitutional Court refers to the ECHR and Strasbourg case law in its jurisprudence. It describes its general approach to the Convention in one of its rulings as follows: "The European Convention for the Protection of Human Rights and Fundamental Freedoms and its Protocols, as earlier stated, were incorporated into the law of Kosovo at the Constitutional level, it being given priority over provisions of laws and other acts of public institutions. This Court must interpret the Constitution and the Convention in a complementary manner bearing in mind the necessity to protect the fundamental rights and freedoms enumerated in both. Many of the countries of Europe which emerged from totalitarian rule over the last number of years have adopted European standards for the protection of human rights. Kosovo has done the same. The constitutional system is one, like others, based on the pillars of democracy, human rights and the rule of law."[29] Initially, most of the referrals to the Court were individual complaints. This led to the development of admissibility criteria according to Article 113 para. 7 of the Constitution and the Law on the Constitutional Court of the Republic of Kosovo.[30] What is more, the Court drew on ECtHR case law not only with regard to substantive rights, but also with regard to the admissibility of individual referrals.

27 For a detailed analysis of the Court's existing and missing competences, see *Doli/ Korenica*, Kosovar Constitutional Court's Jurisdiction (note 26).

28 As of 31 October 2011 the total number of the registered referrals since 2009 is 351, 233 have been decided. 14 of the Decisions issued are key Judgments.

29 Constitutional Court of the Republic of Kosovo, *Ćemailj Kurtiši vs. The Municipal Assembly of Prizren* case no.. KO 01/09, judgment of 18 March 2010, para. 40, available at: http://www.gjk-ks.org/repository/docs/ko_01_09_Ven_ang.pdf.

30 Law no. 03-L-121 on the Constitutional Court of the Republic of Kosovo available at: http://gjk-ks.org/repository/docs/Law_03-L-121_CCK.pdf.

1. Impact on admissibility decisions

a) *Locus standi* and victim status

In the case of "Haxhi Thaçi vs. Kosovo Judicial Council"[31] the Constitutional Court applied the ECtHR approach that the applicant did not have *locus standi* to challenge the constitutionality of the Administrative Instructions of the Kosovo Judicial Council on unification of judicial fees. The reason was that he was not an authorized party under Article 113 para. 1 of the Constitution because he did not have the right to request an abstract review of constitutionality. The Court also elaborated on the victim status of the applicant in view of the requirements of Article 34 of the ECHR. Thus, it declared the referral inadmissible.

b) Status of legal persons and non-exhaustion of legal remedies

In the case of "AAB-Riinvest University vs. the decision No. 01/73 of the Government of Republic of Kosovo"[32] the applicant was a university having the status of a legal person. It challenged a decision of the Government refusing to register it as a university because the decision allegedly violated Article 48 para. 2 of the Constitution, the guarantee of academic freedom, and Article 24 of the Constitution, which guarantees equality before the law. This was the first case where the Constitutional Court applied Article 21 para. 4 of the Constitution accepting that the fundamental rights and freedoms set forth in the Constitution were valid for legal persons. It stated that the applicant was entitled to submit a constitutional complaint involving fundamental rights which were valid for individuals as well as for legal persons.

The Court applied the requirement for individuals that all legal remedies prescribed by law have to be exhausted, as stipulated by Article 113 para. 7 of the Constitution. The Constitutional Court applied the ECtHR standards for exhaustion of legal remedies emphasizing the subsidiary character of the constitutional

31 Constitutional Court of the Republic of Kosovo, *Haxhi Thaçi vs. Kosovo Judicial Council*, case no. 09/09, decision of 19 November 2009, available at: http://www.gjk-ks.org/repository/docs/RESOLUTION_Inadmissibility_of_the_Application.pdf.

32 Constitutional Court of the Republic of Kosovo, *AAB-Riinvest University L.L.C., Prishtina vs. Government of the Republic of Kosovo*, case no. KI 41/09, decision of 21 January 2010, available at: http://www.gjk-ks.org/repository/docs/resolution_case_no_ki _ 41_09.pdf. See also Constitutional Court of the Republic of Kosovo, *Applicant Agron Vula for Constitutional Review Decision of the Municipality of Gjakova not to implement the Decision of the Independent Oversight Board, dated 25 February 2008*, case no. KI57-09, decision of 17 August 2011, available at: http://www.gjk-ks.org/re posito ry/docs/ki_57_09_ang.pdp.

remedy. The Court stressed that the rationale for the exhaustion rule, as interpreted by the ECtHR, was to afford the authorities concerned, including the ordinary courts, the opportunity to prevent or put right the alleged violation of the Constitution. The rule was based on the assumption that the Kosovo legal order would provide an effective remedy for the violation of constitutional rights. Moreover the Constitutional Court reinforced its reasoning that remedies that are available and effective have to be exhausted, quoting Strasbourg case law again. The referral was therefore declared inadmissible for non-exhaustion of the available legal remedies. This case has become a benchmark decision quoted as a classic one in all later cases dealing with the exhaustion requirement.

c) Jurisdiction *ratione temporis*

The applicant in the case of "Shefqet Haxhiu vs. Labour Organization 'Industria e Akumulatorëve'"[33] requested the assessment of the legality of the Regulation on internal organization and systematization of duties and work by his employer. The Constitutional Court found out that the referral was related to a period before the date of the entry into force of the Constitution, and therefore, it maintained that the complaint was prescribed. It did so applying *ratione temporis* ECHR admissibility criteria as applied by the ECtHR in *Blečić vs. Croatia.*[34]

d) Manifestly ill-founded applications

The applicant in "Sevdail Avduli vs. Supreme Court Judgment A. No. 533/2006 of 11 September 2006 and Supreme Court Judgment A. No. 353/2003 of 2 December 2003"[35] claimed that the two decisions of the Supreme Court violated his

33 Constitutional Court of the Republic of Kosovo, *Shefqet Haxhiu vs. Labour Organization "Industria e Akumulatorëve"*, case no. KI 25/09, judgment of 23 June 2010, available at: http://www.gjk-ks.org/repository/docs/vendimi_ki_25_09_ang.pdf; identical is the case No. KI-58/11, *Syle Shlivova for Constitutional Review of the Resolution of the Supreme Court of Kosovo Rev. No. 82/2002*, decision 1 November 2011, available at: http://www.gjk-ks.org/repository/docs/gjk_ki_58_11_ang.pdf.

34 ECtHR, *Blečić v. Croatia*, Application no. 59532/00, judgment of 29 July 2004.

35 Constitutional Court of the Republic of Kosovo, *Sevdail Avduli Against Supreme Court Judgment A. No. 533/2006 of 11 September 2006 and Supreme Court Judgment A. No. 353/2003 of 2 December 2003*, case no. KI 13/09, decision of 17 June 2010, available at: http://www.gjk-ks.org/repository/docs/ki_13_09_eng.pdf. See also: Constitutional Court of the Republic of Kosovo, *Amrush Rexhepi for Constitutional review of the Judgment of the Supreme Court of Kosovo, Rev. No. 256/08, dated 15. November 2010*, case no. KI 12/11, decision of 17 August 2011, available at: http://www.gjk-ks.org/repository/docs/gjk_ki_12_11_ang.pdp; *Azem Ademi vs. The Ministry of Justice*, case no. KI

right to a pension. The Constitutional Court reasoned, using the ECtHR case law and approach, that the Court is not to act as a court of appeal, or a court of fourth instance, in respect of the decisions taken by ordinary courts. It decided that the trial was fair, as there were no indications that the court proceedings were unfair or tainted by arbitrariness. The applicant failed to submit any prima facie evidence of a violation of his constitutional rights. The referral was therefore rejected as manifestly ill-founded. The reasoning in this decision is reiterated in many other similar cases dealt with by the Court.

2. Impact on substantive rights jurisprudence

Besides procedural questions, ECHR standards have also impacted considerably on the interpretation of the substantive rights contained in the Constitution, be it in the merits of judgments or in inadmissibility decisions based on more substantive considerations.

a) Religious freedom

The applicant in the case of "Arjeta Halimi for Constitutional Review of alleged non execution of Judgment of the District Court in Gjilan CN.nr.24/09 of 17 November 2009 and alleged violation of the Applicant's human rights"[36] requested an assessment of the constitutionality of the non-execution of a District Court Judgment, as well as a number of constitutional and Convention rights, particularly, Article 38 (Freedom of Belief, Conscience and Religion) and Article 47 (Right to Education) of the Constitution. The applicant had begun wearing a headscarf in school during the first semester of the tenth grade and she alleged that she was informed verbally by the school management that she would not be allowed to attend school any more unless she removed her headscarf. As she reportedly refused to sign a statement to remove the scarf, she was allegedly asked not to return to school any more. According to the applicant she did not attend school after 15 January 2009.

62/10, decision of 18 March 2011 available at, http://www.gjk-ks.org/repository/docs/gjk_ki_62_10_ang.pdf.

36 Constitutional Court of the Republic of Kosovo, *Arjeta Halimi for Constitutional Review of alleged non execution of Judgment of the District Court in Gjilan CN.nr.24/09 of 17 November 2009 and alleged violation of the Applicant's human rights*, Case No KI 36/11, decision of 30 September 2011, available at: http://gjk-ks.org/repository/docs/KI_36_11_ang.pdf

The Constitutional Court noted as an undisputed fact between the Parties that the applicant had never received any formal decision from the school she was attending that she was banned from it or suspended from continuing her education. Consequently, the Court concluded that it was not convinced by the applicant's argument that she had been forbidden to attend school. Moreover it found that she had not "sufficiently substantiated her claim" as required by the Rules of Procedure. But the Constitutional Court went further than that and also referred to the ECtHR decision in *Dogru vs. France.*[37] This case involved the contentious issue of the wearing of Islamic headscarves in French schools and it elaborated on the margin of appreciation given to states in issues of religious freedom. So based on the margin of appreciation standard, and also on the Constitutional provision on secularity and neutrality of the state in religious matters, the Constitutional Court declared the referral inadmissible also on these grounds.

b) Electoral rights and direct applicability of the ECHR and Article 3 of the First Protocol

The applicant in "Mimoza Kusari-Lila vs. Central Election Commission"[38] was a candidate for the post of mayor in the local elections held on 15 November 2009. She requested an assessment of the constitutionality and legality of the decision of the Central Election Commission (CEC) to certify the results of those elections, without having considered the results of all the complaints and appeals lodged. The applicant relied on Article 45 (Freedom of Election and Participation) and Article 54 (Judicial Protection of Rights) of the Constitution. She considered that the freedom of election and participation had been violated and that her right to be elected had been denied because of the manner of rendering decisions by the Election Complaints and Appeals Committee (ECAC), to which she had complained.

The role of the Constitutional Court in the electoral process is recognized by the Law on General Elections where it is provided in Article 106 para. 1 that the CEC shall certify election results only after complaints have been adjudicated upon by the ECAC and by the Constitutional Court. The Court has no other role in these electoral processes and it cannot revise or overturn the decisions of the

37 ECtHR, *Dogru vs. France*, Application No 27058/05, judgment of 4 December 2008, available at: http://www.echr.coe.int/ECHR/EN/Header/Case-Law/Decisions+and+judg ments /HUDOC+database/.

38 Constitutional Court of the Republic of Kosovo, *Mimoza Kusari-Lila vs. Central Election Commission*, Case No. KI 73/09, decision of 23 March 2010, availableat:http://www.gjk-ks.org/repository/docs/KI%2073_vendimi_ang.pdp.

CEC or the ECAC, unless there has been a violation of the individual rights and freedoms guaranteed by the Constitution. In addition to this legal basis, the Constitutional Court directly applied the ECHR and, in particular, Article 3 of the First Protocol, which provides for the right to free elections. It elaborated on the different nature of the rights to vote in elections and to stand for elections, differentiated by the case law of the ECtHR and the "soft law" of the Council of Europe, particularly of the European Commission for Democracy through Law (Venice Commission). In the end, the case turned on more procedural issues: As had become clear from the evidence given the Court hearing, the applicant's political party, rather than she herself, lodged the appeals to the ECAC and to the Supreme Court. The political party did not submit a Referral to the Constitutional Court as it ought to have done, according to the Law on General Elections. By not submitting a complaint to the ECAC, as a person with a legal interest in a matter, within its jurisdiction, the Applicant did not exhaust the legal remedies provided by law and her referral was rejected as inadmissible.

c) Property rights and fair trial

The subject matter of the referral entitled "Imer Ibrahimi and 48 other former employees of the Kosovo Energy Corporation vs. 49 Individual Judgments of the Supreme Court of the Republic of Kosovo"[39] was the constitutionality of the individual judgments by the Supreme Court. Each of the applicants had sued the Kosovo Energy Corporation (KEK) in the ordinary courts because they were entitled to temporary compensation due to early termination of the employment contract. This compensation should cease when the Kosovo Fund on Pension-Invalidity Insurance was established and functional. KEK terminated the payment stipulated by the Agreements in the summer of 2006 without any notification and despite the fact that the Kosovo Pension Invalidity Fund had not been established at that time.

The Municipal Court in Pristina approved the applicants' claims and ordered monetary compensation. The District Court in Pristina rejected the appeals of KEK and found its submissions ungrounded. The Supreme Court accepted the appeals of KEK, and quashed the judgments of the District Court and the Munic-

39 Constitutional Court of Kosovo, *Imer Ibrahimi and 48 other former employees of the Kosovo Energy Corporation vs. 49 Individual Judgments of the Supreme Court of the Republic of Kosovo,* KI 40/ 09,, judgment of 23 June 2010, available at: http://www.gjk-ks.org/repository/docs/ki_40_09_ang_vendimi_meritor.pdf. For a discussion of the same case from the perspective of interactions between the Constitutional and Supreme Court of Kosovo, see the contribution of *Enver Hasani*, in this volume.

ipal Court and rejected as unfounded the applicants' lawsuits. The applicants complained that their rights had been violated because KEK unilaterally annulled their Agreements, although the condition that the Kosovo Pension-Invalidity Insurance Fund was functioning had not been fulfilled. The applicants further argued that they had not been able to remedy such a violation before the ordinary courts. It appeared from the applicants' submissions that the subject of the complaints was their property rights, as guaranteed by Article 1, Protocol 1 to the ECHR, as well as their right to fair trial, as guaranteed by Article 6 of the ECHR.

The Constitutional Court elaborated that because of the "continuing situation" the four months deadline for submitting a referral should not be imposed. It also elaborated on the purpose of the time limit rule, based on the ECtHR case law and its objectives. In this case and in the Joint Dissent[40] the Constitutional Court elaborated in detail on the time issue. Furthermore, the Court explained the concepts of "possession" according to Article 1, Protocol 1 and the basic Strasbourg case law, of "legitimate expectations", "substantial interest" and "pecuniary interest" and found a violation of Article 46 of the Constitution and Article 1, Protocol 1. As far as the fair trial complaint was concerned, the Constitutional Court applied the Convention standard that the ordinary courts' decision should be reasoned and although not all the arguments were required to be taken into consideration in the light of the circumstances of the case, those that shape the case, being specific, pertinent and important, should not be neglected. Consequently the Constitutional Court found that the Supreme Court fell short of its obligations under Article 6 of the ECHR and Article 31 of the Constitution. It annulled for both reasons a great part of the judgments and remanded them to the Supreme Court for reconsideration in conformity with the Constitutional Court's decision.

40 Joint Dissenting Opinion by Judges Almiro Rodrigues and Snezhana Botusharova, available at http://www.gjk ks.org/repository/docs/ki_47_10_dissenting_opinion_judge_snezhana_botusharova_and _judge_almiro_rodrigues.pdf.

V. Conclusion

The practice of the ECtHR has been greatly beneficial to numerous Constitutional Courts in Europe.[41] The Kosovo Constitution acknowledges these benefits and establishes a normative framework which incorporates and receives ECHR standards. The ECHR and its Protocols are directly applicable in Kosovo and have priority over laws and other acts of public institutions. The decisions which emanate from the ECtHR are a binding interpretive guideline not only for all courts in Kosovo, but also other state organs, and assist them as to how fundamental rights and freedoms must be interpreted and applied in Kosovo.

Already in the first years of its existence, the Constitutional Court has become an important player in the constitutional life in Kosovo. The European Commission stated that the Court "played an important role through the way it exercised its responsibilities" and "has issued a number of key decisions, which made a significant impact".[42] The Court relies extensively on Strasbourg case law in its jurisprudence, not only with regard to substantive rights, but also procedural questions. One can certainly conclude that to date, through its decisions, the Constitutional Court has greatly contributed to the development of the rule of law, democracy and constitutionalism in the Republic of Kosovo.

41 See the contributions in *Wojciech Sadurski* (ed.), Constitutional Justice, East and West, 2002, namely *Lech Garlicki*, The Experience of the Polish Constitutional Court, 281; *Miro Cerar*, Slovenia's Constitutional Court within the Separation of Power, 255; *Renate Weber*, The Romanian Constitutional Court in Search of its Own Identity, 306.

42 European Commission Staff Working Paper, Kosovo 2011 Progress Report, 12.10.2011, SEC (2011) 1207, at 3, 10.

Where Courts Meet: The Effective Protection of the Right to Trial within Reasonable Time in Kosovo in Light of the ECHR and Comparative Experiences

*Peter Pavlin**

Contents

I. Introduction

The right to a trial within a reasonable time and the right to an effective remedy are among the most important human rights in any rule of law state that wants to ensure the *de jure* and *de facto* functioning of its human rights protection system. The two rights are interconnected human rights enshrined in Article 6 para. 1 and Article 13 of the European Convention on Human Rights (ECHR). Any state bound by the Convention has to ensure these two rights within a functioning justice system that really works, and this includes the obligation to put in place mechanisms which offer an effective remedy for violations of the right to trial within a reasonable time. This interconnection of the two rights thus creates a crossroads where all three kinds of courts studied in this book interact: The European Court of Human Rights (ECtHR), domestic constitutional justice, and the ordinary judiciary.

The effective protection of the right to trial within reasonable time is a particularly pressing practical problem in Kosovo. International reports have repeatedly found that the administration of justice and the establishment of the rule of law in Kosovo face serious problems because of severe delays in court proceedings, case backlogs and the like.[1] This has a number of causes, but as we shall see, one reason is that Kosovo currently lacks a legislative framework to deal with delays of justice. Therefore the aim of this paper is to analyse the possible mechanisms to ensure the effective protection of the right to trial within a reasonable time in the Republic of Kosovo in light of the 2008 Constitution of the Republic of Kosovo and the experiences of other ECHR member states.

The paper will first set out the European standards established by the ECtHR and discuss their effect within the legal order of Kosovo (part II). After looking at some comparative experiences from other Council of Europe member states (part III), the paper then discusses possible solutions for complying with constitutional and European standards in Kosovo (part IV). It concludes with a call for cooperation between all three types of courts involved in the effective protection of the right to trial within a reasonable time.

* Secretary, Head of the Division for Punitive Law and for the Protection of Human Rights at the Ministry of Justice of the Republic of Slovenia; external expert advisor to the Government of Kosovo.

1 See for instance *International Crisis Group*, The Rule of Law in Independent Kosovo, Europe Report No. 204, 19 May 2010.

II. Strasbourg standards for effective remedies against delays of justice and their effects within the constitutional order of Kosovo

1. ECtHR jurisprudence on the effective protection of the right to trial within reasonable time

The ECtHR established the systemic connection between the right to a trial within a reasonable time in Article 6 para. 1 on the one hand and the right to an effective remedy in Article 13 ECHR on the other in the leading case of *Kudła v. Poland*:[2] "If Article 13 is, as the Government argued, to be interpreted as having no application to the right to a hearing within a reasonable time as safeguarded by Article 6 § 1, individuals will systematically be forced to refer to the Court in Strasbourg complaints that would otherwise, and in the Court's opinion more appropriately, have to be addressed in the first place within the national legal system. In the long term the effective functioning, on both the national and international level, of the scheme of human rights protection set up by the Convention is liable to be weakened. [...] In view of the foregoing considerations, the Court considers that the correct interpretation of Article 13 is that that provision guarantees an effective remedy before a national authority for an alleged breach of the requirement under Article 6 § 1 to hear a case within a reasonable time."[3]

The ECtHR fleshed out the requirements that follow from this linkage in its 2005 case of *Lukenda v. Slovenia*[4], which is regarded as a "quasi-pilot judgment"[5] on the matter. In this case, the ECtHR held that the legal system of the Republic of Slovenia violated the requirements set by Article 6 para. 1 and Article 13 ECHR. The Court analysed the (then) inefficiency of Slovenia's legal system concerning the rights to trial within a reasonable time and to an effective legal remedy: "Therefore, like an action in the administrative courts and a tort

2 ECtHR, *Kudla v. Poland*, Application no. 30210/96, judgment of 26 October 2000.

3 *Ibid.*, paras. 155-156.

4 ECtHR, *Lukenda v. Slovenia*, Application no. 23032/02, judgment of 6 October 2005.

5 The *Lukenda v. Slovenia* judgment is designated as a quasi-pilot judgment in: *Philip Leach/Helen Hardman, Svetlana Stephenson/Brad K. Blitz,* Responding to Systemic Human Rights Violations: An Analysis of 'Pilot Judgments' of the European Court of Human Rights and Their Impact at National Level, 2010, 26, 86-87. Concerning the terms of pilot judgment and quasi-pilot judgment and their procedures see: *Ibid.*, 9-14 and 34-40; *Council of Europe/Ministry of Foreign Affairs/Ministry of Justice*, The right to trial within a reasonable time and short-term reform of the European Court of Human Rights : Round Table organised by the Slovenian chairmanship of the Committee of Ministers of the Council of Europe, Bled, Slovenia, 21-22 September 2009, 2009, 136; see also *Philip Leach/Jakub Wołąsiewicz/John Darcy*, Pilot Judgment Procedure in the European Court of Human Rights, 3rd Informal Seminar for Government Agents and other Institutions, 2009.

claim, a request for supervision [so-called "supervisory appeal" foreseen as a remedy in Slovenia, P.P.] cannot be regarded an effective remedy within the meaning of the Convention. In the Belinger case the Court found that the efficiency of the constitutional appeal was already problematic in view of the probable length of the combined proceedings. Since the Government have not submitted any new materials concerning the constitutional appeal, the Court considers that, at present, it cannot be regarded as an effective remedy [...] and [...] the Government have failed to establish that an administrative action, a tort claim, a request for supervision or a constitutional appeal can be regarded as effective remedies [...]. For example, when an individual lodges an administrative action alleging a violation of his or her right to a trial within a reasonable time while the proceedings in question are still pending, he or she can reasonably expect the administrative court to deal with the substance of the complaint. However, if the main proceedings end before it has had time to do so, it will dismiss the action. Finally, the Court also concluded that the aggregate of legal remedies[6] in the circumstances of these cases is not an effective remedy [...]."[7]

2. The 2008 Kosovo Constitution and the effective protection of the right to trial within reasonable time

The provisions of the Constitution of the Republic of Kosovo of 2008 on the rights to trial within a reasonable time and to an effective remedy closely mirror the respective ECHR provisions, but display some particularities with regard to the incorporation of Convention standards into domestic law. Firstly, the Constitution has its own fundamental rights catalogue, which states in Article 31 para. 2 (Right to Fair and Impartial Trial) that everyone is entitled to "a fair and public hearing [...] within a reasonable time". Article 32 (Right to Legal Remedies) stipulates that every person has the right to pursue legal remedies against judicial and administrative decisions which infringe his/her rights or interests, in the manner provided by law. Article 31 para. 2 of the Constitution is quite similar to Article 6 para. 1 ECHR, while Article 32 differs slightly from Article 13 ECHR

6 As an aggregate of legal remedies in relation to protection of the right to trial within a reasonable time, the following legal institutes were considered in the case of *Lukenda v. Slovenia*: supervisory appeal which is an administrative matter that is part of the court management (judiciary) in connection with the justice administration (Ministry of Justice), civil law damages (compensation) proceedings before the civil court, suit (action) in an administrative dispute before the administrative court and the constitutional complaint before the Constitutional Court of the Republic of Slovenia.

7 ECtHR, *Lukenda v. Slovenia*, Application no. 23032/02, judgment of 6 October 2005, paras. 64 et seq.

in that it explicitly mentions legal remedies against judicial decisions and uses the wider term of "infringement" of rights and interests. The addition "provided by law" in Article 32 refers to legislative acts adopted by the Assembly of the Republic of Kosovo.

Besides this catalogue of rights, the Kosovo Constitution contains special provisions on the direct application of (some non-ratified) international treaties (since Kosovo is not yet a member of certain international organisations), which are incorporated in the Constitution *in toto*. The ECHR, which Kosovo has not ratified, is one of the treaties explicitly included in Article 22 of the Constitution, which makes the Convention directly applicable within the domestic legal order of Kosovo.[8] Indeed, the provision even explicitly includes ECHR protocols – in general all-inclusive terms.[9] Therefore, the Convention must be applied directly by Kosovo courts and the public administration. Article 22 also specifies that the enumerated instruments have a higher hierarchical rank than acts adopted by the Assembly of Kosovo. Finally, Article 53 of the Constitution on the "Interpretation of Human Rights Provisions" additionally states that "[h]uman rights and fundamental freedoms guaranteed by this Constitution shall be interpreted consistent with the court decisions of the European Court of Human Rights." Therefore, the case law of the European Court of Human Rights is one of paramount sources of all law of Kosovo. Indeed, it is not merely a secondary interpretation tool, since the provisions on the hierarchical status of the ECHR seem to imply a constitutional status for the ECtHR's case law.

In sum, the relationship between the ECHR/ECtHR and Kosovo's legal order can be characterized by the two notions of duplication and constitutionalisation. Duplication results from the fact that the Constitution enshrines the rights to trial within reasonable time and the right to an effective remedy not just in its own fundamental rights catalogue but also incorporates the ECHR *in toto*, which determines, slightly differently, these same rights. Constitutionalisation has three aspects: Firstly, Article 22 of the Constitution means that the ECHR is constitutionalised and additionally, possible relationships and interconnections between its provisions are also constitutionalised. Secondly, the entire corpus of relevant case law of the ECtHR is constitutionalised by virtue of Article 53 of the Consti-

8 For an analysis of the status of the ECHR and ECtHR case law in Kosovo, see the contribution of Snezhana *Botusharova*, in this volume. Article 20 of the Constitution which includes a provision on Delegation of Sovereignty seems to be more of a European Union membership or NATO alliance membership type norm, than a United Nations membership norm, and is in any case probably currently (December 2011) still inapplicable.

9 For example, even protocols that are not ratified by most of the member states of the Council of Europe and can be procedurally or substantively applied within Kosovo are automatically included - like Protocol No. 12 to the European Convention on Human Rights of 2000 on the general prohibition of discrimination.

tution, so this case law is a direct legal source in Kosovo. And thirdly, if by virtue of Article 53 of the Constitution all human rights and fundamental freedoms are to be interpreted in accordance with the case law of the ECtHR, then this case law also covers and seems to be "higher"[10] than the original human rights provisions of the Constitution, even higher than provisions of other human rights treaties enumerated in Article 22. Taking into account these constitutional provisions, it can be stated that from a textual point of view, Kosovo's constitutional order has one of most legally entrenched and detailed systems for the protection of the right to trial within reasonable time and an effective remedy in Europe. This raises the question what consequences the ECtHR case law in this field has in Kosovo's legal order.[11]

3. Consequences of ECtHR case law on the effective protection of the right to trial within a reasonable time in Kosovo's domestic legal order

If applied in light of the aforementioned constitutional provisions, the cited ECtHR case law seems to mean that Kosovo is required to have a detailed domestic regulation on the statutory level for the effective protection of the right to trial within reasonable time. This proposition results from the consideration that whenever the European Court adopts a pilot judgment[12] or finds in some other manner a systemic problem or systemic violations in a ECHR state party, and if

10 This poses some problems for constitutional interpretation, namely, if the European Convention on Human Rights is a common human rights instrument of practically all states in Europe, it is still at least academically a minimum standard; and additionally, can the case law of the European Court of Human Rights really be used for interpretation of other international human rights treaties from Article 22, like the International Covenant on Civil and Political Rights (of the United Nations)?

11 The ECtHR case law in this regard not only affects Council of Europe member states and other states bound by its standards; a possible "transplant" concerning the protection of the right to a trial within a reasonable time also in the law of the European Union can be found in: European Court of Justice, C-385/07 P, *Der Grüne Punkt Duales System Deutschland v. European Commission*, Grand Chamber Judgment of 16 July 2009, especially paras. 167, 177, 188 and 196.

12 See for example the new type of pilot judgment in the recent case of *Rumpf v. Germany* (Application No. 46344/06, 2 September 2010), where amongst others, the Court decided that "in the present case there has been a violation of Article 13 of the Convention on account of the lack of a remedy under domestic law whereby the applicant could have obtained a ruling upholding his right to have his case heard within a reasonable time, as set forth in Article 6 para. 1 of the Convention" (para. 52 of the judgment) and that the Federal Republic of Germany "must introduce without delay, and at the latest within one year from the date on which this judgment becomes final, a remedy or a combination of remedies in the national legal system in order to bring it into line with the Court's conclusions in the present judgment and to comply with the requirements of Article 46 of the Convention. " (para. 73 of the judgment).

the same problem exists in Kosovo (like court backlogs, but also other cases like occupied private immovable property or criminal charges with respect to minor offences), then the Assembly of Kosovo should adopt a detailed and guarantist act to remedy the situation, and other actors (like courts) should directly and in a systemic fashion apply this case law in their entire decision-making processes. Similarly, any other judgment of the ECtHR, which has any relevance on official proceedings in Kosovo should be followed in those individual proceedings, by virtue of the constitutionalisation of the entire corpus of the existing Strasbourg case law as follows from Article 53 of the Constitution.

Moreover, Kosovo's legal system and Kosovo's legal actors should also always follow the so called "soft law" of the Council of Europe, including the "Recommendation CM/Rec(2010)3 of the Committee of Ministers to member states on effective remedies for excessive length of proceedings".[13] This is because such soft law usually recapitulates in a quite (easily) applicable manner the human rights standards stemming from the Convention and the Court's case law. Furthermore, even the Court itself sometimes enshrines this soft law in its case law, like in the recent judgment of *Rumpf v. Germany*.[14] As a result, statements and positions contained in the Recommendation and in the recent judgment in the case of *Rumpf v. Germany* are a detailed and binding standard for any possible regulation, interpretation or decision-making in Kosovo with respect to the right to a trial within a reasonable time and the related right to effective remedy. Of course, a more moderate interpretation of these constitutional provisions may be possible, but this depends on the future developments of authoritative case law of the Constitutional Court of the Republic of Kosovo[15] and of the Supreme Court of the Republic of Kosovo.

13 This Recommendation was adopted by the Committee of Ministers on 24 February 2010 – at the 1077th meeting of the Ministers' Deputies. The accompanying Guide to Good Practice was adopted at the same meeting.

14 ECtHR, *Rumpf v. Germany*, Application no. 46344/06, judgment of 2 September 2010. It is stated in para. 73 of this judgment: "In so doing, the German authorities should also have due regard to the Committee of Ministers' recommendations to the member states on the improvement of domestic remedies of 12 May 2004".

15 See as an example of the possible beginning of this process of interpretation – the judgment of the Constitutional Court of the Republic of Kosovo of 30 October 2010 in the case of *Valon Bislimi Against Ministry of Internal Affairs, Kosovo Judicial Council And Ministry of Justice* (KI 06/10), where the Court started the process of interpretation of Article 53 of the Constitution (especially para. 62 and also paras. 63-67, 52 and some others of this judgment).

III. Comparative overview of the models used in Europe for the effective protection of the right to a trial within a reasonable time

Before discussing problems and possibilities of implementing these standards in Kosovo, we will have a brief look at solutions from other systems bound by the ECHR. We can discern two main models: The acceleratory model and the compensatory models, and variations and combinations of the two.

1. The Austrian/Czech acceleratory model

Austria and the Czech Republic are examples of the acceleratory model. Notably, Article 91 of the Courts Organisation Act of Austria[16] provides for a remedy to expedite judicial proceedings. This procedural institute – the *Fristzetzungsantrag* – was introduced in Austria's legislation in 1989. However, Article 78 of the of the Courts Organisation Act of Austria (*Gerichtsorganisationsgesetz*) still retains the traditional institute of supervisory appeal (*Aufsichtsbeschwerde*) as a mixed matter of court management and justice administration (the Ministry of Justice of Austria can still request explanations and "actions" from presidents of courts about delayed cases amongst others). Article 91 reads:

> "(1) If a court is dilatory in taking any procedural step, such as scheduling or holding a hearing, obtaining an expert's report, or issuing a decision, a party may submit a request to the superior court for this court to impose an appropriate time-limit for the taking of the particular procedural step; unless paragraph 2 of this Article applies, the court is required to submit the request to the superior court immediately, together with its comments, forthwith.
>
> (2) If the court takes all the procedural steps specified in the request within four weeks of its receipt, and so notifies the party concerned, the request is deemed withdrawn unless the party declares within two weeks after service of the notification that it wishes to maintain its request.
>
> (3) The request referred to in paragraph 1 shall be decided in an especially expedite manner by a Panel of the superior court consisting of three professional judges, one of whom shall preside; if the court has not been dilatory, the request shall be dismissed. The decision is final."[17]

16 *Hans Fasching*, Lehrbuch des österreichischen Zivilprozeßrechts, 2nd ed., 1990, 1036-1038, states that this amendment to the Courts Organisation Act of Austria which was adopted in 1989 was needed due to the fact that the supervisory appeal from Article 78 of the said Act does not fulfil obligations from Article 6 para. 1 ECHR about the right to a trial within a reasonable time and accordingly, a new procedural remedy had to be introduced; the supervisory appeal is a matter of court management and provides only for a limited possibility of influencing the speed of the trial.

17 Author's own translation.

In a similar vein, the Czech Courts and Judges Act[18] was amended in 2004 and prescribes in Article 174a that a party to judicial proceedings may file an appeal against the violation of the right to a trial within a reasonable time to the president of the court, who will then hear the case. This president or the president of a superior court may decide that the court should impose an appropriate time-limit for the taking of the particular procedural step.

2. The Italian compensatory model

Italy is an example of the compensatory model, which is not aimed at expediting the proceedings, but rather as monetary compensation after the violation has occurred. The Italian Act No. 89 of 24 March 2001, known as the "Pinto Act"[19], introduced the possibility of lodging a complaint before the Italian courts with respect to excessively long judicial proceedings. It provides only for reparation, namely financial compensation for non-pecuniary and pecuniary damage sustained due to delayed judicial proceedings. The Pinto Act was modified in 2008[20], with respect to the acceleration of administrative proceedings, by prescribing that the request for just satisfaction under the Pinto Act is inadmissible unless the party to judicial proceedings files an urgent request for a hearing before the administrative court.

3. The Slovenian/Polish combined model: Acceleratory and compensatory remedies

Slovenia and Poland opted for a model that combines acceleratory and compensatory remedies. Following the *Lukenda* case cited above[21], a series of ECtHR judgments against the Republic of Slovenia found a violation of the right to trial

18 In Czech language: Zákon č. 6/2002 Sb., o soudech, soudcích, přísedících a státní správě soudů a o změně dalších zákonů (changed in 2011 - 215/2011 Sb.).

19 Act No. 89 of 24 March 2001 – Providing just satisfaction in the case of violation of the right to trial within a reasonable time and amendments to Article 375 of the Civil Procedure Code ("Legge 24 marzo 2001, n. 89, Previsione di equa riparazione in caso di violazione del termine ragionevole del processo e modifica dell'articolo 375 del codice di procedura civile"), Official Gazette No. 78, 3 April 2001, General Part, as modified by the Article 54 of Legislative Decree No. 112/2008, 25 June 2008 and as confirmed by the Act No. 133, 6 August 2008.

20 For a preliminary positive assessment of the solutions from the aforementioned Legislative Decree No. 112/2008 in the context of the *Pinto Act*, see the Decision of the ECtHR in the case of *Daddi v. Italy*, Application no. 15476/09, judgment of 2 June 2009.

21 See above, II.

within a reasonable time. Also, in September 2005, before the ECtHR judgment was issued, the Constitutional Court of the Republic of Slovenia adopted a similar Decision.[22] It decided that the then Administrative Dispute Act of the Republic of Slovenia of 1997 is unconstitutional (contrary to Article 23, para. 1 of the Constitution of the Republic of Slovenia) in respect of some of its provisions for several reasons: Firstly, because the Act does not contain an effective legal remedy against violations of the right to a trial within a reasonable time in cases in which a violation has already ceased. Secondly, because it also does not contain special provisions adjusted to the nature of the right to a trial within a reasonable time that would enable the claimant to claim just satisfaction (in pecuniary terms) in the event that a violation of the right to a trial within a reasonable time has already ceased. Finally, the Constitutional Court held that the remedying of these unconstitutional situations requires more complex legislative regulation, which the Constitutional Court cannot provide in its Decision. The Decision was promulgated and published in the Official Gazette of the Republic of Slovenia after the judgment of the ECtHR in the case of *Lukenda v. Slovenia* was already known and widely publicised.

The legislative solution to this systemic problem followed in 2006 with the "Act on the Protection of the Right to a Trial without Undue Delay"[23], adopted by the National Assembly of the Republic of Slovenia (the Parliament). The Act enables parties to judicial proceedings to use acceleratory remedies for their delayed cases at courts, by using two legal remedies: First, the "supervisory appeal" ("nadzorstvena pritožba") filed at the court which is resolving the case in order to achieve the acceleration of the case's resolution, to be decided by the president of the said court. And secondly, then "motion for a deadline" (rokovni predlog) filed at the superior court if the party to judicial proceedings deems the decision of the president of the original court within the procedure of supervisory

22 Decision of the Constitutional Court of the Republic of Slovenia, No. U-I-65/05, 22 September 2005; published in: Official Gazette RS, No. 92/2005 as of 18 October 2005.

23 In Slovene language: Zakon o varstvu pravice do sojenja brez nepotrebnega odlašanja; published in: Official Gazette RS, Nos. 49/06, 117/06-ZDoh-2, 58/09 and 30/2010 - Decision of the Constitutional Court. The Act was amended to a degree in 2009, similarly as in Poland, but independently. For the critical assessment of the Act and of the Slovenia's Project for the elimination of court backlogs that started in 2005 ("*The Lukenda Project*") see: *Leach/Hardman/Stephenson/Blitz* (note 5), 75-104. For the descriptions and explanations of Slovenia`s relevant constitutional provisions, of the Act of 2006 and relevant national and international case law, see: *Lovro Šturm* (ed.) Commentary of the Constitution of the Republic of Slovenia - Supplement A [Komentar Ustave Republike Slovenije – Dopolnitev A], Fakulteta za državne in evropske študije, Ljubljana, 2011 (*Janez Čebulj*, Commentary of Article 23 of the Constitution 326-337 (margin numbers 1-16), *Aleš Galič*, Commentary of Article 23 of the Constitution 337-338 (margin number 17), 379-384 (margin numbers 76-81), *Franc Testen*, Commentary of Article 15 of the Constitution 203-205 (margin numbers. 9-12).

appeal concerning the acceleration of proceedings to be unsatisfactory. The Act includes all types of judicial proceedings before all courts in Slovenia, including the Supreme Court; however it does not include the Constitutional Court.

Additionally to this acceleratory (expeditory) remedy, a compensatory remedy is also at the disposal of parties to judicial proceedings. This remedy of just satisfaction ("pravično zadoščenje") can be filed after[24] all judicial proceedings have ended and if all previously described acceleratory remedies have been exhausted, within certain prescribed deadlines. It mostly includes the compensation for possible damage, as well as three other types of satisfaction.[25] The compensation for possible non-pecuniary damage ("denarna odškodnina za nepremoženjsko škodo") is limited by this Act to a sum between 300 and 5000 EUR per the entire court case, irrespective of the number of instances where it was adjudicated upon. The compensation for non-pecuniary damage as well as the separately regulated compensation for pecuniary damage ("uveljavljanje premoženjske škode"), in which the amount of reparation is not limited, is based on the principle of strict liability. These combined acceleratory and compensation remedies represent fulfilling, from the Republic of Slovenia's point of view, the general just satisfaction obligation from Article 41 of the European Convention on Human Rights.

Concerning the Republic of Poland, the judgment of the Grand Chamber of the European Court of Human Rights in the case of *Kudła v. Poland*[26] stated amongst others, that that there had been a violation of Article 6 paras. 1 and 13 ECHR in that the applicant had had no domestic remedy to enforce his right to a hearing within a reasonable time. As a systemic response to this judgment, the Polish legislature adopted the "Act of 17 June 2004 concerning the complaint on infringement of a party's right to have a case examined in preparatory proceedings conducted or supervised by a prosecutor and in court proceedings without undue delay"[27]. This Act, which was partially amended in 2009, provides for two types of remedies: acceleratory and compensation remedies that apply to prepar-

24 The ECtHR has decided that this ex-post solution "could have the legitimate aim of simplifying the procedure by, *inter alia*, preventing repeated filing of just satisfaction claims during the pending proceedings." (*Žunič v. Slovenia*, Application no. 24342/04, decision of 18 October 2007, paras. 49-50 and 54).

25 Two other types of just satisfaction, not described in this text, are:
- a written statement of the State Attorney's Office that the party's right to a trial without undue delay was violated,
- the publication of a judgement that the party's right to a trial without undue delay was violated.

26 ECtHR, *Kudła v. Poland*, Application no. 30210/96, judgment of 26 October 2000.

27 Ustawa o skardze na naruszenie prawa strony do rozpoznania sprawy w postępowaniu sądowym bez nieuzasadnionej zwłoki; published in: Journal of Laws, Nos. 179/04 and 61/09.

atory, judicial and civil enforcement proceedings. In accordance with the provisions of this special Act, a party to judicial proceedings may file a complaint that their right to trial without undue delay was violated. The superior court which has to decide upon this complaint may issue an instruction to the relevant court or prosecutor to take appropriate procedural measure within a court-set deadline. The compensation to be paid within these acceleratory proceedings is in principle also statutorily limited – to a sum between 2000 and 20000 Polish Zloty. This type of combined remedy – acceleratory (expeditory) and compensatory – is in accordance with the recommendation from the Grand Chamber judgment of the ECtHR in the case of *Scordino v. Italy (No. 1)*[28], where the Court stated: "Moreover, some States, such as Austria, Croatia, Spain, Poland and Slovakia, have understood the situation perfectly by choosing to combine two types of remedy, one designed to expedite the proceedings and the other to afford compensation."[29]

4. Croatian combined and refurbished model: From the Constitutional Court to the courts of regular jurisdiction

Starting in 1999, the Constitutional Court of the Republic of Croatia began to develop the constitutional complaint into a legal remedy for protecting the right to trial within a reasonable time. In 2002, the Constitutional Act on the Constitutional Court of the Republic of Croatia[30] was significantly changed. Its then Article 59a (now Article 63) explicitly regulated the use of the constitutional complaint for delayed court proceedings – even if previous proceedings have not been finished. The Constitutional Court may impose a deadline on the regular court in which certain procedural actions should be taken, as well as order the payment of compensation to the claimant. However, the Constitutional Court became a victim of its success, since it had to deal with too many constitutional complaints with respect to presumed violation of the right to a trial within a reasonable time. The Court thus adopted on 24 February 2005 a special "Report of the Constitutional Court of the Republic of Croatia to the Parliament of Croatia

28 ECtHR, *Scordino v. Italy (no. 1)*, Application no. 36813/97, Grand Chamber judgment of 29 March 2006.

29 *Ibid.*, para. 186, citing further case law, for instance *Slaviček v. Croatia*, Application no. 20862/02,decision of 4 July 2002; *Fernández-Molina González and Others v. Spain*, Application no. 64359/01, decision of 8 October 2002; *Michalak v. Poland* Application no. 24549/03, decision of 1 March 2005; and *Andrášik and Others v. Slovakia* Application nos. 57984/00, 60237/00, 60242/00, 60679/00, 60680/00, 68563/01 and 60226/00, decision of 22 October 2002.

30 Official Gazette of the Republic of Croatia, No. 29/02.

on realisation of constitutionality and legality and on noted occurrences of unconstitutionality and illegality in the year of 2004".[31] In the Report, the Constitutional Court proposes to amend the legislation on court organisation and to transfer the existing jurisdiction on constitutional complaints with respect to violation of the right to trial within a reasonable time from the Constitutional Court to regular courts. The Croatian Government accepted this idea in 2005, and drafted the new Courts Act, which was adopted by the Croatian Parliament in late 2005.[32] As proposed, the Act relegated the jurisdiction to regular courts (Articles 27 and 28 of the Courts Act). However, this decision was heavily criticised, namely by the highly respected former President of the Constitutional Court Jadranko Crnić, because the reform created a dual jurisdiction or "bilocation": As it stands, regular courts can decide on delay issues in accordance with Articles 27 and 28 of the Courts Act, and at the same time the Constitutional Court retained the same jurisdiction in the unchanged Article 63 of the Constitutional Act on the Constitutional Court.[33]

IV. Possibilities in Kosovo for complying with the requirement of effective protection of the right to trial within a reasonable time

Having looked at the potential models adopted elsewhere, we now turn to possible solutions for Kosovo, taking into account its legal system, especially the guarantees and limitations contained in its 2008 Constitution. Kosovo has not legislated specifically and in detail on the right to trial within reasonable time and to an effective remedy. We will thus explore a number of potential solutions to the problem of implementing the requirements of the two rights.

1. The Constitutional Court solution

One possibility for protecting the two rights would be through constitutional complaints before the Constitutional Court of Kosovo. The Constitutional Court already has the jurisdiction to decide upon constitutional complaints filed by individuals claiming violations of their human rights or fundamental freedoms, ac-

31 Item No: U-X/835/2005.

32 In Croatian language: Zakon o sudovima, Official Gazette of the Republic of Croatia, Nos. 150/05, 16/07, 113/08, 153/09, 116/2010, 122/2010, 27/2011 and 130/2011.

33 *Jadranko Crnić*, (Un)constitutional absurdities of (non)reasonable time in the application of Article 29 of the Constitution - on the "bilocation" of jurisdiction [(Ne)ustavni apsurdi (ne)razumnog roka u primjeni članka 29. Ustava – o "bilokaciji" nadležnosti], Hrvatska pravna revija, No. 3/2008, 1-8.

cording to Article 113 para. 7 of the Constitution and according to Articles 46-50 of the Act No. 03/L-121 on the Constitutional Court of the Republic of Kosovo of 2008.[34] The problem here is that Article 113 para. 7 requires the exhaustion of all legal remedies provided by law before complaints are admissible, which is currently impossible precisely in cases of delays. The Court would thus have to adopt the position that no exhaustion of other (presumably inefficient) legal remedies is needed in cases of severe delays in the ordinary courts. This could be justified with the argument that there are no special remedies that could possibly be exhausted in cases of violations of the right to a trial within a reasonable time. Such a position would thus also be in line with case law of the ECtHR.

This solution, if developed by the Constitutional Court itself, would be quite systemic and bold – not in the sense of judicial activism[35], but in the sense of developing this solution within the context of Kosovo's young and human rights oriented Constitution and of the still developing institutions of Kosovo's legal system. Still, when considering the Croatian experience, such jurisprudence might quickly lead to an overload of cases at the Constitutional Court if not complemented by other mechanisms. Hence other more sustainable and permanent solutions must be found.

2. The Ministry of Justice solution

When looking for a potential role for the Ministry of Justice of the Republic of Kosovo in solving judicial delay problems, one has to realize that it is probably one of the weakest Ministries of Justice in Europe when assessed from a competences' viewpoint. The Constitution gives it few competences, and notably judicial administration[36] is not the task of the Ministry, but of the Kosovo Judicial

34 Official Gazette of the Republic of Kosovo, No. 46, 15 January 2009.

35 For a criticism of the late 1990's judicial activism of the Constitutional Court of the Republic of Slovenia, which, due to historic and legal system familiarity, may be comparable to the Kosovo's Constitutional Court, see: *Miro Cerar*, Slovenia's Constitutional Court within the Separation of Power, in: Wojciech Sadurski (ed.), Constitutional Justice, East and West: Democratic Legitimacy and Constitutional Courts in Post-Communist Europe in a Comparative Perspective, 2002, 227-233. For a discussion on the issue of the "arbitrary Constitutional Court" that in its judicial activism role exceeds it powers and violates a principle of legal certainty and on the solution to this issue in an extreme situation (the solution being the amendment of 25 July 2000 to the electoral system part of the Constitution of the Republic of Slovenia) see equally *Cerar*, ibid., 230-232.

36 The usual term for this competence is: court management. This provision therefore means that independent courts of Kosovo do not operate court management matters on their own, but an external body – the Kosovo Judicial Council performs this, or at least that it should – nearly *in toto*. For a recent systematic description of institutes of court management and justice administration in the Republic of Slovenia see *Zoran Skubic*, Evolving

Council by virtue of Article 108 para. 5 of the Constitution. The Ministry also cannot have any jurisdiction over matters of justice administration[37] due to the wide enumerated powers of the Kosovo Judicial Council in Article 108 of the Constitution. Therefore, the Ministry of Justice cannot be an intermediary between the parties to judicial proceedings and courts that process their supposedly delayed cases. Neither can the Ministry of Justice be established as a sort of an *ex officio* monitoring authority over matters that are part of the court management (judicial administration). So, in this unique system of extremely strict separation of powers, there seems to be little possibility for the Ministry of Justice to have any operational role concerning the right to a trial within a reasonable time. Where it could play a part is in ensuring sufficient budgetary resources for the courts during negotiations on the Government of Kosovo level.

3. The Kosovo Judicial Council solution

As has been seen, the Kosovo Judicial Council, which is the self-administration body of the judiciary, is tasked with judicial administration and might thus perform some functions in matters of court management. These functions could include intermediary and monitoring powers concerning individuals' claims about the violation of their right to a trial within a reasonable time, or the Council could perhaps perform them even *ex officio*. Yet there is no legislative or otherwise official specific rule on this, and no legally enforceable claim for individuals.

4. The regular courts solution

The regular[38] courts of Kosovo, which include the Basic Courts, the Court of Appeals and the Supreme Court of Kosovo, presently lack a specific legislative

Justice: The Constitutional Relationship Between The Ministry Of Justice And The Judiciary And A Short Overview Of Recent Developments In The Area Of Court Management In The Republic Of Slovenia, International Journal For Court Administration 7 (2011), 1.

37 Judicial administration usually means that part of the executive (!) power that deals with administrative matters (logistics, financing, monitoring, some personnel/employment issues, some service issues, like preparing judges' official identity cards, prescribing official judicial attires etc.) with relation to the independent and separate judicial power, within the usual framework of the principle of checks and balances, which is a part of the fundamental constitutional principle of separation of powers.

38 Regular courts of Kosovo in this text designate courts of general jurisdiction and do not include specialised courts and especially not the Constitutional Court of the Republic of

basis to hear claims for violations of the right to trial within reasonable time. The new Act on Courts of the Republic of Kosovo of 2010[39] simply states in Article 7 para. 2 second sentence: "Every natural and legal person has the right to a fair trial within a reasonable timeframe." Since this general provision from the new Act on Courts is not accompanied by any effective procedural acceleratory or compensatory remedy for its enforcement, it is *de facto* of a declaratory nature.

There used to be a legal base in Kosovo's earlier judicial organisation legislation, namely in Article 61 para. 1 subpara. 6 of the Regular Courts Act of the Socialist Autonomous Province Kosovo of 1976[40], which stated: "The Provincial Secretariat[41] of Justice and General Administration [...] examines directly or through the president of the superior court complaints against the work of courts for reasons of denial of justice, delays of work and other reasons." This remedy was similar to and copied from Austria's traditional institute of supervisory appeal (*Aufsichtsbeschwerde*) in Article 78 of the Courts Organisation Act of Austria. But this "remedy" was under-regulated and thus one of the most inefficient "remedies" in practice, only exceptionally providing just satisfaction to parties of judicial proceedings. It was *de facto* in the hands of the judiciary itself, which decided whether to provide sufficient information to the then Secretariat and when to accelerate judicial proceedings, even if the *dominus litis* of these semi-administrative proceedings was supposed to be the Secretariat. After this mostly negative experience and the advent of new ECtHR case law, most of the successor states of former the Yugoslavia statutorily adopted some other, more detailed remedy or even a special Act, like Slovenia[42] or Montenegro.[43]

Kosovo, which is an independent constitutional body (Article 112 para. 2 of the Constitution of the Republic of Kosovo).

39 Act No. 03/L-199, as of 22 July 2010, Official Gazette of the Republic of Kosovo, No. 79/2010.

40 Regular Courts Act of the Socialist Autonomous Province of Kosovo of 1976 (Official Gazette of the SAP Kosovo, Nos. 47/76, 20/77, 21/78 - Officially Consolidated Text and 2/89). The provision remained in force during UN administration, c.f. UNMIK Regulation No. 1999/05, UNMIK Regulation No. 1999/24 and UNMIK Regulation No. 2000/59. Since the enactment of the Kosovo Republic Act on Courts, Official Gazette of the Republic of Kosovo, No. 79/2010, the provision is not in force any more, as its Article 42, para. 1 repeals the former Regular Courts Act of the Socialist Autonomous Province of Kosovo of 1976.

41 This older institutional terminology means: The Ministry of Justice and General Administration.

42 See the aforementioned Slovenian Act on the Protection of the Right to a Trial without Undue Delay of 2006.

43 See: Act on the Protection of a Trial within a Reasonable Time, Official Gazette of Montenegro, No. 11/2007. In Montenegrin language: "Zakon o zaštiti prava na suđenje u razumnom roku".

The Kosovo Assembly is in a position to enact such a special or general judiciary related Act to deal directly with complaints of parties to judicial proceedings about violations of their right to a trial within a reasonable time. An appellate remedy against possible decisions of Presidents of courts or special judicial panels on these claims/complaints could also be envisaged. Or the matter of these complaints should be dealt with directly by superior courts, but an appellate remedy even against their decisions should still be envisaged. Bearing in mind the problems with the earlier regulations, these remedies should be detailed and explicit.

III. Conclusion

The Kosovo Constitution, the direct applicability of the ECHR, the binding case law of the ECtHR, and soft law by the Council of Europe require Kosovo to provide for detailed regulation on a remedy against delays in judicial proceedings. The Constitutional Court can temporarily fill this gap, but the legislature should soon deal with this issue to find a permanent solution and to bring Kosovo law in line with European standards. In the meantime, the Constitutional Court and ordinary courts need to handle delayed cases in a spirit of cooperation. Indeed, the effective protection of the right to trial within reasonable time is an interface between Kosovo's regular courts and Constitutional Court and the Strasbourg court that requires particular sensitivity and cooperation between all jurisdictions concerned – in the interest of the individual citizens and legal persons who come to seek justice and place their trust in official legal means of dispute-settlement.

The Relationship between the Constitutional Court and the Supreme Cassation Court in Serbia

*Ivan Čukalovič**

Contents

I. Introduction

It is interesting to analyze the relationship between the Constitutional Court and the Supreme Cassation Court of Serbia because it is illustrative of the changing Serbian approach to rule of law and constitutionalism. Notably, the current institutional framework reflects recent constitutional reforms: The numerous jurisdictions of both courts have been significantly changed by the enactment of the new Constitution of Serbia in 2006[1] and by the new Law on Regulation of Courts in 2008.[2] Both acts assign the control of constitutionality, as well as the protection of human and minority rights, to the Constitutional Court. The Constitutional Court is an independent state organ, whose decisions are final, executive and binding on everyone. The Supreme Cassation Court sits atop of the ordinary court system and performs different adjudicative functions. However, it is linked to the Constitutional Court in functional, procedural and – more peculiarly – in personal terms.

We will analyze the relationship of the two courts in three steps: First, we will set out the development and the present status of constitutional justice in Serbia (part II). Then we will give an overview of the Serbian justice system and the Supreme Cassation Court (part III). The last part analyzes the relationship between the two courts in a functional, procedural and personal perspective (part IV).

II. Evolution and present status of constitutional justice in Serbia

1. Historical development

The position of the Constitutional Court has undergone significant changes in past constitutional reforms. Today, it is the only organ of that kind in Serbia and, as such, the default carrier of the protection of constitutionality, and, to a certain extent, legality in the entire territory. This was not always the case, but is the result of the restructuring of the autonomous regions in the Constitution of the Republic of Serbia of 1990. The 1990 Constitution abolished the constitutional or legislative authority of the autonomous regions, which resulted in the abolition

* Judge at the Constitutional Court of Kosovo; Professor of Law, University of Kragujevac, Republic of Serbia.

1 Constitution of the Republic of Serbia, published in the Službeni glasnik (Official Gazette of the Republic of Serbia) RS, No. 98/2006 of 10 November 2006.

2 A new organizational scheme of courts was established by the Law on Court Organization; see Official Gazette of the Republic of Serbia No. 116/2008, 104/2009.

of their constitutional courts. Consequently, the 1990 text deleted the provisions of the Constitution that addressed the relations towards the constitutions and laws of those regions, and towards their constitutional courts.

Another change over time was due to the general conception of the Constitution, which appears to be of a formal nature at a first glance, but in fact evidences fundamental changes in Serbian statehood: In the 1974 Constitution of Serbia, the analogous organ is called "The Constitutional Court of Serbia", while the constitutions of the Republic of Serbia from 1990 and 2006 use the term "The Constitutional Court". This linguistic change affected all organs of the Republic. In other words, the Constitutions of 1990 and after do not emphasize that the organs are those of the Republic of Serbia, as is done in the Constitution of Serbia from 1974. The important legal background to this wording is that the constitutions from 1990 and 2006 are written as complete constitutional documents of an independent state, while the Constitution from 1974 has been set out as the Constitution of one federal unit within the Socialist Federal Republic of Yugoslavia. Some of the significant differences between the 1990 – 2006 Constitutions and the 1974 Constitution are:

1) The Constitutional Court is now the carrier of constitutionality, and to a certain extent, legality in the whole territory of Serbia, as a result of the change in the character and jurisdictions of autonomous regions.

2) New jurisdictions: the banning of political parties and deciding in electoral disputes requires changes in operation and the procedure before the Constitutional Court.

3) Deleting the initiative abilities of the Constitutional Court.

4) Along with increasing the number of judges, important novelties are the limited mandate of judges (nine years), and the fact that one person may be elected twice only.

2. The Constitutional Court under the 2006 Constitution

The constitutional provisions, namely Article 166, on the Constitutional Court emphasize that the Constitutional Court is an autonomous organ of the Republic of Serbia and presupposed carrier of constitutional protection. "Presupposed" signifies that, in the Constitution itself, the Constitutional Court has been appointed as the guardian of constitutionality and legality, as well as human rights. That position puts it beyond the classical functions of the justice system, but also distinguishes it in principle from the legislator. But admittedly the work of the Constitutional Court also contains elements typical for the judicial system, and its decisions can have the effect of "negative legislator". [3] In light of this, the

3 Certain authors point to the role of the Constitutional Court as the "negative legislator", especially when the Constitutional Court decides what is unconstitutional. Along with this, the Constitutional Court could also be seen as the "shadow positive legislator" when,

Constitutional Court of Serbia is generally perceived as an organ beyond the scheme of the traditional branches of government. This could also be seen from the fact that the institutionalization of the Constitutional Court as such has often been disputed in the literature, from both groups of authors: those that support a division of authority, and those that support unity of authority. The 2006 Constitution of the Republic of Serbia does not give a complete abstract definition of the current Constitutional Court's position. But it refers to all elements and attributions relevant to the Court from which its status can be discerned. The Constitution defines the protection of the constitutional order and some aspects of legality as the main task of the Constitutional Court (Article 167).

a) Jurisdiction

The Court's jurisdiction is defined by Article 167 of the Constitution, according to which the Constitutional Court decides firstly on cases of abstract norm control, namely on the

> "1) compatibility of laws and other general acts with the Constitution, with general rules of international law and with ratified international treaties;
>
> 2) compatibility of ratified international treaties with the Constitution;
>
> 3) compatibility of other general acts with laws;
>
> 4) compatibility of statutes and other acts of autonomous regions and units of local government with the Constitution and laws;
>
> 5) compatibility of general acts of organizations that have delegated public authority, political parties, unions, non-governmental organizations, and collective agreements, with the Constitution and laws".[4]

Furthermore, the Constitutional Court decides on disputes between public bodies and some other matters, namely about

> "1) conflicts of jurisdiction between courts and other state organs;
>
> 2) conflicts of jurisdiction between the organs of the republic and provincial
>
> bodies or bodies of local self-government units,
>
> 3) conflicts of jurisdiction between provincial bodies and bodies of local self-government units,

while establishing that a certain act is unconstitutional, it indirectly points to the possible solution of the problem. See for instance *Wojciech Sadurski*, Constitutional Justice, East and West: Introduction, in: Id., Constitutional Justice, East and West, 2002, 1, 9 et seq. with further references.

4 On the role of international law, and namely the European Convention of Human Rights, in Serbian domestic law, see *Vidan Hadzi-Vidanovic*, in this volume.

4) conflicts of jurisdiction between the organs of different autonomous regions or different regions of local self-government,

5) election disputes for which no court has jurisdiction according to law,

6) other affairs, according to law."

Finally, the Court is also competent for bans of political parties, trade unions, non-governmental organizations and other political organizations. This extensive list of competences represents an expansion of the Constitutional Court's jurisdiction, compared to the Constitutions of 1990 and 1974, which is a direct result of the acceptance of political pluralism in the Serbian political system. The 2006 Constitution made some textual changes compared to that of 1990: Regarding the competence to ban political parties, the 2006 Constitution takes up and modifies a provision from the 1990 text (old Article 125 para. 6), the difference being that under the old law the Court decided about the banning of "other political organizations" (besides political parties), while the new text now specifies that the Constitutional Court decides on banning of trade unions and NGOs along with political parties. The 1990 Constitution already foresaw that the Constitutional Court decides on electoral disputes that were not in the jurisdiction of courts or other state organs (Article 125 para. 7), while the 2006 Constitution holds that the Court decides on election disputes for which no court has jurisdiction according to law. Comparative examples for such powers concerning party bans and election disputes can be found in the constitutional court systems of, *inter alia*, the Federal Republic of Germany and Austria, which served as an example for solving these questions in the 2006 Constitution of Serbia.

b) Procedure

The Constitution of Serbia contains only basic solutions on the procedure before the Constitutional Court and is relatively short in this respect compared to earlier constitutional provisions. The procedure for ex-post norm control regarding constitutionality or legality is regulated in Article 168, while norm control prior to entry into force is regulated in Article 169. The text contains some rules on standing before the Court. Namely, it stipulates that the procedure for the control of constitutionality and legality of an act of public authority can be initiated by state organs, organs of territorial autonomy or organs of local government, at least 25 of the National Assembly members, as well as the Constitutional Court itself. In addition, every natural or legal person has the right to initiate the procedure for constitutionality or legality assessment. This latter aspect means that there is a sort of general initiative, an *actio popularis*.

In addition, Article 170 institutes a constitutional appeal, which may be lodged against individual general acts (i.e. acts made by an individual body that concern its own powers and jurisdictions only) or actions performed by state bodies or organizations exercising delegated public powers which violate or deny human or minority rights and freedoms guaranteed by the Constitution, if other legal remedies for their protection have already been applied or not specified. This means that the constitutional appeal has been prescribed as a subsidiary legal remedy. This is relevant for the relationship to the Supreme Cassation Court, as elaborated upon below.

Some questions regarding the procedure remain unresolved by the Constitution:[5] For instance, it is unclear who exactly can instigate the procedures other than norm control, for example the banning of political parties or election disputes. It seems that standing has been granted to State organs[6], and the Constitutional Court itself. Other organs and organizations[7] could initiate the procedure, if, by their estimation, their rights and interests are directly violated by the act whose legality and constitutionality are being questioned.

c) Composition

There have been significant changes in the organization of the Court, and even more in the status of its President and the judges. The Court now has 15 judges, while according to the 1990 Constitution it had nine. Earlier, the office as Constitutional Court judge was permanent and ended in the case of resignation, retirement, criminal conviction to prison term, or loss of capability to perform duties. The important novelty in the 2006 Constitution is the choice for a limited mandate – nine years, and with the additional restriction that one person can be appointed no more than twice. Further changes regarded the appointment and dismissal of judges, where the rules were changed with the intention of harmonizing them with the European manner of electing the Constitutional Court judges. The reform was inspired by the Italian model, where the Constitutional Court is also made up of 15 judges, five appointed by the President of the Republic, five elected by parliament in a joint session by a two-thirds majority of votes, while five are elected by the members of the Italian Supreme Court and the Supreme Administrative Court. According to the 1990 Constitution of Serbia, the

5 For a weaknesses in the Serbian Constitutional Court's jurisdictions, see also the contribution of *Vidan Hadzi-Vidanovic*, in this volume.

6 By the terms of the Constitution, they are all State organs, which causes certain dilemmas.

7 There are no specifications on their nature.

President and judges of the Constitutional Court were proposed by the President of the Republic, and the selection was made by the National Assembly. According to the 2006 Constitution, all three branches of power now have a say: Five Judges of the Constitutional Court are elected in the National Assembly, five are appointed by the President of the Republic, and five by the General Chamber of the Supreme Cassation Court. This has important implications for the relationship of the two courts, which we will elaborate upon after an analysis of the Supreme Cassation Court's position and function in the justice system of Serbia.

III. The Supreme Cassation Court in the justice system of Serbia

1. The organization of the judiciary in general

The legal system of the Republic of Serbia comprises a complex framework of justice institutions and other actors, such as courts, public prosecutors, public defenders, protectors of citizens[8], law faculties and others. The constitutional changes made in 2006 were an important step towards an independent, efficient and responsible justice system. They have paid particular attention to providing guarantees for court independence and to realizing that independence in practice. The Constitution provides notably for the self-administration of the courts. This implies that the High Judicial Council, the self-administrative body of the courts, plays an important role in the appointment of judges, alongside the parliament: The State Assembly appoints judges on the proposal of the High Judicial Council to a temporary, three year long function. Afterwards, the High Judicial Council appoints the judges to permanent judicial office and also decides on promotions or changes of office. The ratio of this arrangement is that appointments should be based on objective criteria and capabilities, and not on political deliberations. The High Judicial Council is considered to be an objective authority ensuring this aim.

As regards the court structure, the judicial authority in the Republic of Serbia, according to the 2006 Constitution (Article 143), belongs to general and special jurisdiction courts. Formation, organization, jurisdiction, regulation and structure of courts are regulated by the Law on Court Regulation.[9] There is a prohibition

8 Also referred to as "ombudsman" or "public advocate", the protector of citizens protects human rights by checking the allegations of the appealer, criticizing the acts of public organs, and publishing the results of those inquiries in the media, but different from courts and organs of public management, he has no authority to put the questioned acts out of power.

9 See the Law on Court Regulation, in Official Gazette of the Republic of Serbia, Rs. 116/2008 of 22 December 2008.

on establishment of temporary, severe or irregular courts. The highest court in the Republic is the Supreme Cassation Court, and the seat of this court is in Belgrade (Article 143.4 and 143.5 of the Constitution). The general courts are divided according to their jurisdiction into a civil and penal branch, while the special courts comprise numerous different jurisdictions according to the subject matter they adjudicate, such as trade, administrative, police and religious issues.[10] As far as functional jurisdiction is concerned, courts are divided into first degree courts, appellate courts (which also decide on some important first instance matters), and the Supreme Cassation Court.

2. The Supreme Cassation Court

The Supreme Cassation Court generally hears appeals against judgments from lower courts, but generally does not decide on the merit of the case, that is, it does not solve the contentious legal question. Rather it only decides on the legality of the verdict, and quashes and remands it for a retrial if it is found to be illegal. This limited review function partly motivated the rather peculiar designation as "Supreme Cassation Court", which is a result of the constitutional reform, conducted in 2006, that abandoned the previous term "Supreme Court". A major reason for this terminological choice was to create a – rather artificial – discontinuity regarding the highest court instance, in order to indicate a change of structure and a reduction of political control over the institution. The term "Supreme Cassation Court" is rare in comparative law. Highest state courts are usually the "cassation court" or the "supreme court", depending on the role they play in certain legal traditions. Cassation courts, mainly drawn from the French model, have the main purpose to control the legality of judicial decisions; if they are illegal, the court annuls – or "cassates" – them. Supreme courts have more powers, and can notably revise the decisions of lower courts. Yet often the terms "supreme" and "cassation" are held more for traditional rather than functional reasons. Joining the two terms together seems rather unnecessary and contradictory. Regarding Serbia's legal tradition, it would be more appropriate to use the term "Supreme Court".

As far as the status and functions of the Supreme Cassation Court are concerned, the Constitution of 2006 did not change the prior set-up fundamentally, all the more so as it remains largely silent on the Court. Article 143 para. 4 simp-

10 The full list includes the following specializations: 1. Trade; 2. Economic; 3. Military; 4. Administrative; 5. Labor; 6. Social; 7. Customs; 8. Tax; 9. Agrarian; 10. Juvenile; 11. Police; 12. Marital status; 13. Religious, and others.

ly states that "The Supreme Cassation Court is the highest court in the Republic of Serbia", which could go without saying, because it results from the name itself. The important decisions are left to the Law on Court Regulation, which defines the Court's jurisdiction and divides it into "jurisdiction in trial" and "jurisdiction beyond trial", or contentious and non-contentious functions. Regarding the first competence, the Court decides on three types of cases: extraordinary legal means lodged against the decisions of the lower courts; conflict of jurisdictions between courts, if another court does not have the jurisdiction for it; and delegation of the jurisdiction of courts in order to conduct proceedings more efficiently, or for other important reasons. The jurisdiction beyond trial comprises three essential attributions: The Court establishes general legal positions of the Court in order to have a unique practice of law; supervises the application of laws and other regulations, as well as work of the courts; and plays a role in the appointment of Constitutional Court judges. Both the function of overseeing the equal application of the law and of appointing judges concern the relationship to the Constitutional Court, to which we turn now.

IV. The Relationship between the Constitutional Court and the Supreme Cassation Court

1. Functional aspects

From an abstract point of view, the functions of the two Courts are defined, and differentiated, by their respective jurisdiction: The Constitutional Court decides about the compatibility of acts of public authority with the Constitution, while the Supreme Cassation Court ensures the legality and the uniform application of statutory law. But obviously there are several jurisdictional points of interaction between the two: Some of the Constitutional Court's competences include a control of legality, such as the jurisdiction to decide on the compatibility of other general acts *with laws* as well as the compatibility of statutes and other acts of autonomous regions and units of local government with the Constitution *and laws*. There is some functional overlap here. A second overlap may be seen in the function of the Supreme Cassation Court to ensure the equal application of law and the unification of legal practice, and to this end, issues general positions to guide the lower courts. Of course, this refers to uniformity in ordinary law on first sight, but the Constitutional Court's general competence to uphold the Constitution also implies a certain unifying function in the sense that all nation-wide practice must be in conformity with the Constitution. This relationship between the Supreme Cassation Court and the Constitutional Court in respect of equal and uniform application is not regulated by the Constitution.

2. Procedural aspects

The precise relationship between the two courts depends largely on the procedures before the Constitutional Court. There are a number of procedural crossroads where the courts interact: Firstly, the Constitutional Court is authorized to decide conflicts of competence between all courts in the Republic of Serbia and other state organs. This also applies to jurisdictional conflicts in which the Supreme Cassation Court is involved. Thus in this jurisdiction of the Constitutional Court we can discover a first link between the two courts. For now, in practice, there is no case law on this matter, but it is possible that these cases will occur in the future. A second point of procedural interaction directly between the two courts results from the rule that every legal or physical entity can initiate the procedure for assessing the constitutionality and legality. This implies that the right of initiative also belongs to the Supreme Cassation Court, i.e. it can initiate itself a control of constitutionality. For now, in practice, there is again no case law on this matter, but that may change.

However, the most important procedural interface between the two courts is the constitutional appeal. This means that individual citizens can refer judgments of the Supreme Court of Cassation to the Constitutional Court for review. The Constitutional Court then has jurisdiction to decide on the conformity of the acts of this Supreme Cassation Court with the Constitution, laws, general rules of international law, and ratified international treaties (Article 168 of the Constitution of Serbia). This includes the power to quash these last instance judgments, which bears a potential for conflict. However, this can be avoided by a clear distinction of the procedural roles of the courts and the function of the constitutional appeal to benefit individual citizens. The procedure is a legal remedy established in the interest of citizens, for protection of their basic human rights and freedoms, but it is a restricted legal means: It requires a precise range and goal of the appeal and is not a regular legal remedy. It is rather a means that can be submitted only and exclusively to protect basic human rights and freedoms established by the Constitution, not the rights guaranteed by a law or any other act to a certain person. Constitutional appeal "is not a means to express ordinary life's burdens, but an irregular legal remedy whose goal is to protect the most precious human freedoms".[11] Hence, it is clearly foreseen that the constitutional appeal is destined as a subsidiary means of protecting the constitutionally guaranteed human rights and freedoms. This is further procedurally ensured by the requirement that citi-

11 *Dragan Bataveljić*, Ustavno pravo Republike Srbije, II tom, Pravni fakultet Kragujevac, 2007, 195. Translation I.C.

zens exhaust ordinary legal remedies before they address the Constitutional Court.

With all stated, it should be pointed out that the decision of the Constitutional Court on the constitutional appeal must not bring this Court into a position of a supreme court in relation to regular courts and other State organs, that is, in a position of an organ of supreme supervision. The competence for constitutional appeal must not bring the Constitutional Court in the position of the highest court organ in the country (in relation to regular courts and other state organs). Subsidiarity of the constitutional appeal means that citizens cannot "overleap" regular – constitutionally and legally guaranteed – paths of protection of their interests. Subsidiarity of a constitutional appeal ensures that it is not just "yet another" regular means of legal protection, lest the constitutional appeal itself loses the character of "ultimate, extraordinary legal means" that should be used only to protect the most valuable, constitutionally guaranteed human rights and freedoms. Currently, there are a great number of constitutional appeals before the Constitutional Court, which are in the phase of being reviewed.

3. Personal aspects

Finally, the relationship between the two Courts also has a personal dimension, i.e. the appointment and dismissal rules of the judges. As mentioned, the Supreme Cassation Court has a say in the appointments, and also in the dismissal, of the constitutional judges: While the National Assembly chooses five out of ten judges proposed by the President and the President chooses five out of ten judges proposed by the National Assembly, the General Chamber of the Supreme Court appoints five of the ten candidates proposed by the High Judicial Council and the State chamber of prosecutors. This leads to a rather complex mechanism which interlinks all three branches of power in a system of mutual checks and balances. In this system, the Supreme Cassation Court, and the ordinary courts' representative body, has a significant influence on the composition of the Constitutional Court.

In practice, this means that there is a strive for a better selection of judges of the Constitutional Court, giving greater significance to judicial practice (in this particular case, the Supreme Cassation Court), when electing the judges of the Constitutional Court. Earlier solutions favored the legislative and executive, that is, the Assembly of the Republic of Serbia, together with the government. The effects of the current solution are that now there is significantly more cooperation in the relation between the Constitutional Court and the Supreme Cassation

Court. The constitutional reform also resulted in an increased number of professional judges at the Constitutional Court, and fewer politicians and professors.[12]

The Supreme Cassation Court's influence also extends to the cessation of duty of a Constitutional Court judge. According to Article 174 of the Constitution, a judge can be dismissed also if he/she violates the ban on conflict of interests, permanently loses the working capability for the Constitutional Court judge, is convicted to a prison sentence or for an offence which renders him/her unworthy to be a Constitutional Court judge. What matters to us, is the provision of Article 174 para. 3, which determines that all institutions authorized to propose judges can equally demand their dismissal, upon which the National Assembly decides. This implies, according to one interpretation, that the Supreme Cassation Court, through its General Council or the Supervision Board, can initiate the procedure for dismissing the Constitutional Court judge of his/her duty.

V. Conclusion

This article had the aim of clarifying the relation between the Constitutional and the Supreme Cassation Court of the Republic of Serbia. This relationship is governed by the Constitution enacted in 2006, which brought some significant changes and has enlarged the Constitutional Court's competences. The main interface of the two courts is the constitutional appeal procedure (Article 170 of the Constitution). Another point of interaction between the two is rather peculiar to the Serbian system: Namely, the Supreme Cassation Court plays an important role in the selection of Constitutional Court judges. Some matters in this relationship, such as dismissal of the Constitutional Court judges, need further clarification through interpretation, and in practice the courts still do not have cases on certain questions, leaving those matters still in the domain of theory. However, it is obvious that the new position of both Courts, as well as the standards that have been used in their creation, have brought the Serbian legal system closer to other European models.

12 For considerations on the independence of the court, see the contribution of *Vidan Hadzi-Vidanovic*, in this volume.

The European Convention on Human Rights in the Serbian and English Constitutional Orders: A Comparative Analysis

*Vidan Hadzi-Vidanovic**

Contents

I. Introduction

The European Convention on Human Rights (ECHR), like any other international treaty, leaves it up to the discretion of its contracting parties to find the most suitable manner in which its provisions are to be given legal effect within their internal legal systems. While variations are numerous, it seems that the prevailing attitude among state parties to the ECHR is that the internal justiciability and the remedies offered by the domestic courts for violations of the Convention rights are the best way to secure the observance of their international human rights obligations. On the other hand, such an approach by the states is also of great importance for relieving the overburdened Strasbourg system of the cases that can be resolved at the national level.

I have decided to look at the issue of domestic application of the Convention through the comparison of two very different legal traditions: the English and the Serbian one. The former, firmly based on a dualist approach to international law with the strong notion of parliamentary sovereignty might seem to be burdened, on the face of it, by nationalist attitude to international obligations,[1] legislative rigidity and disempowered courts.[2] The latter sounds like a polar opposite. With a monistic, international-friendly approach to international law, and with the clear possibility of judicial review of the decisions of all the branches of the government, including the legislative one, the Serbian legal system appears to be more open to international human rights standards. It also seems to be more responsive in remedying the insufficiencies of domestic legislations affecting indi-

* PhD candidate, The University of Nottingham School of Law; associate, Belgrade Centre for Human Rights.

1 For the general discussion on dualist theory and "nationalist introvert" approaches to international law see: *Antonio Cassese*, Modern Constitutions and International Law, Recueil des Cours 192, 1985, 343. See also, in general: *Christian Tomuschat*, Der Verfassungsstaat im Geflecht der internationalen Beziehungen, Veröffentlichungen der Vereinigung der Deutschen Staatsrechtslehrer, vol. 36 (1978), 9. With regard to the UK system: *Thomas Erskine Holland*, Studies in International Law, 1898, 199.

2 This follows from Dicey's famous sentence: "The principle of Parliamentary sovereignty means neither more nor less than this, namely, that Parliament thus defined has, under the English constitution, the right to make or unmake any law whatever; and, further, that no person or body is recognized by the law of England as having a right to override or set aside the legislation of Parliament." *Albert Venn Dicey*, An Introduction to the Study of the Law of the Constitution, 10th ed., 1959, 39–40. Less "scientific", but not less true is the analysis of Anthony King: "For most of the first six decades of the twentieth century, the judges were dogs that seldom barked or even growled. They did not, because they could not, declare acts of parliament unconstitutional. They did not, because they could not, declare them inoperable. They seldom even criticized them on the ground that they violated one or more of the principles of the rule of law." *Anthony King*, The British Constitution, 2007, 115. See further: *ibid*, 115 et seq; *Alison Young*, Parliamentary Sovereignty and the Human Rights Act, 2009, 2 et seq.

vidual rights and liberties. In Part II of this study I will offer a closer look at these different starting positions of the two systems and at their relative approximation after the adoption of the 1998 UK Human Rights Act (HRA).[3] Despite this "approximation", it will be seen that, from the perspective of positive law, the Serbian system is more "Convention-friendly" and that Serbian courts seem to have more power than the English courts in rectifying violations of the Convention.

This legal analysis, performed largely from the perspective of the pure theory of law, will be tested in Parts III and IV against the actual practice of English and Serbian courts in observing and applying the European Convention. As it will be seen, despite the formal shortcomings of the English system and nominal superiority of the Serbian one, the Convention, against the odds, seems to have a much cosier life in the former than in the latter system. Here, I will have to abandon a purely legal approach and turn to some extralegal factors that might have influenced such a state of affairs. These factors are different and they range from the very different legal and political traditions of the two countries, through the different approaches to legal education, to those factors which could be branded as largely psychological ones: the dedication to human rights of the English jurists and the relative lack of it among Serbian professionals; the will of the English judiciary to uphold the rights of citizens, and the dubious determination of Serbian senior judges. Most important, however, is the courage of one generation of English senior judges to refuse to side too often with ministers and other governmental officials, and the lack of such courage among their Serbian colleagues.

II. Serbia and the UK: Two different international legal philosophies

The relationship between municipal and international law is traditionally explained with reference to two divergent theories. The first is dualist theory. According to this theory, international and municipal law are two separate legal systems and hence the incorporation of international law into the domestic legal system is required in order to give it effect. Only incorporated international treaties are justiciable before the courts of law and applicable in administrative proceedings. The other is the monistic theory which sees international and municipal law as a part of the same system and gives the rules of international law not only ef-

3 Human Rights Act, 1998 c. 42.

fect from the moment of their ratification, but also primacy over the rules prescribed by municipal law.[4]

1. The Serbian Constitution and international law

I have already written with Marko Milanovic in 2006 about the position of international law in the Serbian constitutional system, and I will offer here only a short summary of our thoughts expressed in the 2006 article.[5] The Serbian legal system clearly opts for the monistic theory with some slight modifications regarding the hierarchical relations between the rules of international law, the Constitution and municipal laws, and bylaws.[6] According to Article 16 para. 2 of the Serbian Constitution, generally accepted principles of international law and ratified international treaties are an integral part of the Serbian legal system and are directly applicable. This means that administrative bodies and the courts of law can deliver their decisions on the grounds of an international treaty. The participants in the proceedings are also entitled to base their claims on the provisions of an international treaty.[7] Moreover, Article 18 para. 2 of the Serbian Constitution stipulates that human rights guaranteed by international treaties are directly applicable in the Serbian legal system, while Article 18 para. 3 states that the provisions on human and minority rights are to be interpreted with the view to advance the values of a democratic society in accordance with international human rights standards and in accordance with the practice of the international institutions responsible for the monitoring of the enforcement of human rights.

All of this means that individuals under the jurisdiction of Serbian authorities can invoke the provisions of the European Convention on Human Rights (ECHR) at any stage of any type of proceedings, and that Serbian administrative bodies and the courts of law are obliged not only to consider such claims, but to consider them in accordance with the established practice of the European Court of Human Rights (ECtHR). This approach ensures, at least formally, the highest degree of harmony between the internal and international system for the protection of human rights. It also requires a good knowledge of international human

4 For the general discussion on dualist and monist approaches to the relationship between international and municipal law see: *Peter Malanczuk*, Akehurst's Modern Introduction to International Law, 7th ed, 1997, 63 et seq.; *Anthony Aust*, Handbook of International Law, 2005, 80 et seq.; *Malcolm Shaw*, International Law, 6th ed., 2008, 129 et seq.

5 *Marko Milanovic/Vidan Hadzi-Vidanovic*, Međunarodno pravo i ljudska prava u Predlogu Ustava Srbije, Srpska Pravna Revija 1 (2006), 62-73.

6 See Article 16(2) and Article 194(4) and (5) of the Serbian Constitution.

7 *Ibid.*

rights practice of all participants in the proceedings – judges, advocates, prosecutors, police officers and other executive and administrative organs.

2. The English legal system and international law

In contrast to the Serbian legal system, the English legal system generally follows the dualist theory in treating the interrelationship between international and municipal law.[8] The dualist approach in English law is best seen through the operation of international treaties.[9] In order to become a part of the national legal system, international treaties to which the United Kingdom adheres as a sovereign state must be incorporated, normally through Parliament's exercise of its legislative functions (promulgation of a statute).[10] Otherwise, exceptionally, cabinet ministers can change certain aspects of law through the exercise of delegated legislative powers.[11] Obviously, the need for incorporation arises only if the national law is not in accordance with international obligations adhered to by the signing of a treaty.

The traditional explanation for the need of incorporation of a treaty into the domestic legal system streams from the notion of separation of powers.[12] In English law, the power to enter into international treaties lays with the executive branch of the government without Parliament's substantial involvement.[13] If international treaties – the performance and the making of which is the responsibility of the executive – were to be given a direct effect in the internal English legal system, it would infringe on the Parliament's absolute superiority in exercising its legislative functions.[14]

As a consequence of such approach, international treaties cannot be invoked before English courts if they are not given legal effect through incorporation in

8 *Aust* (note 4), 81; *Shaw* (note 4), 139; *John Alder*, General Principles of Constitutional and Administrative Law, 4th ed., 2002, 102.

9 International custom is, unlike treaties, considered to be an integral part of common law and there is no need for its incorporation. See: *Chung Chi Cheung v. R* (1939) AC 160, 168. However, if the custom is contrary to the statutory provisions or there is prior precedent resolving the matter which contradicts the custom, that custom would not apply. See: *Mortensen v. Peters* (1906) 8 F(J.C.) 93.

10 A-*G for Canada v. A-G for Ontario* (1937) AC 326, 347.

11 See for explanation: *A.W Bradley/K.D. Ewing*, Constitutional and Administrative Law, 15th ed., 2011, 621 et seq.

12 *Murray Hunt*, Using Human Rights Law in English Courts, 1997, 8; *Malanczuk* (note 3), 65; *Alder*, (note 7), 117. For the case law see: *Maclaine Watson v. DTI* (1988); *The Parliament Belge* (1879).

13 *Bradley/Ewing* (note 11), 317.

14 See the following section.

the national legal system.[15] As for any other treaty, the same stood for the ECHR before its incorporation through the adoption of the HRA.[16] Since 2000 when the HRA came into force, the substantial provisions of the Convention and its Protocols ratified by the UK, with the exception of Article 13 of the ECHR,[17] have been incorporated in municipal law. In applying the HRA, English courts are invited by Section 2 of the Act to take into consideration the practice of the ECtHR, but they are not obliged to do so,[18] and some would suggest that the English courts are even encouraged to develop their own human rights jurisprudence independently from that developed in Strasbourg.[19]

3. The role of courts compared

A considerable difference between the Serbian and English legal system is the power of the courts to challenge the authority of the legislative body. The Serbian Constitutional Court has several means to challenge acts adopted by the National Assembly, as well as bills that are still in the process of adoption, before their promulgation by the President.[20] First, state organs, bodies of autonomous territorial entities, municipalities, as well as a minimum number of Members of Parliament (MPs) (25) can request the initiation of the procedure for determining the conformity of laws and other general acts with the Constitution and international obligations.[21] The Constitutional Court can also decide to determine the constitutionality of an act *proprio motu.*[22] Further, any legal or natural person has a right to submit the initiative invoking the procedure with the same effect,[23] but the Court has complete discretion whether to take such initiative into considera-

15 *Rayner (Mincing Lane) Ltd v. Department of Trade* (1990) 2 AC 418, 499.

16 For the opinion on the matter see: *R v. Home Secretary ex parte Brind* (1991) 1 AC 696.

17 Another ECHR provision omitted from the HRA is the one from Article 1 of the ECHR. The provision was rightfully excluded from the Act since it is generally understood to contain an inter-state obligation. For the explanation on the exclusion of these two provisions see: *K.D. Ewing*, The Human Rights Act and Parliamentary Democracy, Modern Law Review 62 (1999), 84-85.

18 *R v Secretary of State for Environment, Transport and the Regions* (2001) 2 All E.R. 929, 982.

19 *Douglas W. Vick*, The Human rights Act and the British Constitution, Texas International Law Journal 37 (2002), 354; *David Feldman*, The Human Rights Act 1998 and Constitutional Principles, Legal Studies 19 (1999), 191-192. For criticism of such an approach see: *Ewing* (note 17), 86.

20 See Article 167(1), 168 and 169 of the Constitution. On the Constitutional Court's jurisdiction, see also the contribution of *Ivan Čukalovič*, in this volume.

21 Art. 168(1) of the Constitution.

22 *Ibid.*

23 Art. 168(2) of the Constitution.

tion.[24] Finally, one third of MPs have a right to demand that the Court determine the constitutionality of an adopted bill, before its promulgation by the President of the Republic of Serbia.[25] Interestingly, the initiator of the individual constitutional complaint procedure cannot ask for determination of constitutionality of the general acts if his rights have been violated solely by that act.[26] This is one of the two shortcomings of the judicial review of legislation adopted by Serbia, and the present author is currently involved in one case before the Constitutional Court where an effort was made to initiate the proceedings for determination of unconstitutionality of an act through the constitutional complaint mechanism. The case, concerned with the rights of transsexuals, was still pending in late 2011.

Another important shortcoming of the judicial review of legislation in Serbia is that the Constitutional Court can only determine unconstitutionality of an act and put it out of force.[27] It cannot change the act or offer an interpretation which would be consistent with the Constitution or international obligations, and it cannot submit the proposal to the National Assembly about ways to amend an act in a way which is consistent with the Constitution. The decision of the Constitutional Court can therefore, at best, create *lacuna*, but it cannot remedy the shortcomings of the law.

Contrary to the Serbian system, the English system is firmly based on the principle of parliamentary sovereignty.[28] The traditional view is that "Parliament makes law and the judges apply the law."[29] Judges are, therefore, subordinated to Parliament, and if the judiciary usurps Parliament's law-making prerogatives, Parliament can overturn that decision.[30] This position is firmly based on the belief that only the Government, or more precisely the members of the House of Commons, are democratically elected representatives of the people who have the sole responsibility to legislate in accordance with the people's will. The same cannot be said for the judges who are appointed by the Crown.[31] The interaction

24 See Article 53 of the Constitutional Court Act, Official Gazette 109/2007.

25 Art 169 of the Constitution. Considerable shortcoming of the provision is that the President of the Republic of Serbia, who is probably in the best position to determine if there are reasons for suspicion that a bill is not in conformity with the Constitution or international obligations before he promulgates it, and who on several occasions delayed or refused to promulgate bills on these grounds, is not empowered to submit a bill to the Constitutional Court for consideration.

26 Article 170.

27 Article 58 of the Constitution.

28 One needs to note, however, the significant infringement that British parliamentary sovereignty endured after the UK's accession to the EU. See: King,(note 2), 98-99.

29 *H. Barnett*, Britain Uncovered: Government and Constitution Explained, 2002, 40.

30 *Ibid.*

31 *Ibid.*

between the courts and the Parliament in England has, however, always been much more complex than this simple statement can reveal.

The courts were always invited to "interpret" the law,[32] and through the development of common law even to create law where certain situations were not covered by acts of Parliament.[33] Of course, Parliament could always overrule such a decision by promulgating a statute, but the fact remains that the courts in England are much more than simple appliers of legislation. This is probably most visible in the area of human rights protection in which the courts – many years before the adoption of the HRA – tended to interpret statutes in conformity with the provisions of the European Convention. This sometimes, effectively, meant the creation of a new principle or a considerable amendment of the text (but not of the spirit) of the statute.[34]

This feature has been even more pronounced since the adoption of the HRA. According to Section 3 of the HRA, "[s]o far as it is possible to do so, primary legislation and subordinate legislation must be read and given effect in a way which is compatible with the Convention rights." As noted by many, this extended the "role of construction of the courts" since they now operate under the presumption that the legislator intended to promulgate the law in accordance with the European Convention. Courts may be required to construe the interpretation of the act to be in conformity with the Convention even if there is no ambiguity in legislation.[35] In this way the court might depart from the will of Parliament, but it can do so only insofar as such intention could reasonably be attributed to Parliament in enacting Article 3 of the HRA.[36] But the court cannot adopt an interpretation which is inconsistent with the fundamental feature of the legislation. Parliament has reserved the right to enact legislation contrary to the Convention.[37] The High Court and superior courts can make a declaration of incompatibility,[38] but the Lords (now the judges of the Supreme Court) tend to avoid making such declarations.[39] Moreover, the declaration has no "operative or coercive

32 *Derbyshire County Council v. Times Newspapers Ltd* [1993] 3 All ER 65, 77-79; *Buchanan v. Babco* (1977); *Brind v. Secretary of State for the Home Department* (1991).

33 This power of the courts goes as far as the creation of new criminal offences, an unthinkable feature in any civil law system. See for example *Shaw v. Director of Public Prosecution* (1962) AC 220.

34 See *infra* III.

35 *Ghaidan v. Godin Mendoza* (2004) UKHL 30, (2004) 2 AC 557.

36 *Ibid.*

37 *Bradley/Ewing* (note 11), 409-410.

38 See Section 4 of the HRA.

39 *Bradley/Ewing* (note 11), 409-410.

effect", and does not prevent the courts from relying on the incompatible law in the future.[40]

Based on the preceding considerations, several important differences between the Serbian and English approach to the implementation of the European Convention can be identified. First, while the ECHR forms an integral part of the Serbian legal system and is directly applicable before Serbian courts of law, the ECHR had to be incorporated into the English legal system in order to become justiciable. Now both Serbian and English courts can declare that there was a violation of conventional rights, rather than of some other right stemming directly from the national legislation. Another difference is the binding nature of the Strasbourg jurisprudence. Serbian courts are bound to follow it, while English courts are not. They just need to take it into consideration. Following this, one would expect heavy reliance on the ECtHR practice in Serbian courts' decisions and the absence of such reliance before the English courts, especially before the adoption of the HRA. One could also expect a number of decisions of the Serbian courts where the violation of *conventional rights* has been established (or dismissed), and the same would stand for the English courts after the adoption of the HRA. Finally, it would be normal to expect greater consistency of the Serbian practice with the jurisprudence of the ECtHR in comparison to the situation in England. With regard to judicial review, it would seem that the Serbian Constitutional Court has significant power to overrule legislation by the National Assembly, while the power of the English courts seems significantly impaired with regard to that.[41] On the basis of these considerations, one would expect the Convention's omnipresence in Serbian legal life and its superior power in action, in contrast to its much more timid and unimposing life on the British island. But, the proportions largely stand in reverse, as I will now discuss.

III. The ECHR and English courts

As already noted, the European Convention was not incorporated into the English legal system until the very end of 20th century. Considering the firm dualist approach with regard to international treaties and a strong doctrine of parliamentary sovereignty dominating the English legal system, one could expect the complete absence of the European Convention from the considerations of the English

40 *Ewing* (note 17), 88.
41 See: *Gerhard van der Schyff*, Judicial Review of Legislation: A Comparative Study of the United Kingdom, The Netherlands and South Africa, Berlin, 2010, 3.

courts.[42] However, the history of the ECHR and the practice of its monitoring bodies before the English courts is not as simple as this general remark would suggest.

1. The early life of the Convention in English courts

The first decision of the European Court involving the United Kingdom as a wrongdoing state came in 1975,[43] while the first reference to the European Convention made by the English courts came a year later, in 1976.[44] Since then, all the way to the adoption of the HRA, the English courts embarked on an uncertain journey of tackling the tensions between English law and the European Convention, often bringing much inconsistency and uncertainty into the matter.

Before a very short survey of this practice is offered, one must resolve the issue of the legal basis for the consideration of the ECHR prior to its incorporation in the English law. There are several lines of reasoning that can explain this. First, the ECHR was applicable when its provisions represented customary international law,[45] but also when they could have been regarded as an element of public policy.[46] The Convention was also applicable when there was no clear precedent resolving the matter, to the extent that its provisions could have been regarded as customary rules.[47] All of these approaches should be observed from the perspective of the development of the common law.[48] But the Convention was also used as an interpretative tool in cases where either statute or the common law affected the rights and liberties of individuals.[49] This interpretative function was based on the assumption that "the Crown, in taking its part in legislation, would do nothing which was in conflict with treaties."[50] Finally, the Con-

42 With the same effect see: *Paul Roberts*, Criminal Procedure, the Presumption of Innocence and Judicial Reasoning under the Human Rights Act, in: Helen Fenwick/Gavin Phillipson/Roger Masterman (eds.), Judicial Reasoning under the UK Human Rights Act, 2007, 384.

43 *Golder v. United Kingdom*, (1975) 1 EHRR 524.

44 *Hubbard and Others v. Pitt and Others* (1974) QB 142 according to: *Donald Wilson Jackson*, The United Kingdom Confronts the European Convention on Human Rights, 1997, 126.

45 See note 8. See also: *Jones and Lee v. Miah and Miah* (1992) 24 HLR 578.

46 *P.J. Duffy*, English Law and the European Convention on Human Rights, International and Comparative Law Quarterly 29 (1980), 599, 605.

47 *Ibid.*, 599.

48 *Hunt* (note 12), 128.

49 *R v. Secretary of State for Home Affairs, ex parte Bhajan Singh* (1975) 3 WLR 225.

50 *Ibid.*

vention has been considered as a part of European Community law, which, unlike the Convention, was fully incorporated into English law.[51]

The case which is usually cited as a groundbreaking case of the English courts with regard to their observance of the European Convention is *Bhajan Singh*,[52] in which Lord Denning offered his opinion about the place of the Convention in the considerations of the English courts. Here, Lord Denning referred to his previous reasoning in *Birdi v. Secretary of State for Home Affairs*[53] in which he laid down the basic principle of the interpretative function of the Convention in the English legal system as already described above, but also went as far as to say that an act of Parliament incompatible with the Convention could be declared invalid by the superior courts. Lord Denning in *Singh* maintained his position on the interpretative function of the Convention, but withdrew his opinion which allowed judicial invalidation of a statute due to incompatibility with the Convention, stating that "[i]f an Act of Parliament contained any provisions contrary to the convention, the Act of Parliament must prevail. But I hope that no Act ever will be contrary to the Convention. So the point should not arise."

The limits of the ECHR in English law were further determined in the *Malone* case where it was established that the Convention rights are not directly justiciable before the English courts.[54] Sir Robert Megarry, an acting judge in this case, gave a lengthy and well-reasoned opinion further explaining the influence of the Convention rights and the practice of the ECtHR on English law where no statute has been enacted, although the issue at stake was of such importance and complexity to require the existence of such statute (phone tapping was at stake in this particular case). The judgment thoroughly looks at the ECtHR case law related to the matter, but regardless, Sir Megarry refused to allow the Convention's influence on matters clearly left to Parliament to legislate on.

As a consequence, the English courts did not allow for claims invoking the violation of Convention rights. Rather, they looked at the possibilities to find a legal basis for adjudicating the case derived from the domestic legislation, sometimes going as far as to invoke Magna Carta provisions, as was the case in *Begum and Phansopkar*.[55] But the courts continued to give great attention to the European Convention wherever it was possible to construe the existing legisla-

51 *Hunt* (note 12), 128.

52 See *supra*, note 49.

53 Unreported.

54 *Malone v. Commissioner of the Police of the Metropolis* (no. 2) 2 AIIW.R. 620 (1979).

55 *R v. Secretary of State for the Home Department, Ex parte Phansopkar; R v. Secretary of State for the Home Department, Ex parte Begum*, [1976] QB 606, [1975] 3 All ER 497, [1975] 3 WLR 322, 139 JP, United Kingdom: Court of Appeal (England and Wales), 11 July 1975.

tion in accordance with it, sometimes with more, and sometimes with less success and dedication. The fact remains though that the parties in the proceedings continuously invoked the Convention and the Strasbourg case law, thus forcing the courts to consider them even if they were unwilling to apply the principles contained within.

2. The Convention and the Human Rights Act 1998

After the adoption of the HRA – probably the greatest constitutional reform of the English legal system in the past several centuries – things changed significantly. Not only did the English courts get the mandate to adjudicate on violations of conventional rights, but they also acquired long-awaited power to challenge the legislators in both discrete (through interpretation) and quite blatant (through declaration of incompatibility) fashions. Additionally, the English courts have been required to "take into account" judgments, decisions, declarations and advisory opinions of the ECtHR in interpreting the Convention rights. This, however, does not mean a complete adherence to the European Court's practice.

First, it is entirely possible for the English courts to develop a practice which would ensure greater protection of a specific right than that offered by the ECtHR, since the Convention only guarantees a bare minimum of rights.[56] To depart from the practice of the European Court in order to limit the protection would be, however, at least difficult. Although there were some isolated cases where English courts refused to follow the jurisprudence of the European Court,[57] the ECtHR practice carries substantial weight in directing the decisions of the English courts, especially in the higher instances.[58] The issue was largely resolved by Lord Bingham who reasoned that, although not strictly binding, the clear and constant practice of the European Court should be followed by domestic courts.[59]

This, however, is not always entirely possible, even if it is the best intention of the English courts to follow the ECtHR practice. Most obviously, the ECtHR itself sometimes avoids giving clear pronunciation on some legal matters by in-

56 *Thomas Burghental*, The Domestic Status of the European Convention on Human Rights, Buffalo Law Review 13 (1963-1964), 354.

57 *R v Spear and another R v Boyd R v. Williams and other appeals and applications* – (2002) All ER (D) 271 where the House of Lords held that courts martial do not lack independence and impartiality in deciding criminal cases contrary to the practice of the European Court. See in: *Bradley/Ewing* (note 11), 407.

58 *Bradley/Ewing* (note 11), 407.

59 *R (Ullah) v. Special Adjudicator* (2004) UKHL 26; (2004) 2 AC 323. See in: *Bradley/Ewing* (note 11), 407.

voking a well-known doctrine of the margin of appreciation. This vague concept has the potential to mislead national courts into the development of their own practice which might well be contrary to that of the ECtHR.[60] Another problem inevitably arises from what we can call, "the interpretation of interpretation". When applying the reasoning of the ECtHR, English courts are in the position to reinterpret it in order to grasp its meaning and needless to say, the legal result of such interpretation can be quite different from the one that the ECtHR really had in mind, especially when the ECtHR practice is in itself inconsistent. This can easily be seen from the long awaited Grand Chamber Judgments in the *Al-Skeini and Al-Jedda* cases.[61] Here, the House of Lords allegedly misread the practice of the ECtHR with regard to the extraterritorial application of the Convention[62] and was later effectively overruled by the ECtHR.[63]

Finally, a few words need to be said about the preparedness of the high courts to issue non-binding declarations of incompatibility. It was argued in the opening years of the HRA that the courts will make a considerable effort to interpret the statues in the way which would bring them into conformity with the ECtHR and that they will avoid, as much as possible, the declarations. This has become a fact during the decade-long practice of the English courts with regard to the application of the HRA. By 2010, only 26 declarations of incompatibility had been issued, 18 of which have become final (in whole or in part) and none of which are subject to a final appeal.[64] This is obviously not a significant number, but the fact that the government responded to these declarations without delay and that declarations resolved some very urgent human rights issues in the English legal system, shows that, if there is a will, even the non-binding suggestions of judiciary can influence the legislature to adhere to human rights standards, even in the atmosphere of strict parliamentary sovereignty, as is the case in the UK.

60 For the analysis see: *Lammy Betten*, The Human Rights Act of 1998: What It Means: The Incorporation of the European Convention on Human Rights into the Legal Order of the United Kingdom, 1999, 78 et seq.

61 ECtHR, *Al-Skeini and Others v. UK*, Application no. 55721/07, judgment of 7 July 2011 and *Al-Jedda v. UK*, Application no. 27021/08, judgment of 7 July 2011.

62 See: *R (on the application of Al-Jedda) (FC) v. Secretary of State for Defence*, [2007] UKHL 58 and *Al-Skeini and others v. Secretary of State for Defence*, [2007] UKHL 26.

63 For the analysis see: *Marko Milanovic*, European court Decides Al-Skeini and Al-Jedda, EJIL Talk, available at: http://www.ejiltalk.org/european-court-decides-al-skeini-and-al-jedda/.

64 See: Responding to human rights judgments: Government Response to the Joint Committee on Human Rights' Fifteenth Report of Session 2009-10, Ministry of Justice, London, July 2010, 5. See for the list of declarations: *ibid*, 42.

3. Explaining the vitality of the Convention in English courts

It is very hard to offer a systematic explanation how the ECHR achieved such a prominent place in the English legal system (even prior to the adoption of the HRA) without making dangerous generalisations. Of course, one could rush into a conclusion that such a development was only natural in the land of John Locke whose ideas had a global influence on the contemporary notion of rule of law and civil liberties; the land of the Magna Carta; the land which had a decisive influence in creating the European Convention and was the first to ratify it.[65] But one must not forget that, despite the "domestically born" Lockean "natural rights" doctrine,[66] human rights in Britain were, until as late as 1960s, understood as the privileges granted by the almighty Parliament, and not the rights inherent in every human being.[67] One must also not forget that the Magna Carta was not for everyone, but for the barons and lords,[68] and that the path from this document to the HRA was as long as 800 years.[69] Further, one must also not forget that the "cradle of democracy", as Britain is often called, is also the land of the Bloody Sunday, the "Operation Demetrius"[70] and the "Five Techniques" of interrogation.[71] Equally, if one focuses on the activities of the judges in questioning the acts of Parliament, one must not forget that Britain, as much as it adheres to the system of judicial precedents is also a land where the legal system and judicial reasoning was for a long time firmly based on the Diceyan premise of absolute parliamentary sovereignty.[72] Finally, Britain is currently a country in which pejorative phrases such as "the dictates from Strasbourg", construed to describe the unpleasant rulings of the European Court, are most audible.[73] It is

65 For Churchill's personal input and the British input into the creation of the European Convention see: *Steven Green*, The European Convention on Human Rights: Achievements, Problems and Prospects, Cambridge, 2006, 14, 18; *Ed Bates*, The Evolution of the European Convention of Human Rights: From Its Inception to the Creation of a Permanent Court of Human Rights, 2010, 7, 33 et seq.

66 For the problems surrounding Locke's notion of natural rights see: *A. John Simmons*, Lockean Theory of Rights, 1992, 90 et seq.

67 *King* (note 2), 118-119.

68 *Peter Linebaugh*, The Magna Carta Manifesto: Liberties and Commons for All, 2008, 22; *Geoffrey Robertson*, Crimes Against Humanity: The Struggle for Global Justice, 1999, 2-3. See also: *Anne Pallister*, Magna Carta: The Heritage of Liberty, 1971.

69 For the evolution of the idea of human rights in England see: *Linebaugh* (note 68).

70 See in: *Donald Wilson Jackson*, The United Kingdom Confronts the European Convention on Human Rights, 1997, 36-37.

71 See *ibid.*, 37 et seq. See also: ECtHR, *Republic of Ireland v. United Kingdom*, Application no. 5310/71, judgment of 18 January 1978, paras. 96-104 and 106-107.

72 *King* (note 2), 117.

73 The outcry was most recently reinvigorated by the ECtHR ruling that British law, namely the Forfeiture Act of 1870 and the Representation of the People Act of 1983 which bars

also a country in which there is a strong movement, supported by (a part) of the current Government, to abolish the HRA and introduce the British Bill of Rights with the goal to distance British protection of human rights from the European Court.[74]

Despite all of this, one can safely say that the British legal system evolved towards the rule of law and the protection of human rights more or less steadily over centuries – a process of uninterrupted evolution which was not experienced by any other country in the world. The British (unwritten) Constitution went through some dramatic changes over these centuries, but all of these changes were steps of progress in strengthening the rule of law and the enlargement of civil liberties within the British legal system. It can be safely said that the idea of the universal human rights is indisputably a part of the British DNA. But one must not rush to the conclusion that because of this it was easy to give effect to the ECHR in the British legal system. On the contrary, this was one of the main barriers to such a development for half a century. "In essence, the United Kingdom's long history of freedom was put forward to argue that its sovereign parliament could be trusted with the nation's rights, unlike the political bodies of other countries."[75] On the other hand, however, this almost natural link between the idea of human rights and British jurists (and people in general) led some to believe that "you have to look long and hard before you can detect any difference between the English common law and the principles set out in the Convention at least if you view the convention through English judicial eyes."[76] In other words, since the principles of the ECHR are perceived to be identical to the principles of English law irrespective of the existence of the ECHR, it was relatively painless to digest Strasbourg approaches since they, in essence, were nothing new for an Englishman.

This attitude towards the Convention, coupled with the recognition that the "common law is too weak and vulnerable" to offer a satisfactory protection of human rights,[77] the understanding that parliamentary sovereignty is eroded by the ever-growing influence of the executive branch of the Government over Parliament,[78] and the will to offer the protection of human rights to the citizens at home, rather than abroad, certainly enabled the Convention's relatively smooth

prisoners from voting in elections, is contrary to the European Convention. See *Hirst v. United Kingdom*, Application no. 74025/01, judgment [GC] of 6 October 2005.

74 For the news on the debate see: http://www.guardian.co.uk/law/british-bill-of-rights.

75 *Van der Schyff* (note 41), 18. See also: *James Young*, The Politics of the Human Rights Act, Journal of Law and Society 26 (1999), 29-30.

76 Lord Donaldson in: *R. v. Secretary of State ex parte Brind* [1990] 1 All ER 469, 477.

77 *John Alder*, General Principles of Constitutional and Administrative Law, 4th ed., 2002, 426.

78 *Ibid.*, 460. Also: *Van der Schyff* (note 41), 18-19.

"domestication". It is also significant that the British courts always observed the Crown's international obligations with utmost seriousness, and developed the doctrine according to which there is an assumption that the legislation adopted after the entry into force of a relevant treaty is in conformity with that treaty and hence interpreted in accordance with it.[79] Some would add to these factors the political and social circumstances in 1980s Britain which were marked, on one side, with the non-existing effective opposition to the Conservative (with capital C) government, "authoritarian" style of the Thatcher government, and on the other, the "romantic revolt" of the British people which craved for "democracy, justice, the right to consultation, responsiveness and transparency."[80] Another factor that might have played a role was the educational superiority of the senior British judges. As noted by Robert Stevens, the senior judges of the time were "extremely well educated, extremely bright, politically quite sophisticated … and very talented, perhaps more talented than the other branches of government".[81] This new generation of judges assumed its social responsibility and moulded (but not abandoned) doctrinal Diceyan principles for the sake of upholding more rudimentary principles on which British society and its legal system rested, namely the principle of personal liberty and human rights.

As can be seen, the assumption of an almost natural adherence of the British courts and the Government in general to the European Convention, based on the British democratic tradition and Britain's devotion to the rule of law and human rights, although not without problems, is not entirely wrong even if it is often made on the ground of superficial considerations. British legal and political tradition undoubtedly played a major role in the Convention's tiptoeing into the English (and British) legal system and the increased role the English courts assumed in upholding and protecting individual rights. I will now turn to the experience of Serbian courts, the courts that operate in a rather young and fragile democracy, and will dedicate some space to their efforts to enrich the Serbian legal system with the idea of human rights.

79 This approach stems from the assumption that Parliament would normally not intend to contradict assumed international obligations. See: *Garland v. BREL* [1983] AC 251 at 277; *Pan American World Airlines Inc v. DoT* [1976] 1 Lloyds Rep 257, 261; *A-G v. BBC* [1981] AC 303, 354; *A-G v. Guardian Newspapers Ltd* [1987] 1 WLR 1048, 1096; cf. *Blackburn v. A-G* [1971] 1 WLR 1037, 1039.

80 *King* (note 2), 120-121.

81 As quoted in *ibid.*, 121.

IV. The ECHR and Serbian courts

Based on the face value of the Serbian constitutional norms, as already suggested, the Serbian legal system seems to be much more open to both judicial review of legislation and the direct application of international obligations in domestic proceedings than is the case with the British system. The state of affairs in practice is, however, quite different. Although the situation is far from grave, one might be disappointed with the findings and the opinion that will be presented here.

1. The relative under-utilisation of the Convention in Serbian courts

The European Convention is rarely invoked by the parties in the regular proceedings before the Serbian courts. Serbian legal tradition, despite the monistic approach in the current Constitution, tends to observe municipal and international law as two quite separate legal systems. As a consequence, Serbian legal professionals are not well accustomed in applying international legal principles in domestic proceedings and there is a considerable lack of knowledge of international practice. This is obviously a dangerous generalisation, and it must be said that some legal professionals in Serbia are very eager and ready to invoke international norms at any stage of the national proceedings.

Unlike in the regular proceedings, the European Convention has a very prominent role in the constitutional complaint proceedings, and the Constitutional Court increasingly pays attention to the Convention and the practice of the ECtHR. This, however, does not mean that the Constitutional Court has so far made the most of the Convention, especially from the perspective of using the Convention as the ultimate legal basis for the delivering of its decisions.

The practice adopted by the Constitutional Court of the Republic of Serbia with regard to the declaration of violations of the conventional rights is one of *identification* with the constitutional rights. It seems that in the early cases before the Constitutional Court there was some confusion with regard to the place of the Convention in domestic human rights adjudications. In the *Dimovic* case, for example, the Constitutional Court held that "since the Constitution is the highest legal act of the Republic of Serbia by which the right to freedom and security is guaranteed, the right which is also guaranteed by Article 5 of the Convention, the Constitutional Court deliberated on the alleged violation of the right in concern in accordance with the provision of Article 27(1) of the Constitution and the provisions of the Criminal Procedure Act."[82] From the wording of the decision one might conclude that the Court held that constitutional rights, due to the superiority of the Constitution over international obligations as established by Article 194 of the Constitution, take priority over conventional rights. This, however, is not the case. The issue is more the Court's exercise of mental and judicial economy and it simply means that as long as the conventional rights are not different in content from the rights guaranteed by the Constitution, the Court will proceed with considering only violations of constitutional rights.[83] In addition, the Serbian Constitution covers a much wider scope of human rights than the European Convention, most notably due to the incorporation of economic and social rights, which have been declared by the Constitutional Court to be fully justiciable.[84] In situations in which these rights are invoked, the Court cannot rely on the ECHR. It can, however, seek the guidance of other international human rights instruments,[85] something that the Court has so far consistently failed to do.[86] This is especially worrisome, considering that some of the basic economic and social rights, such as the right to water or right to housing, did not find their way into the Constitution.

2. The domestic use of ECtHR case law

The invocation of the European Convention by the Serbian Constitutional Court has become regular practice. Unfortunately, it cannot be inferred from the reasoning offered by the Court precisely how much attention has been given to the legal principles developed through the Strasbourg case law, since the invocation of the case law is comparatively rare. The Court, as a rule, does not fail to take into consideration cases which were directly concerned with the legal problems in Serbia and it tends to fully accept the findings of the ECtHR in such cases.[87]

82 *Ivica Dimovic*, Constitutional Complaint, UZ-687/2008, 25 12 2008.

83 See for example *Vojin Biljic*, Constitutional Complaint, Case No. UZ 1866/2009, 18 February 2010; *Dragoljub Zajkeskovic et al.*, Constitutional Complaint, Case No. UZ-2260/2010, 30 September 2010.

84 Consolidated opinions of the Constitutional Court with regard to the Constitutional Complaints Matters, adopted on 10 October 2009.

85 For example, the International Covenant on Economic, Social and Cultural Rights or the conventions of the International Labour Organisation.

86 See, for example: *Snezana Jakovljevic*, Constitutional Complaint, Case no. UZ-1862/2009, 19 November 2009 where the right to work was at stake.

87 See, for example, *Natasa Abramovic*, Constitutional Complaint, Case no. UZ-1896/2009, Decision of 9 December 2010. The Court quotes the Judgment of the ECtHR delivered in the *Vincic and others v. Serbia*, Application nos. 44698/06, 44700/06, 44722/06, 44725/06, 49388/06, 50034/06, 694/07, 757/07, 758/07, 3326/07, 3330/07, 5062/07,

Also, one can easily establish that the Constitutional Court increasingly cites cases from the ECtHR's general practice, especially if it has been invoked by the applicants.[88] It, however, regularly fails to deliberate on these decisions in more detail, which certainly diminishes the level of coherence of its judgments and does not offer many clues to practitioners who may not be well informed about Strasbourg case law.

The Court also does not seem to be quick to accept Convention based initiatives for review of the constitutionality of general acts. Only 2 out of 37 initiatives that relied on both the constitution and the European Convention have been taken into consideration by the Court.[89] Interestingly, however, in one of these cases concerned with the right to property, the Court established that the law under consideration violated not only the Constitution, but also the "confirmed international treaties".[90] In reaching this conclusion, the Court relied on Article 1 of Protocol 1 to the Convention, but it did not elaborate much on its understanding of this very complex provision, nor on the practice of the ECtHR.[91] The Court, so far, has not had any case for the determination of constitutionality of proposed legislation. Also, 22 initiatives were submitted to the Court without any reference to international law and the European Convention.

Looking at this snapshot, one can conclude that the things are slowly moving toward greater respect and adherence to the direct application, or at least consideration of the ECHR and the Strasbourg case law in Serbia. However, considering the freedom and indeed the obligation that Serbian courts have with respect to the application of international human rights standards, there is still a long way to go before one could assess their practice, even at the Constitutional Court level, as well reasoned, firmly based on the European Court's case law, coherent, and directed toward the highest possible standard of protection of human rights.

8130/07, 9143/07, 9262/07, 9986/07, 11197/07, 11711/07, 13995/07, 14022/07, 20378/07, 20379/07, 20380/07, 20515/07, 23971/07, 50608/07, 50617/07, 4022/08, 4021/08, 29758/07 and 45249/07, judgment of 1 December 2009.

88 See, for example: *Milan Radojcic*, Constitutional Complaint, Case no. UZ -1429/2008, Decision of 16 July 2009.

89 See: Case nos. IU-95/2006, IU-68/2006. Mind that this does not include initiatives that challenged general acts other than the acts of Parliament.

90 See Case no. IU-95/2006, Decision of 17 March 2011.

91 *Ibid.*

3. Public attitudes and legal culture as determinants of Convention use

There are several factors that need to be taken into consideration when trying to explain the under-utilisation of the Strasbourg case law and the direct application of international instruments on human rights by the Serbian courts, including the Constitutional Court. Without giving priority to any of them, these factors can be summarised in several categories: the overall attitude of the Serbian public, including legal professionals, towards human rights; the perception of the general public with regard to the rule of law as a principle for the functioning of an organized society; and legal education and the place of human rights within it.

Thanks to the systematic research performed by a Serbian based academic NGO, the Belgrade Centre for Human Rights, we have the luxury of observing these factors through the prism of empirical data. According to this data, it is notable that a significant part of the Serbian population saw human rights either as an instrument of blackmail used by powerful states against smaller ones (including Serbia),[92] or as a "paper law" invoked by politicians when it serves their own interests.[93] It is also notable that nearly half of the Serbian population in 2004 and 2005 considered that the protection of human rights falls under the domain of the exclusive domestic jurisdiction of Serbia.[94] It must be noted that the figures indicating the perception of human rights as an alien ideology and the international intervention in the protection of human rights as unacceptable has more or less steadily dropped over the years. Despite that, one must conclude that the Serbian population, in the opening years of Serbian democratisation and participation in international human rights institutions, did not look favourably upon human rights and international intervention with regard to the protection of human rights.

This obviously did not give an admirable start to Serbia in its process of integration into the European and universal human rights institutions. The poor starting position was additionally burdened with the Serbian population's attitude towards the rule of law in general. In 1998 nearly 46% of the Serbian population perceived that the law is what powerful or "smart" people say it is.[95] Constitu-

92 For 1998 – 11%, for 2000 – 8%, for 2001 – 11%, for 2002 – 14%, for 2003 – 8%, in 2004 – 9%, in 2005 – 7%. See in: Ljudska prava u pravnoj svesti gradjana Srbije i Crne Gore, Belgrade, 2005, at 9.

93 In 1998 – 25%, in 2000 – 18%, in 2001 – 19%, in 2002 – 22%, in 2003 – 11%, in 2004 – 14% and in 2005 – 13%. See: *ibid.*

94 In 2004 – 49% and in 2005 – 38%. *Ibid.*, at 10.

95 Human Rights in Yugoslavia, 1998: Legal Provisions, Practice and Legal awareness in the Federal Republic of Yugoslavia Compared to International Human Rights Standards, Belgrade, 1999, 323.

tional or international legal components played an even lesser role.[96] Despite the fact that between 2003 and 2005 only one third of the population claimed that it successfully exercised all of its human rights, 90% of population did not seek remedy for violations.[97] When asked to which institution they would complain about the human rights violations they suffered, 25% opted for the domestic courts and only 12% for the international human rights bodies.[98] Interestingly, however, 37% of the population stated that it would turn to "influential people" such as politicians, people with money or political connections.[99] Law and the legal system were at best perceived as secondary instruments of disputable relevance for the achievement of human rights protection. International institutions, on the other hand, fell even further behind.

These results are understandable when one takes into consideration the Serbian legal tradition which was predominantly based on authoritarian rule of absolutist rulers with only short spells of democratic processes. To this, one needs to add the constitutional instability of the former Socialist Yugoslavia which changed its constitutions no less than 4 times in a span of fewer than 30 years (1946, 1953, 1963 and 1974) with even more frequent comprehensive constitutional amendments (1967, 1968, 1971, 1981 and 1988).[100] When one adds to this the remarkable number of constitutional changes that took place prior to the Second World War (1835, 1838, 1869, 1888, 1901, 1903, 1921 and 1931), one may pose a legitimate question as to the significance of the Constitution as the highest legal instrument in the Serbian legal tradition.

Serbia also has a long history of a judiciary that was anything but independent, impartial and free from political influence.[101] The judges were systematically intimidated by the ruling elite prior to the democratic changes in 2000 and these direct and indirect pressures led the best educated judges to leave the judiciary.[102] In replace, the new ones were elected mostly on the ground of political obedience.[103] Although the situation has changed significantly, the present situa-

96 *Ibid.*
97 *Supra* note 92, 46-47.
98 *Ibid.*, 47. Note that this is despite the fact that nearly 60% of population thought that judges are predominantly bad and under the influence of politicians. *Ibid*, 25.
99 *Ibid.*, at 47.
100 See in: *V. Dimitrijevic*, The 1974 Constitution as a Factor in the Collapse of Yugoslavia, or as a Sign of Decaying Totalitarianism, in: N. Popov (ed.), The Road to War in Serbia: Trauma and Catharsis, 2000, 399.
101 See: The Situation of the Judiciary in Serbia after Milosevic: Where Does It Stand, Where Does It Go?: Presentation by Serb Judges and Discussion, OSCE, Warsaw, 2000.
102 *Ibid.*, 5.
103 *Ibid.*

tion is far from perfect.[104] Considering the shortcomings of the Serbian judicial system, one can at least try to understand (but not to accept) the lack of courage among Serbian judges in challenging the authorities, the courage which was so vital for the resurrection of the English judiciary in the 1980s.

Finally, one needs to take into consideration the fact that international human rights became a part of the curriculum in the Serbian law schools only in the late nineties. Even today, international human rights are a compulsory undergraduate subject only in one law school in the country.[105] Other schools offer either a separate facultative undergraduate course on human rights[106] or a compulsory course within a specific undergraduate module on public international law (but not as a part of other modules, most notably the judicial module).[107] It is impossible to deduce from the curriculum of some schools if human rights have any place in their educational program.[108] None of the law schools offers a dedicated master module on human rights law, although some schools offer comprehensive and compulsory courses on international human rights in general and European human rights in particular within specific master modules.[109] Neither international law nor international human rights law are a part of the Serbian bar exam.[110]All of this points to the obvious lack of capacity of Serbian legal professionals to pursue more vigorously the implementation of the principles of the European Convention.

Of course, when one takes into consideration that there were 3514 pending applications against Serbia before the ECtHR in 2010,[111] and 3999 decisions on

104 See European Commission Serbia 2010 Progress Report, 9, available at http://ec.europa.eu/enlargement/pdf/key_documents/2010/package/sr_rapport_2010_en.pdf. See also: Human Rights in Serbia 2010, Belgrade, 2011, 102 et seq.

105 See The Curriculum of the Union University School of Law, at: http://www. pravnifakultet.rs/studije/osnovne.html.

106 See The Curriculum of the University of Nis Faculty of Law, at: http://www.prafak .ni.ac.rs/index.php?option=com_content&view=article&id=56&Itemid=151&lang=cir.

107 See The Curriculum of the University of Belgrade Faculty of Law, at: http://www.ius. bg.ac.rs/Studije/novi%20nastavni%20program%20osnovnih%20studija%20od%202011-12.htm.

108 See, for example, The Curriculum of the University of Kragujevac Faculty of Law, at: http://www.jura.kg.ac.rs/index.php/sr/dokumenti/download-document.htm?gid=1299; The Curriculum of the University of Novi Sad Faculty of Law, at: http://www.pf.uns .ac.rs/index.php?option=com_content&view=article&id=468&Itemid=183.

109 See The Curriculum of Master Studies for the European Law Module, Union University School of Law, at: http://www.pravnifakultet.rs/studije/master.html. For the sake of fairness, it needs to be said that this school also offers a dedicated master module on the rights of the child. See at: http://www.pravnifakultet.rs/studije/master-prava-deteta.html.

110 See: *Zakon o pravosudnom ispitu ("Sl. glasnik RS", br. 16/97); Pravilnik o polaganju pravosudnog ispita ("Sl. glasnik RS", br. 14/98); Pravilnik o programu pravosudnog ispita ("Sl. glasnik RS", br. 51/97).*

111 See: European Court for Human Rights, Analysis of Statistics 2010, 2011, 51.

individual constitutional complaints before the Serbian Constitutional Court from 2006 to 2011, one can safely say that things are moving forward. It will, however, take much more than statistics to prove that international human rights standards, and more specifically the rights enshrined in the European Convention, are taken with the utmost seriousness by Serbian judges and are regularly employed, in an appropriate and fully informed manner, by Serbian legal professionals.

IV. Conclusion

On the face of common knowledge the findings of this paper are not, in any way, revolutionary. One could have expected that the English courts show much more appreciation and knowledge in dealing with the European Convention than the Serbian courts do. After all, the UK has been around since the ECHR's inception, while Serbia is yet to enter into the second decade of its membership in the Council of Europe. But when one considers that the English courts were not only barred from implementing the Convention directly, but also severely restrained by the principle of parliamentary sovereignty to challenge the authority of the legislator until 2000 when the HRA came into force, one could expect that the difference in the approach would not be dramatic. It unfortunately still is, with the English courts clearly paying much more attention to the Convention and the Strasbourg practice than the Serbian ones. Of course, the Convention is evermore present before the Serbian courts, especially at the highest level, but it seems that neither the practitioners nor the judges are prepared to make greater use of the Convention. It is, in the end, up to the advocates to use all possible means to pursue the interests of their clients, and the Convention is certainly a powerful weapon in any lawyer's arsenal. On the other hand, the courts need to show more courage in using powers given to them by the Constitution, with the aim of becoming the true protectors and promoters of human rights.

It is the proposal of this paper that human rights are such fundamental principles in the contemporary world that formalities of law are not sufficient barriers to or safeguards for their implementation in the domestic legal systems. No provision can prevent their advance if there is a sincere adherence to the idea of human rights, just as no provision can guarantee their sensible protection if human rights are seen as alien ideology. A single message of this paper is, therefore, if there is a will, there is a way.

The Case of Albania: The Relationship between Constitutional Justice and the High Court under the Influence of the ECHR

*Xhezair Zaganjori**

Contents

I. Introduction

The relationship between constitutional justice and the highest ordinary court, or to be more precise, between the decision making activities of these two extremely important mechanisms of the democratic state, is a very delicate and sensitive issue – particularly in new and still unconsolidated democracies. They do not have the appropriate practice or experience in the implementation of the fundamental principles of the rule of law and of fundamental human rights and freedoms. At first sight the problem appears to be rather easy to solve, since almost every state constitution has clearly defined and separated the functions performed by both courts. The Constitutional Court guarantees the respect for the Constitution and makes its final interpretation, while the High Court is placed at the top of the pyramid of the judicial system, whose main function is to give justice. From this viewpoint, the High Court controls the way in which material and procedural law has been implemented by the lower courts, which, on the other hand, have the duty to interpret and implement the Constitution and the normative acts enacted on the basis of and for its implementation.

In practically every system that has adopted the centralized constitutional review, based on the positivist theory of Hans Kelsen about the rigorous hierarchy of the norms of law, the occurrence of interferences or "collisions" between the constitutional and judicial functions and competences, especially between Constitutional Court and High Court, can often be observed. It is certain that the range and nature of these "collisions" mainly depend on the jurisdiction and competences that the Constitution of each country has assigned especially to the Constitutional Court. Accordingly, major problems have been particularly observed in cases when it has been provided for that the Constitutional Court can be put into motion even through complaints by individual persons. The main problem identified in these cases is often the opinion that the Constitutional Court has the duty to review only the constitutionality of laws and not the constitutionality of court decisions, despite the fact that the latter may have seriously breached fundamental human rights.

Because of the relations established in many law systems, it might happen quite often for the constitutional courts to be labeled as the third or fourth superior instance of judgment. As examples could be mentioned: the case of Italy due to the advanced incidental control; the case of Spain due to the so-called *amparo* applications; the case of Hungary and Macedonia due to the *actio popularis* applications; the case of Germany due to the so-called *Verfassungsbeschwerde*.

Regardless of these labels[1], it is rightly pointed out that in constitutional judgment, the self-restriction or avoidance of exaggerated activism by the judge has a special importance. Certainly, he should do his best to accomplish the constitutional obligations assigned to him, taking into consideration and having quite clear and right ideas about the demarcation line between his functions and the functions performed by the courts of ordinary jurisdiction.

However, it should be underlined that despite the nature of the problems arising between the Constitutional Court and the High Court, it should be taken into account that in a democratic government, and in the framework of fundamental principles of the rule of law, their obligations, goals and objectives remain the same. They are related to the implementation and interpretation of the Constitution and other normative acts enacted on the basis of and for its implementation in such a way to ensure, to the greatest possible extent, the organization and functioning of the state based on the principles of democracy and the effective protection of the fundamental human rights and freedoms. Therefore, the "conflicts" or the "problems" arising between the Constitutional Court and the Supreme Court should be treated and solved in this spirit. The European Convention on Human Rights (ECHR) and the enhanced jurisprudence of the European Court of Human Rights (ECtHR) provide a valuable guide in this direction. As will be mentioned below, the reason for this lies not only in the general obligation that the Albanian state has to respect the standards of the ECHR, but also in the privileged position of international law, especially of this Convention, in the Constitution of the Republic of Albania.

In this article, we discuss the relationship between the Constitutional Court of Albania and the High Court in the light of the ECHR and Strasbourg case law. The paper will first set out the normative framework which governs the relationship between the Constitutional Court and High Court, based on the constitutional text (part II). After that, we will address the practical working relationship and discuss essential case law (part III). We will conclude with some general remarks (part IV).

* Professor of Law at the Faculty of Law, Tirana University, and the School of Magistrates; Judge at the Constitutional Court of Albania since 2003.

1 *Louis Favoreu*, Constitutional Review in Europe, Parliamentary law and legal policies 46 (2008), vol. 5.

II. The normative framework governing the relations of the Constitutional Court and the High Court in Albania

The problems between the decision making of the Constitutional Court and the High Court are encountered quite often, even in the Albanian situation of recent years. Taking into consideration the relatively large number of individual complaints addressed to the Constitutional Court of Albania concerning violations of the constitutional right to due process of law, it has been frequently restated that this Court is tending to be turned into a fourth instance of judgment. As a result, there have been many debates and opinions regarding the relation that should exist between the decision making of the Constitutional Court and the High Court.

1. The general framework

To begin with, Article 124 of the Constitution sets forth that the Constitutional Court guarantees respect for the Constitution and makes its final interpretation, whereas Article 135 states that the judicial power is exercised by the High Court, as well as by the other courts of appeal and courts of first instance. Article 141 para. 1 of the Constitution provides for the right of the High Court to unify or amend the judicial practice through a unifying decision of its Joint College. In everyday practice, the Constitutional Court and High Court closely cooperate with each other on the basis of different constitutional provisions assigned to them.[2]

One of the most important forms of this cooperation is the incidental control exercised by the Constitutional Court according to Article 145 para. 2 of the Constitution.[3] The High Court has used this opportunity in some cases, particularly in view of its interest and obligation to guarantee to the best possible extent the independence of the judicial power, as well as to unify judicial practice. Out of 15 applications for incidental control addressed by the High Court since the adoption of the Constitution in 1998 (until November 2011), nine have been accepted by the Constitutional Court. But the most delicate problem and the major concerns with regard to the relation between the Constitutional Court and the High Court are especially evident in cases where the Constitutional Court adjudicates individual complaints alleging the infringement of the standards of due

2 *Denar Biba*, Constitutional Court and the ordinary courts, Parliamentary law and the legal policies 46 (5) (2008), 47.

3 Article 145 para. 2 reads: "If the judges believe that a law is unconstitutional, they do not apply it. In this case, they suspend the proceedings and send the question to the Constitutional Court".

process of law, in reliance on Articles 42 and 131/f of the Constitution. When examining these kinds of applications, the Constitutional Court controls the observance of the due process of law by the courts of ordinary system, including here even the decision making of the High Court. Let us take a closer look at this aspect.

2. Individual complaints and due process control

It should be highlighted that since the adoption of the Constitution in 1998, the Constitutional Court has perceived and applied the constitutional requirement of due process of law only as a procedural guarantee,[4] almost totally equating it to the standards of Article 6 ECHR. Surely, this control is not exercised as a purpose in itself, but as closely related to the claim regarding the violation of another right or freedom sanctioned by the Constitution. Moreover, some other elements that have not been explicitly guaranteed in the framework of Article 6 ECHR have been considered as constituting part of the due process of law in the procedural meaning, such as the elements related to freedom and security of the individual, the principle *nulla poena sine lege*, the principle *ne bis in idem*, etc. Nonetheless, there have been many discussions and criticisms with regard to the appropriate understanding and application of the principle of due process of law from the substantial point of view. Another reason is the fact that the wording of Article 42 para. 1 of the Constitution of Albania is clearly similar to that of Amendments V and XIV of the Constitution of the U.S.A.[5] In the U.S.A. due process of law has been given a substantial meaning, rather than a procedural one.[6]

3. The importance of ECHR standards

It should also be noted that during the examination of individual complaints for undue process of law, a precious help for the Albanian situation has been and

4 Article 42 (1) reads: "The liberty, property, and the rights recognized in the Constitution and by the law may not be infringed without due process."

5 Amendment V has stated *inter alia* that "No person…shall be compelled in any criminal case to be witness against himself, nor be deprived of life, liberty, or property, without due process of law…." Whereas, Part 1 of Amendment XIV has stated *inter alia* that "… nor shall any State deprive any person of life, liberty, or property, without due process of law."

6 *John E. Nowak/Ronald D. Rotunda/J. Nelson Young*, Constitutional Law, 2nd ed. 1983, 425-430.

continues to be the rather privileged position of international law in the Constitution of Albania, especially of the ECHR. This can be clearly and particularly seen in Articles 5, 116, 121, 122, 123 and 17 para. 2 of the Constitution. Article 5 explicitly mentions the obligation of the Republic of Albania to apply international law that is binding upon it. Article 116, ranking the normative acts that are effective in the territory of the Republic of Albania, places ratified international agreements immediately after the Constitution and before the laws adopted by the Assembly of Albania, whereas article 122 para. 2 declares that international agreements ratified by law have priority over the country laws that are incompatible with it. Most importantly, Article 17 para. 2 of the Constitution, which deals with the possibility of limiting fundamental rights and freedoms, clearly sets forth that "these limitations [...] in no case may exceed the limitations provided for in the ECHR." So, it can be easily concluded that as to limitations, the ECHR is placed above the Constitution, or at least at the same level. In this respect it can be said that the Albanian judge, including here even the constitutional judge and that of the High Court, should consider the ECHR as a referral point and pay attention to the dynamic case law of the ECtHR, notably the case law related to Article 6 of the Convention.

4. Effect of Constitutional Court decisions

Finally, it should be underlined that the Constitutional Court, when repealing ordinary court decisions, including those of the High Court, neither repairs the right that has been violated, nor resolves the case on its merits, as it is the case in many other homologous courts. The case is remanded to the court which has committed the violation in order to redress it and resolve the litigation in question. However, the complaint to the Constitutional Court must remain an effective remedy that meets the standards of Article 13 ECHR. In one of its recently taken decisions against Albania, the ECtHR has reiterated that the Constitutional Court is not an effective remedy, given the many applications concerning the non-execution of final court decisions, which is an important component of the first paragraph of Article 6 of the Convention.[7]

7 ECtHR, *Gjyli v. Albania*, Application no. 32907/07, judgment of 29 September 2009.

III. The relationship in practice: A survey of the case law

Out of the total number of applications admitted by the Constitutional Court since 1998 (up to November 2011), approximately 100 had to do with violations of due process of law by the High Court and approximately 80 of them with violations by decisions of the first instance and courts of appeal. The main problems identified as violations of the due process of law by the High Court are mostly related to the right of defense, the principle of impartiality of the court, the right of access to court, the reasoning of court decisions, and the implementation of the Constitutional Court decisions.

1. Violation of the right of defense

In a series of its decisions, the Constitutional Court has specifically stressed the great importance of the right of defense in court trials, particularly in criminal proceedings. It noted the close relation of this element with other elements of due process of law, especially with the principle of equality of arms. As to the relation with the High Court, Constitutional Court decisions have pointed out the following components of the right of defense.

a) Right of defense in the absence of counsel in criminal proceedings

The Constitutional Court has stressed the need to guarantee the right of defense during the criminal proceedings before the High Court even in cases when, although the court notifications have been carried out correctly, the defense counsel does not appear in the court hearing and the prosecutor's appeal aggravates the position of the accused. The adoption of such a standard brings about certain difficulties in the everyday work of the High Court, and furthermore, a kind of paradoxical situation (the defense counsel receives all the necessary notifications, but he simply does not show up). However, what is important for the Constitutional Court is to guarantee the most qualified defense for the accused individual, even through an officially appointed defense counsel, in a court trial which ultimately is going to discuss how the material and procedural law should be applied by the lower courts for the litigation in question.[8] In addition to the adoption of

8 Constitutional Court of Albania, decisions nos.21/05; 23/05; 24/05; 5/08; 7/09; 16/09: "[W]ithout the assistance of a defense counsel, the process could not usefully contribute to the examination of the legal issues representing the essence of the litigation [...] The examination by the High Court of the points of law not only fully justifies the representa-

this standard, the need to take effective measures which could reduce the abuse of duty and could help to ensure a better work discipline for the lawyers has been rightly put forward. Such measures could be the imposition of fines against lawyers who do not appear without reason in the court hearings, the approval of or additions to the Lawyers' Ethical Code, the taking of disciplinary measures by the National Bar Association, up to the repeal of the lawyer's license.

b) The right of defense during examination of applications for revision by the High Court

There have been frequent cases where the High Court, in the "consulting room,"[9] has admitted the applications for revision of the final civil or criminal court decisions, remanding the case for re-examination to the court of appeal or the first instance court, at a time when the other party has not received any kind of notification or does not have the possibility to submit its claims. In such instances, the Constitutional Court has held that if the respective college of the High Court, summoned at the consulting room, thinks that the application for revision is legally founded, it should provide the interested parties with the possibility of putting these arguments forward for discussion in a court hearing and render the court verdict only later.[10]

c) Right of defense of the accused tried *in absentia*

For years, the Constitutional Court and the High Court have upheld different opinions about cases of the accused tried *in absentia,* when it comes to the restrictions imposed on the officially appointed defense counsel or on the defense counsel assigned by the family. Like the Italian criminal system, the Constitution of Albania recognizes the possibility to try a person who is evading justice *in ab-*

tion by a lawyer in the court hearings, but also, it becomes indispensable in order to guarantee an effective and professional defense in favor of the accused".

9 Consulting Room is a judicial panel composed of five judges of the High Court, who decide on the admissibility or non-admissibility of the submitted applications. If the judges deem that the concrete case has problems regarding the interpretation and application of material and procedural law, then this room decides to pass the case to the plenary session. Otherwise, it decides on the non-admissibility of application. Approximately 90% of the total number of applications are declared as non-admissible by this panel.

10 See Constitutional Court of Albania, decisions nos. 17/05; 6/07; 13/07; 4/09.

sentia.[11] Accordingly, Article 48 para. 3 of the Criminal Procedure Code recognizes the right of the families of the accused tried *in absentia* to assign a defense counsel, whereas Article 410 para. 2 of the same Code states that the defense counsel can lodge an appeal against the decision given *in absentia* only if he or she is provided with an authorization issued and complied in conformity with the law. In 1999, the Joint Colleges of the High Court[12] stated that the right of appeal is an exclusive right of the accused, and as such, it should be exercised only by him and his defense counsel if he is provided with a special power of attorney issued specifically for that purpose. In contrast, in 2000 the Constitutional Court called attention to the right of the officially appointed defense counsel or the defense counsel assigned by the family to lodge an appeal against the court decision.[13] Afterwards, the Joint Colleges of the High Court reaffirmed their position, clearly evading the decision of the Constitutional Court on that matter.[14] At the same time, the Constitutional Court re-iterated its position and stressed the *erga omnes* character of its decisions, as well as the obligation of the High Court not to put in doubt its conclusions, since otherwise it might leave room for a "dangerous precedent" to be created. [15]

As it stands now, there is still lack of clarity about this issue. The problem becomes really complicated when the accused tried *in absentia*, after being detained by the competent organs, requests to lodge an application for revision with the High Court. The reasons for lodging such application might be a "lack of knowledge" about the decisions given in *absentia*, at a time when his right to lodge an application for revision with the High Court has been exhausted by the officially appointed defense counsel or by the defense counsel assigned by his family. The High Court and the Constitutional Court have once more indirectly "provoked" each other through the respective decisions.[16] Under these circumstances, I think that a possible decision of the ECtHR on this matter would be expected with great interest. The question of the accused tried *in absentia* is truly important and the standards established by the Court of Strasbourg in its decision *Sejdovic v. Italy* are especially relevant to this end.[17]

11 Article 33 of the Constitution has explicitly stated that 1) Everyone has the right to be heard before being sentenced. 2) A person who is evading justice may not take advantage of this right.

12 High Court of Albania, decisions no. 47/99 and 354/99.

13 Constitutional Court of Albania, decision no.17/2000.

14 High Court of Albania, decision no.182/2000.

15 Constitutional Court of Albania, decisions no.77/2000 and 5/2001.

16 See decision (application) for incidental control of the High Court, dated 6 February 2009, and decision of the Constitutional Court no. 30/2010.

17 ECtHR, *Sejdovic v. Italy*, Application no. 56581/00, judgment of 10 November 2004.

2. Violation of the principle of "impartial court"

With the aim of guaranteeing the individual elements of due process of law, the Constitutional Court emphasized in a number of cases the need to respect the principle of "impartial court," even in the court proceedings held by the High Court. In these cases, the Constitutional Court has been mainly focused on guaranteeing the objective elements of impartiality, thus the obligation to remove biased judges from certain cases. Accordingly, it has requested the removal of some judges from the trial panel, reasoning that they do not offer the necessary guarantees for the objective aspects of impartiality.[18] The decisions consider the issue of respect for the principle of impartiality in the High Court firstly with regard to the vertical level, which implies the dismissal from adjudication of the particular case of the judge of the High Court who, in one way or another, had expressed himself about the same case in one of the other instances of judgment. The second case concerns the horizontal level, which implies dismissal from the case if the judge of the High Court has previously expressed himself on the same case while performing the same duty.

In the first instance, the problem seems rather simple. The Constitutional Court has considered as a violation of the principle of impartiality the fact that one or some members of the panel of the High Court, summoned in a court hearing or in the consulting room, had expressed themselves about the same case when performing the duty of judge in a lower instance court or another function as prosecutor, expert, lawyer etc. The second case seems to be more difficult and complicated in the everyday practice, given the relatively small number of judges, namely 17 members (actually, their number varies from 11 to 14 judges due to the ongoing problems regarding the appointments and to disagreements between the President of the Republic who makes the proposals and the Assembly, that should vote them by a simple majority). Initially, the Constitutional Court has tolerated the cases when the same judge of High Court had taken part firstly in the consulting room and later on at the court hearing held by the panel of judges. However, especially after the decision of the ECtHR in *Driza v. Albania*,[19] the Constitutional Court has reiterated the necessity to respect the principle of impartiality at horizontal level, in all the court proceedings held by the High Court for the same case.

In this context, the Constitutional Court stressed that, besides the individual considerations in each particular case, in specific cases, special importance is

18 Constitutional Court of Albania, decisions no. 16/03; 17/08; 21/08; 23/08; 4/09; 23/09; 30/09; 32/09; 1/10; 10/10.

19 ECtHR, *Driza v. Albania*, Application no. 33771/02, judgment of 13 November 2007.

given to the principle of functionality of the institution. This means that, when for the sake of rigorous implementation of the principle of impartiality in adjudication at the High Court, all the judges (or such a number of them that would have made impossible the adjudication of the case at this level) would have to be dismissed, i.e. an institutional blocking would result, then the sitting of an otherwise pre-engaged judge could be tolerated, in order to enable this Court to render a decision on the particular case. It is also worth mentioning here that in some of its recent decisions, the Constitutional Court has restated the importance of the implementation of this principle even during the examination of applications for revision at the High Court, especially in cases when the revelation of new essential evidence is advanced as an argument for revision. It has been pointed out that, regardless of having to do with a separate process of examination of the application for review held by the panel of judges in the consulting room, in the end, the judges are going to express their opinion about the reopening or not of the same case, which has been previously and conclusively decided by them.[20]

3. Violation of the right of access to court

The Constitutional Court has clearly made evident that the right to have access to a court as an element of the due process of law in the context of Article 42 of the Constitution and Article 6 ECHR does not only include the right to open the court proceedings, but also the right to have a final solution for the dispute, because access to the court must be substantive and not formal.[21] With reference to the violation of this right by the High Court, the most typical cases to be mentioned are as follows:

a) Inaccurate calculation of time limits by the High Court

The cases of miscalculation concern the time limits governing the lodging of a lawsuit in the first instance court, an appeal in the appellate court against the decision of the first instance court, or a recourse to the High Court against the decision of the appellate court. These represent the simplest cases of the denial of the right of access to the court ascertained by the Constitutional Court.[22] In view of that, the decision of the Constitutional Court on the evaluation of the time limits

20 Constitutional Court of Albania, decision no. 1/2010; 21/2010.
21 Constitutional Court of Albania, decisions no.14/09; 30/2010; 5/2011.
22 Constitutional Court of Albania, decisions no. 4/2005; 22/2006.

for lodging the applications for review is of special interest, because the provisions of the Civil Procedure Code contradicted themselves, which gave the High Court the opportunity to adopt different stands. More concretely, Article 445 of this Code conditioned the lodging of the application for review with a one year period from the rendering of the final verdict, whereas Article 496 provided for the one year time limit for lodging the application for review, a time limit which begins upon the publication of the reasons for this review. The Constitutional Court held that the time limit for lodging the application for review should begin upon rendering the final verdict that contains the reasons for this review. Any different interpretation of the provisions of the Civil Procedure Code would deny to the applicants the right of access to the High Court.[23]

b) Judicial protection against measures implementing UN Security Council sanctions

The most interesting case in the relation between the Constitutional Court and the High Court on this matter is the case named after the applicant "Albanian International Investment – Development Ltd.", headquartered in Albania. The Sanctions Committee of the UN had included this company on the list of persons related to terrorism. The respective resolution of the UN Security Council orders *inter alia* the blocking of bank accounts and the sequestration of the property of this company. In 2004, the Minister of Finances of Albania issued the respective order, which, like any other administrative act, was challenged by this company before the Tirana Judicial District Court. This court sent the case to the High Court to decide the question of jurisdiction. In 2006, the Civil Panel of the High Court reached the conclusion that this case did not fall under the jurisdiction of the domestic judiciary.

The company in question appealed to the Constitutional Court, which stated *inter alia* in its decision that "[a]ccording to Article 42 para. 22 of the Constitution, everyone has the right to a fair and public trial to protect his constitutional and legal rights, freedoms or interests." On this basis, the Constitutional Court reiterates that "the rule of law presumes that any interference of the executive authorities in the individuals' rights [...] should be object of an effective control exercised by an organ that could guarantee impartiality and independence."[24] In conclusion, contrary to the High Court opinion, the Constitutional Court held

23 Constitutional Court of Albania, decision no. 20/2008.
24 Constitutional Court of Albania, decision no.10/2007.

that the Albanian ordinary courts enjoy jurisdiction, since in the particular case the subject matter at issue was the administrative act, the decision of the Minister of Finances on the sequestration of property and blocking of bank accounts, and not the resolution of the Security Council.

It should be noted here that a short time afterwards the very same conclusion as that of the Constitutional Court with regard to the question of jurisdiction was reached by the Court of First Instance (CFI) and the European Court of Justice (ECJ) of the European Union in the case Al Kadi and Al Barakat. Even in this case, the appellants alleged a violation of the right to due process of law and the right of property by EU Regulations, adopted in reliance on the respective resolutions of the UN Security Council regarding the blocking of bank accounts and sequestration of property of persons related to terrorism. Indeed the same applicant, Mr. Al Kadi, was one of the main shareholders of "Albanian International Investment – Development." It is very interesting to note that both courts of the EU, in pursuance of Articles 230 para. 4 and 308 of the Treaty of the European Community, assumed jurisdiction to adjudicate the case, because the object of review in this case were not the resolutions of the Security Council, but only the respective regulations of EU that have applied these resolutions in the community area. Regarding the merits, the CFI found no violations of the right to due process of law and the right of property, whereas, on the contrary, the ECJ reached the conclusion that the respective Regulations of the Council of the European Union adopted in reliance on the Resolution of the Security Council had violated the appellants' rights to due process of law and the property right.

c) Lack of lawyer's signature in the application for revision lodged with the High Court

Recently, the Constitutional Court declared as incompatible with the Constitution some decisions of the High Court which refused to examine applications for revision because they were not signed by a lawyer as provided for by Article 435 para. 22 of the Criminal Procedure Code. In order to protect to the best possible extent the individuals' rights in criminal proceedings, the Constitutional Court emphasized in a number of its decisions that it is the duty of the administrative staff of the High Court to formally verify the existence of a lawyer's signature in the application for revision lodged with the court, as well as to notify the accused or his lawyers about this legal obligation.[25]

25 Constitutional Court of Albania, decision no. 38/2010; 5/2011; 8/2011; 10/2011.

4. Violations of due process with respect to the reasoning of High Court decisions

The Constitutional Court upholds that even the reasoning of court decisions, including here the High Court decisions, both in the sense of logical sequence of arguments and the harmony between the reasoning part and the disposition of decision, is an important element of due process of law.[26] The obligation to give reasons has been explicitly stipulated in Article 142 para. 1 of the Constitution.[27] As to this problem, the main concern in the relation with the High Court remains the reasoning of inadmissibility decisions rendered by the colleges of the High Court in the consulting room. It is very interesting to note here that the ECtHR, referring to the Albanian cases, has put the emphasis on the need that such decisions be reasoned.[28] However, the ECtHR has determined that the problem of reasoning of the court decision depends on the specific nature of the particular case. The Court assesses that even a *de plano* formulation held in the consulting room of the High Court or by the selective panel of three judges of the Constitutional Court might be considered as a reasoning.[29]

However, in my opinion even the consulting room decision should have a minimum reasoning, which is necessary either for the effectiveness of the appeal (Article 13 ECHR), or for the sake of an ongoing examination of the case by another mechanism, respectively from the High Court to the Constitutional Court or from the Constitutional Court to the ECtHR. During the last years, the Constitutional Court was able to respond quite well with regard to this issue, providing a sufficient reasoning even for the inadmissibility decisions of the selective panel of three judges. In contrast, the High Court keeps on making *de plano* reasoning of the inadmissibility decisions in the consulting room, giving rise to many problems and difficulties in the further examination of the case, particularly by the Constitutional Court. Finally, I would like to underline that the Constitutional Court has considered as indispensable the reasoning of inadmissibility decisions on the applications for review examined by the colleges of the High Supreme Court in the consulting room. This has been considered as especially important in cases where the revelation of new, previously unknown evidence is alleged.

26 Constitutional Court of Albania, decision no. 35/2005.

27 This article has set forth that: "Judicial decisions shall be reasoned."

28 ECtHR, *Driza v. Albania*, Application no. 33771/02, judgment of 13 November 2007.

29 ECtHR, *Marini v. Albania*, Application no. 3738/02, judgment of 18 December 2007.

5. Violations of the standard "court established by law"

The most difficult and complicated problem in relations between the decision making of the Constitutional Court and the High Court has been related to the cases (although very few in practice) where, in the framework of due process of law, the Constitutional Court has ascertained violations by the High Court of the standard "court established by law." In almost all of these cases, the Constitutional Court has encountered difficulties while reaching the respective conclusion and decisions, which are often adopted only by a majority of votes. The Constitutional Court upheld that the respective college of the High Court has shown a kind of partiality in assessing the evidence, giving them a different meaning or making an interpretation in contradiction with the conclusions reached by the first instance court and court of appeal on the same evidence. This reasoning of the Constitutional Court is mainly based on the argument that the High Court is a court of law, and as such has the duty to control how the material and procedural law has been applied by the lower courts, without having the right to accept new evidence or to give them a different meaning from that given by these courts.[30]

6. Enforcement of Constitutional Court decisions and implementation of ECtHR rulings by the High Court

The title of this sub-section may seem rather paradoxical, since everyone should have an obvious idea that the Constitutional Court decisions have general binding force and are final. Moreover, Article 145 para. 2 of the Constitution explicitly stipulates that these decisions are binding on all courts.[31] It should be noted that in general terms the Constitutional Court decisions have been accepted and correctly applied by the High Court, despite some occasional objections. The exchange of views and experiences among judges of both courts in conferences, workshops or round tables has been very fruitful to this end. Furthermore, in some rare cases, when during the re-examination of the case the High Court has upheld the same stand ignoring the Constitutional Court decision, the Constitutional Court has been obliged to render a new decision, recalling the *erga omnes* character of its decisions and the obligation to fully apply them.[32]

30 Constitutional Court of Albania, decisions 31/2005, 7/2009, 32/2009 etc.
31 Article 145 para. 2: "Decisions of the Constitutional Court are binding on all courts".
32 Constitutional Court of Albania, decisions no.5/2001, 15/2003, 14/2009.

Regarding this problem and its links to the ECHR, the Xheraj case[33] is of particular interest, since it deals with the execution of the ECtHR decisions in the Albanian situation, more specifically with the issue of reopening the judicial proceedings in criminal cases after the Strasbourg decision. In the Xheraj case, the ECtHR assessed *inter alia* the violation of Article 6 para. 1 of the Convention (it has upheld the opinion that there was a violation of the principle of legal certainty, since Albanian courts had accepted the prosecutor's request for the leave to appeal out of time). In this decision, the ECtHR recommended to the Albanian competent authorities that the most appropriate form of redressing the violated right was the reconfirmation of the quashing of the decision by the Albanian authorities. Afterwards, Xheraj lodged an appeal with the High Court, which held the case to be inadmissible, reasoning that the Criminal Procedure Code does not yet provide that a Strasbourg decision is a ground for reopening court proceedings.[34] Furthermore, after being called upon by the appellant, the Meeting of Judges[35] of the Constitutional Court held the case inadmissible, reasoning that it should be the High Court, which, in reliance on the ECtHR decision, should find a way to reopen the judicial proceedings which had convicted the appellant for the crime of murder.[36] In this decision, the Constitutional Court, taking into consideration that the Codes of Procedure are often complementary to each other, recommended to the High Court to take into consideration the recent amendments to Article 494 of the Civil Procedure Code, according to which a respective decision of the ECtHR is a ground to reopen the judicial proceedings in civil cases.

However, the High Court in the next step again held the case to be inadmissible.[37] Under these circumstances, after having been called upon once again by the appellant, the Constitutional Court decided to examine the case in a court hearing and unanimously decided to repeal the respective decision of the High Court. The court reiterated once more the obligation of the High Court to admit the application for review and to reopen the judicial proceedings against Xheraj, following the ECtHR decision.[38] On this occasion, the Constitutional Court reminded the High Court of the *erga omnes* character of its decisions and the possibility that such situation could violate "the essence of the functioning of the

33 ECtHR, *Xheraj v. Albania*, Application no. 37969/02, judgment of 1 December 2008, para. 82.

34 High Court of Albania, decision no. 417/2010.

35 In this case, the Meeting of Judges decides on the admisablity or non-admisability of the submitted application, if this has not been done by the panel of the Constitutional Court composed of three judges.

36 onstitutional Court of Albania, decision no. 22/2010.

37 Supreme Court, decision 1042/2010.

38 Constitutional Court of Albania, decision 20/2010.

rule of law". It should be appreciated that the High Court, via its decision taken in the consulting room, dated 16 November 2011, has decided that, in principle, reasons for this revision do exist. Therefore, it has decided to pass this case to the plenary session of the High Court.

IV. Conclusion

The relationship between the decision making of the Constitutional Court and the High Court in Albania is mainly focused on the individual complaints regarding due process of law in the context of Articles 42 and 131/f of the Constitution. According to the Constitution, individuals can address the Constitutional Court only for this category of issues. Regardless of the observations and discussions with reference to the meaning of fair court trial as stated by the aforementioned constitutional provisions, the jurisprudence of the Constitutional Court of the Republic of Albania has treated this process only from the procedural aspect and not from the material one. To this end, the central point of referral for the Constitutional Court jurisprudence with regard to the individual complaints has been and continues to be Article 6 ECHR and the jurisprudence of the ECtHR on this provision. The reason for this lies not only in the general obligation that the Albanian state has to respect the standards of the ECHR, but also in the privileged position of international law, especially of this Convention, in the Constitution of the Republic of Albania.

In this framework, the Constitutional Court has played a very active role in defining the main standards of due process of law in the Albanian legal system, taking into consideration the fact that the Convention has provided for minimal standards only. In order to achieve this aim, the Court has declared as unconstitutional many ordinary court decisions, including here even High Court decisions. The cases have been remanded to respective courts for re-examination, so that they take into account constitutional problems that have been considered as violation of due process of law. Special attention rested on the establishment and respect of standards of due process of law in criminal proceedings. The main part of Constitutional Court decisions finding violations of due process of law by the High Court have to do with the right of defense in the court trial, respect of the standard of impartial court, violations of the right of access to the court, respect of the standard "court established by the law," and the obligation to give reasons for the rendered decisions. In spite of some hesitations, the decisions and the standards established by the Constitutional Court have been accepted and reflected in the decision making of the High Court. Furthermore, this decision making has been very helpful even for the High Court, in its efforts to achieve one of the most important duties, the unification of judicial practice.

The Position of the European Convention on Human Rights in the Hungarian Legal Order

*Pál Sonnevend**

Contents

I. Introduction

The European Convention on Human Rights is the most important constitutional document in Europe. It is the foundation of a common European constitutional law and a minimum that all European states must respect. Indeed, it is not an exaggeration to call the Convention the European Human Rights Constitution,[1] or fundamental rights constitution,[2] or to call the Convention a constitutionalising process.[3] The enforcement mechanism before the European Court of Human Rights is probably the most effective one compared to other international law instruments protecting human rights. Besides this international law enforcement mechanism, however, the effectiveness of the protection largely depends on how member states treat the guarantees of the Convention in their respective domestic legal orders.

There are basically three distinct but interrelated questions that must be answered to assess the national treatment of the Convention. First, can individuals invoke directly the Convention in ordinary Court proceedings? Second, does the Convention take precedence over contrary national legislation? And third, does the Convention enjoy a constitutional rank either directly or as a standard of interpretation of the respective Constitution?

Looking at the practice of the members of the Convention, it is hard to find a legal order where the Convention cannot be invoked directly by individuals. More difficult is the resolution of a possible conflict with a national statute. In several countries – like Switzerland, Lichtenstein, Belgium, Luxemburg, the Netherlands and Spain – the Convention enjoys supremacy over national statutes. In others – like in Italy, Sweden, Denmark, Finland and Norway – the Convention only has the rank of an ordinary statute.[4] This means that in case of a conflict the rule of *lex posterior* would apply and therefore statutes adopted later than the promulgation of the Convention would prevail. As regards the constitutional rank of the Convention, the Constitution of the Netherlands provides for

* Professor of law, Eötvös Loránd University Budapest; former constitutional advisor to the President of Hungary László Sólyom.

1 *Jochen Frowein*, Der Europäische Menschenrechtsschutz als Beginn einer europäischen Verfassungsrechtsprechung, Juristische Schulung (1986), 845.

2 *Frank Hoffmeister*, Die Europäische Menschenrechtskonvention als Grundrechtsverfassung und ihre Bedeutung in Deutschland, Der Staat (2001), 349, 353 et seq.

3 *Christian Walter*, Constitutionalizing (inter)national Governance, German Yearbook of International Law 44 (2001), 170.

4 *Giuseppe Martinico*, National Judges and Supranational Laws: Goals and Structure of the Research, in: Giusepppe Martinico/Oreste Pollicino (eds.), The National Judicial Treatment of the ECHR and EU Laws, 2010, 11 et seq.

the supremacy of the Convention even over the Constitution[5], and Austria regards the Convention explicitly as part of the Austrian Constitution.[6] It is also possible to interpret fundamental rights of the Constitution in light of the Convention, as foreseen explicitly by Article 10 para. 2 of the Spanish Constitution.[7]Article 53 of the Constitution of Kosovo goes even further as it requires consistency with case law, since Article 53 provides that "human rights and fundamental freedoms guaranteed by this Constitution shall be interpreted consistent with the decisions of the European Court of Human Rights."

The present article will first address the questions as to whether the Convention is a directly applicable law in Hungary and what rank it has in the domestic hierarchy of norms (part II). In order to do so, it will refer briefly to the position of international treaties in the Hungarian legal order in general and then focus on the Convention itself. Following that, it will continue by discussing the procedural obstacles in the way of enforcing the guarantees of the Convention in ordinary domestic courts and in the Constitutional Court (part III).

The Article reflects developments in the Hungarian legal order until 2011. From 1 January 2012 a new Basic Law replaces the present Constitution.[8] Since the relevant language of the Basic Law is comparable with that of the prior Constitution,[9] it can be expected that the doctrinal framework of the rules pertaining to the position of the Convention will not change fundamentally after 1 January 2012. Accordingly, the discussion below will outline the situation up until 2011 and then address the possible changes following from the Basic Law at the end of the article.

5 *Peter Van Dijk/Fried van Hoof/Arjen van Rijn/Leo Zwaak* (eds.), Theory and Practice of the European Convention on Human Rights, 4th ed., 2006, 27.

6 Art. II. 7 Bundesverfassungsgesetz vom 4. März 1964 (BGBl. 59/1964).

7 Article 10 para. 2 of the Constitution of Spain: „The norms relative to basic rights and liberties which are recognized by the Constitution shall be interpreted in conformity with the Universal Declaration of Human Rights and the international treaties and agreements on those matters ratified by Spain."

8 On the constitutional reform leading from socialism to democracy and rule of law in 1989, see *Georg Brunner*, Structure and Proceedings of the Hungarian Constitutional Judiciary, in: Laszlo Sólyom/Georg Brunner (eds.), Constitutional Judiciary in a New Democracy. The Hungarian Constitutional Court, 2000, 67 et seq.

9 See below, IV.

II. The status of the European Convention on Human Rights in Hungary

1. International treaties in the domestic legal order

As part of international law, the status of the European Convention on Human Rights was governed until 2011 by Article 7 para. 1 of the Constitution and the rules pertaining to its application. Article 7 para. 1 stipulates that "[t]he legal system of the Republic of Hungary accepts the generally recognized rules of international law, and shall ensure the harmony between domestic law and the obligations assumed under international law." This language – in many respects similar to Article 10 para. 1 of the Italian Constitution – has been consistently interpreted by the Constitutional Court as establishing a clear dualist relationship between international law and domestic law. Customary international law is deemed to be transformed in its entirety into the Hungarian Legal order by Article 7 para. 1 of the Constitution,[10] whereas international treaties only become part of the Hungarian legal order if they are included in a statute of Parliament or other piece of national legislation. Without such transformation, no international treaty can create rights or obligations for individuals.[11] To date, the transformation of international treaties is governed by Act Nr. L of 2005, and this Act envisages a mechanism comparable to Article 59 II of the German *Grundgesetz* (Basic Law):[12] The binding force of international treaties can be accepted either by the President of the Republic or the Foreign Minister. This, however, presupposes an authorisation by Parliament or the Government, respectively. The authorisation is given in an Act of Parliament or a Government decree, which also promulgate the international treaty into the national legal order.

In spite of this strict dualist approach the Hungarian legal order is rather friendly towards international treaties once they are duly promulgated by domestic legislation. Although the Constitution is silent on questions of hierarchy between domestic law and international treaties, this friendly approach follows from the Constitutional Court Act that in effect provides supremacy to interna-

10 53/1993.(X. 13.) AB, ABH 1993, 323, 327.

11 7/2005. (III. 31.) AB, ABH 2005, 83, 88.

12 Article 59 para. 2 of the Basic Law of Germany: „Treaties that regulate the political relations of the Federation or relate to subjects of federal legislation shall require the consent or participation, in the form of a federal law, of the bodies responsible in such a case for the enactment of federal law. In the case of executive agreements the provisions concerning the federal administration shall apply mutatis mutandis." For a commentary see *Martin Nettesheim*, Article 59 GG, in: Maunz/Dürig/Herzog/Scholz/Herdegen/Klein (eds.), Grundgesetz Kommentar, January 2009.

tional treaties promulgated by statute[13] over conflicting national legislation. The Constitutional Court is entitled under Section 1 c) of the Constitutional Court Act to review the conflict of a national piece of legislation with an international treaty promulgated into the Hungarian legal order. Should a treaty promulgated by statute conflict with a domestic statute or a lower ranking norm, the Constitutional Court is obliged by virtue of Section 45 (1) of the Act to declare the domestic law null and void. Even international treaties promulgated by government decree can be granted supremacy over statutes, should the Court so decide under Section 46 (1) of the Act. This generous approach only applies to international treaties in conformity with the Constitution: the constitutionality of treaties can be reviewed before their conclusion by the Court[14], and domestic laws promulgating international treaties can also subject to *ex post facto* norm control.[15] Therefore international treaties must conform to the Constitution, but in most cases take precedence over national legislation.[16]

2. The applicability of the Convention and of the jurisprudence of the European Court of Human Rights in the Hungarian legal order

The Convention was promulgated in the Hungarian legal order by Act Nr. XXXI of 1993, and therefore, in theory, it can be invoked by individuals. This does not apply directly and in general to the judgments of the European Court of Human Rights as such. The above mentioned Act Nr. L of 2005 on the procedure applicable to international treaties foresees in its Section 13 (4) the promulgation of judgments of international courts. The language of Section 13 (4), however, only refers to judgments made in an inter–state procedure, which is a fairly rare case in the practice of the European Court of Human Rights. Further, in view of Section 13 (4) of the Act only such judgments shall be promulgated where Hungary was a party in the case. Consequently, judgments of the European Court of Human Rights in individual complaint procedures where Hungary was not a party can only be referred to as interpreting the provisions of the Convention. It is unclear, however, whether from the perspective of the Hungarian constitutional order this role of the jurisprudence of the Court is merely of non-binding, inspiring

13 Section 7 (3) of Act Nr. L. of 2005 defines international treaties that require promulgation by statute of Parliament, and a closer look reveals that there remains hardly any room for promulgation by Government decree.

14 Section 1 a) of the Constitutional Court Act.

15 4/1997. (I. 22.) AB, ABH 1997, 41.

16 *MolnárTamás*, 7. § [nemzetközi jog és belső jog; jogalkotási törvény], in: András Jakab (ed.), Az Alkotmány kommentárja, 2009, 375 et seq.

character,[17] or whether the case law of the Court should deemed to be defining the scope and content of the respective rights, and as such has a binding force.[18]

The picture is somewhat different with regard to the parties of a case decided by the European Court of Human Rights, at least in criminal cases. The Code of Criminal Procedure[19] makes it possible to reopen a case should a human rights body established by international treaty find that the criminal procedure or the binding judgment in the case violated one of the provisions of said treaty, provided the Republic of Hungary accepted the jurisdiction of the international human rights body in question. Reopening of the case is, however, not possible should the international human rights body have established a violation of the requirement of deciding the case within a reasonable time.[20] These provisions are framed broadly to be able to cover other human rights institutions – like the Human Rights Commission of the UN – but they clearly apply to the European Court of Human Rights. It is rather unfortunate, however, that the Code of Civil Procedure does not provide for a similar opportunity. This is especially problematic since administrative court procedures are also governed by this Code, and so the judgments of European Court of Human Rights cannot ultimately lead to the annulment of unlawful acts of public administration. Because of this, an important area of possible human rights violations by the state enjoys less effective protection.

III. What court can enforce the Convention over conflicting statutes?

As can be seen above, the Hungarian legal order is rather friendly towards international treaties, and this naturally applies to the European Convention on Human Rights as well. Should it come to specific cases, however, individuals may find it difficult to enforce the Convention against conflicting statutes. Equally, the Constitutional Court seems to be unwilling to grant the rights of the Convention a constitutional status.

17 This seems to be the traditional understanding. Cf. *Christoph Grabenwarter*, Europäische Menschenrechtskonvention, 2nd. ed. 2005, 98, with further references.

18 This approach seems to follow from the Commentaries attached to the Charter of Fundamental Rights. Cf. The comments on Article 52. (3) [2007] OJ C 303/33.

19 Section 416 (1) g) and (3).

20 On this aspect see also *Peter Pavlin*, in this volume.

1. Procedural obstacles to enforcing the Convention

As indicated above, the Constitutional Court can review the conformity of Hungarian laws with international treaties, and as such, also with the Convention. This opportunity is, however, of little help for individuals seeking protection on the basis of the Convention. The Constitutional Court Act reserves the right to petition such a review to certain state organs, and amongst these, we do not find the courts or individuals.[21] Even if the President of the Supreme Court is entitled to seek review of laws conflicting with international treaties, this sort of procedure seems to be of an abstract nature: the president of the Supreme Court is not petitioning as a judge in a pending case but as the head of the highest judicial organ of the country. Consequently, a decision of the Constitutional Court upon the petition of the president of the Supreme Court does not necessarily have an impact on the parties in a dispute.

It appears that the only way to enforce the Convention would be if the ordinary courts enjoyed the power to petition the concrete, incidental norm control of a national law that seemingly contradicts the Convention. Such concrete, incidental norm control is open for the review of the constitutionality of laws under Section 38 of the Constitutional Court Act, which authorises the ordinary courts to suspend a pending procedure and ask for the review of a law applicable in the case if they find that law to be unconstitutional. Yet Section 38 is reserved for the review of constitutionality, and conflicts with international obligations cannot become subject of a motion of a court under Section 38. As a result, ordinary courts are bound to apply the applicable Hungarian laws, and interpret them in conformity with the Convention as far as possible. Such a harmonious interpretation is a constitutional mandate repeatedly confirmed by the Constitutional Court.[22] Should, however, a harmonious interpretation not be possible because of the express language of the Hungarian law in question, the Convention cannot have a practical effect in the specific case.

21 According to Section 21 (3) Constitutional Court Act, review on the basis of Section 1 c) of the Act can be petitioned by:
a) the Parliament, its standing committees or any MP,
b) the President of the Republic,
c) the Government or its members,
d) the President of the State Audit Office,
e) the President of the Supreme Court,
f) the Chief Prosecutor.

22 53/1993. (X. 13.) Ab, ABH 1993, 323, 327; 4/1997. (I. 22.) AB, ABH 1997, 41, 51.

2. The Convention as part of constitutional standards?

Hungarian legal literature pays little attention to the possibilities of enforcing the Convention and its jurisprudence in ordinary court procedures.[23] Whenever the effect of the Convention upon the domestic legal system is addressed, the central question is whether or not the Convention shall be considered as a binding standard of interpretation of constitutional rights, whereas in this context no clear distinction is made between the text of the Convention itself and the practice of the European Court of Human Rights. The question so put is answered almost unanimously in the negative. Representative of this is the view of the first President of the Constitutional Court, who argues that reference to the Strasbourg case law is merely of auxiliary nature besides the reasoning of the Constitutional Court, and such reference might also emphasize the importance of a specific rule of the Constitution.[24]

This is relevant, because should the violation of rights of the Convention be regarded as one of the fundamental rights of the Constitution, this would enable the Constitutional Court to provide effective protection either on a motion of an ordinary court, or upon a constitutional complaint.[25] This could be achieved if the fundamental rights of the Constitution had to be interpreted in harmony with the Convention.[26] This is, however, not the case. Although especially the recent decisions of the Constitutional Court thrive to make reference to the case law of the Strasbourg Court, the Hungarian Court never went as far to infer binding constitutional standards from the Convention. Only once has the Constitutional Court found that the understanding of the freedom of expression by the European

23 *Pál Sonnevend,* Offene Staatlichkeit, Ungarn, in: Armin von Bogdandy/Peter Huber, Ius Publicum Europeaum II, 2008, 393, 397 et seq.; *László Blutman,* A nemzetközi jog használata az alkotmányértelmezésnél, Jogtudományi Közlöny (2009/)7–8., 301, 309 et seq.; *Tamas Molnár* (Fn. 16) 379; *Attila Vincze* 32/A. § [Az Alkotmánybíróság], in: András Jakab (ed.), Az Alkotmány kommentárja, 2009, 1134.

24 *Sólyom/Brunner* (note 8), 1317.

25 Constitutional complaints may be submitted under the present Constitution and the Act on the Constitutional Court after the final judgment in the case. The subject matter of such a procedure is solely the constitutionality of the legislative act applied in the case, but not the actual judgment of the ordinary court. In that sense, the constitutional complaint procedure is about norm control. The extra benefit of a constitutional complaint compared to an *ex post facto* norm upon an *actio popularis* is that decisions of the Constitutional Court made upon a constitutional complaint may declare the unconstitutional law in question to be inapplicable in the specific case. As a result, the petitioner may seek reopening his case in the ordinary courts, now without applying the unconstituional law. Such a remedy is not available on the basis of an *actio popularis*. See Brunner (Fn. 8), 84 et seq.

26 This is a solution followed by the German Bundesverfassungsgericht, BVerfGE 111, 307, 315 et seq, although Karlsruhe does not consider itself to be bound to give full effect to the Convention, rather it talks about assistance in interpretation (Auslegungshilfe).

Court of Human Rights is "forming and binding the Hungarian jurisprudence."[27] Yet this statement had no consequences in later decisions and the Court continued to refer to the practice of the Convention without declaring them to be binding in the interpretation of the Constitution.

This picture is not changed by a decision of the Court that actually gave effect to a judgment of the European Court of Human Rights. In *Bukta and others v. Hungary*[28] the European Court of Human Rights ruled that the subjection of public assemblies to a prior–authorisation procedure does not normally encroach upon the essence of Article 11 of the Convention.[29] But when an immediate response, in the form of a demonstration, to a political event might be justified, a decision to disband the ensuing, peaceful assembly solely because of the absence of the requisite prior notice, without any illegal conduct by the participants, amounts to a disproportionate restriction on freedom of peaceful assembly.[30] Shortly after this judgment the Constitutional Court decided on the constitutionality of the Act Nr. III of 1989 on the right of assembly in its Decision Nr. 75/2008.[31] This Decision actually comes to the same conclusion as Strasbourg. Yet the Hungarian Court merely refers to the *Bukta* judgment in a brief paragraph, and the same paragraph also quotes the jurisprudence of the German Bundesverfassungsgericht (Federal Constitutional Court). The substantive argument is solely based on Article 62 para. 1 of the Constitution. It appears that the Court did not want to tie its hands for the future, even if it was ready to follow the path of interpretation drawn by the European Court of Human Rights,[32] and even if the Constitutional Court is deciding about a statute the application of which was reviewed by the European Court of Human Rights.

Recently published analyses attempt to vest the jurisprudence of the European Court of Human Rights with a certain binding force for constitutional interpretation. It is argued that the Constitutional Court actually qualified this jurisprudence in its above cited Decision 18/2004[33] as guidance for the interpretation of the Constitution.[34] It is also noted, however, that such a binding force cannot be attached to singular judgments of the European Court of Human Rights, rather to

27 18/2004. (V. 25.) AB, ABH 2004, 303, 306. The Constitutional Court referred to a series of judgments in this context, Hungary was not party to any of them.

28 ECtHR, *Bukta and others v. Hungary*,Application no. 25691/04, judgment of 17 July 2007.

29 Ibid. para. 35.

30 Ibid. para. 36.

31 75/2008. (V. 29.) AB, ABH 2008, 651.

32 Ibid. 663 et seq.

33 See above note 27.

34 *Vincze* (note 23), 1134

the interpretation of the different rights of the Convention.[35] It appears that these views overestimate the importance of a single sentence of a Decision of the Constitutional Court that never had consequences in jurisprudence.

IV. Conclusion

In sum, the European Convention on Human Rights formally enjoys a high rank in the Hungarian legal order: it can be invoked by individuals in court proceedings and theoretically it takes precedence over conflicting national statutes. Yet such precedence is hard to enforce in the specific case, and the Constitutional Court has been unwilling to regard the rights of the Convention as a binding guidance for the interpretation of the fundamental rights of the Constitution. The heart of the problem is apparently the fact that conflicts with international treaties are not regarded to be a direct constitutional question, since the precedence of treaties is only expressed in the Constitutional Court Act. Naturally, the Constitutional Court Act could not provide for such precedence, should that not follow from Article 7 of the Constitution itself. Yet neither legal scholarship, nor judicial practice has ever created that link. Under these circumstances, ordinary courts could regard Article 7 of the Constitution as irrelevant for their procedure and so not transform the question of conformity with the Convention into a constitutional question.

This situation may change with the entry into force of the new Hungarian Constitution (named Basic Law) on 1 January 2012.[36] The Basic Law seems to be more friendly towards international law than the present Constitution. Whereas the old Article 7 of the Constitution only requires harmony between international obligations and the Hungarian legal order,[37] the new Article Q seems to grant expressly precedence for international law over conflicting Hungarian laws. Article Q para. 2 provides that "Hungary shall ensure harmony between international law and Hungarian law in order to fulfill its obligations under international law." On the face of it, this language does not do more than declare explicitly what has previously followed from Article 7 of the Constitution. Nevertheless, the express language of Article Q para. 2 will now make it clear for both ordinary courts and the Constitutional Court that precedence of international treaties over conflicting national statutes is a constitutional rule. This will enable

35 *Blutman* (note 23), 310.

36 Magyarország Alaptörvénye, Magyar Közlöny 43/2011. 10656 et seq. The Basic Law was adopted by the Hungarian Parliament on 18 April 2011 and was published in the Official Journal on 25 April 2011.

37 For the language of Article 7 of the Constitution see above, II.

ordinary courts to transform conflicts with the Convention into a constitutional question, and so ask for a concrete, incidental norm control of laws that seem to contradict the Convention. This may open the possibility of enforcing the supremacy of the Convention against conflicting national statutes, and the Constitutional Court may be more inclined to consider the Convention and its practice in the interpretation of the Basic Law.

Constitutional Justice between Courts, Citizens and Politics: Lessons Learned from the Transition Experience in Hungary and Beyond

*Péter Paczolay**

Contents

I. Introduction

The institution of judicial review belongs undoubtedly to the heritage of American constitutionalism, and in Europe it has been implemented in a different legal context. Judicial review by an independent judiciary as a mechanism for constitutional enforcement has a different role in the American constitutional system where its idea originated, and where courts since *Marbury v. Madison* have been controlling the acts of legislatures. During the twentieth century, and mainly after World War Two, European democracies have set up constitutional courts to promote emerging constitutionalism, to help frame a new legal system and to replace the former authoritarian ones (e.g. Austria, Germany, Italy, Spain, Portugal, and more recently further east in Europe). These European constitutional courts, unlike the Supreme Court in the United States, represent the centralized type of judicial review, where one single judicial organ has the jurisdiction to adjudicate on the constitutionality of laws.[1] The difference from the American model had already been anticipated by Alexis de Tocqueville in the first part of the 19th century:

> "The Americans have given their courts immense political power; but by obliging them to attack the laws by judicial means, they have greatly lessened the dangers of that power. If the judges had been able to attack laws in a general and theoretical way, […] they would have played a prominent part on the political scene. […] But when a judge attacks a law in the course of an obscure argument in a particular case, he partly hides the importance of his attack from public observation. His decision is just intended to affect some private interest; only by chance does the law find itself harmed."[2]

The European model and context have given constitutional courts a more visible political role in transition processes. The creation of these new institutions of constitutional justice, distinct from and sometimes opposed to the established judicial organs, embodied the democratic transition and was often considered as a way of leaving old structures, and sometimes also old elites, behind. In recent decades, this has been particularly true in the post-communist transition in Central and Eastern Europe, of which Hungary is an often cited example. Other transition states have had their own experiences with constitutional justice; all have acceded to the European Convention on Human Rights (ECHR), and many joined the EU. In states still aspiring to EU membership, such as Albania and

* Professor of Law; President of the Constitutional Court of the Republic of Hungary; former Vice-President of the European Commission for Democracy through Law (Venice Commission).

1 On the difference between the American and European model of constitutional review, see *Mauro Cappelletti*, Judicial review in the contemporary world, 1971.

2 *Alexis de Tocqueville*, Democracy in America. Part I, edited by J. P. Mayer, 1988, 102.

Serbia, constitutional courts play an increasingly important role, as discussed in this book. It is in this context that constitutional justice also emerged in Kosovo, in a special, though not entirely unique, situation. The special context is obvious: after a decade of UN administration over Kosovo, a new independent state was born. While the formation of new states in Central and Eastern Europe is not an unusual development in the last two decades, what is more exceptional in Kosovo is its internationalized governance structure, which is maybe only comparable to Bosnia-Herzegovina. Thus, despite the quite early establishment of Constitutional Courts in the former Yugoslavia, the foundation of the Constitutional Court of Kosovo provides a new challenge, which is discussed in this collection.

The purpose of the present paper is to conclude the book with reflections on the role of constitutional justice between citizens, courts and politics in light of the Hungarian transition experience. This experience has lasted for 20 years, and we may now ask how constitutional justice was initially designed and how it developed over time, how it has related to citizens and other courts, and how it interacts with politics. Hence, the present paper consists of three main parts. Firstly, it provides an overview of the development and normative framework of constitutional justice in Hungary, also with a view to the similarities with and differences from the respective progress in Kosovo. Secondly, the paper focuses on the issue of individual access to constitutional justice, which is a key feature of more recent constitutional developments and a meeting point of different types of courts, domestic as well as European. The third part raises certain issues concerning the relationship between law and politics in judicial review in the light of current reforms in Hungary.

II. Constitutional justice in transition: The Hungarian experience

1. Establishment of the Constitutional Court in Hungary

In the process of political transition in 1989, the institution of the Constitutional Court (hereinafter referred to also as 'the CC') was considered as a rather insignificant item of a comprehensive political deal. The Constitutional Court and the idea of judicial review itself were unknown in the Hungarian constitutional tradition. As Hungary did not have a written (chartal) constitution until 1949 when a Soviet-type constitution was adopted, the thousand-year long tradition of the unwritten constitution excluded the principle of the supremacy of a written constitution. In 1989, neither "Europe" in general nor the Council of Europe, which was monitoring the developments in democracy and rule of law, regarded constitutional jurisprudence as a condition of the democracy in Hungary. Nevertheless, the CC started first among the new institutions of the rule of law. The first five justices of the CC were elected by the Parliament on 23 November 1989 and the constitutional justices held their first session on 2 January 1990. The CC enjoyed great freedom in determining its position in the constitutional structure, including its political weight and role and also its legal competence, since its creators had rather ambiguous ideas about the functions of a constitutional court and the role it should play in the process of political transition. Historical circumstances thus had a strong influence and determined in principle the set-up of the new institution.[3]

After the early Polish experience, Hungary was the second country to reject Communist rule in an unchanged international environment. In this respect, its constitutional reform process differed considerably from the drafting process of the Kosovo constitution, where the main issue was the creation of a new sovereign state, not "only" changing the political regime. Thus external experiences definitely played a more important role in the constitution-making process.[4] In contrast, the negotiations in Hungary starting in summer 1989 involved domestic representatives of the governing party and representatives of the opposition known as the Opposition Roundtable (ORT). The ORT declared at the trilateral political negotiations held on 15 September 1989 a willingness to set up the CC and integrate it in the text of the Constitution if the parties came to an agreement on the Constitution in its entirety.[5] The negotiations regarding the CC focused on three main issues: The circle of petitioners initiating the CC's procedure, its "strong" competencies (including notably the right of annulment of legislation), and the procedural rules on the election of constitutional justices to ensure, *inter alia*, their independence. The first drafts of the Constitutional Court Bill proposed by the Ministry of Justice did not give authorization to citizens to submit petitions on a posterior constitutional review, but limited such petitions to selected organizations or officials. In contrast, one of the main requirements presented by the ORT (declared also as a precondition for the agreement about the text of

3 On the history of the Hungarian Constitutional Court see *Peter Paczolay* (ed.), Twenty years of the Hungarian Constitutional Court, 2009; *Georg Brunner*, Development of a Constitutional Judiciary in Eastern Europe, Review of Central and East European Law 6 (1992), 535 et seq.; *László Sólyom / Georg Brunner*, Constitutional Judiciary in a New Democracy: The Hungarian Constitutional Court. Ann Arbor 2000.

4 See on the Kosovo process eg *John Tunheim*, Rule of Law and the Kosovo Constitution, Minnesota Journal of International Law 18 (2009), 371 et seq.; *Michael Riegner*, The two faces of the internationalized pouvoir constituant: Independence and constitution-making under external influence in Kosovo, Goettingen Journal of International Law 2 (2010), 1035 et seq

5 See *Gábor Halmai*, The Transformation of Hungarian Constitutional Law from 1985 to 2005, 1-18, in: András Jakab/Péter Takács/Allan F. Tatham (eds.), The Transformation of the Hungarian Legal Order 1985-2005, 2007; *Peter Paczolay*, Hungarian constitutional law 1989–2005, in: *ibid.*, 19-25.

the draft) was to entitle any person to submit a petition on posterior abstract constitutional review. This position prevailed and thus gave birth to the *actio popularis* in Hungarian constitutional law.

The other main requirement of the ORT was that constitutional review and the right of annulment should also be extended to parliamentary statutes. The Ministry draft had only foreseen that the CC should refer statutes it deemed unconstitutional to Parliament, but eventually the ORT's condition was met and the CC granted the right to annul all types of legislation. The third requirement of the ORT was the regulation of appointment and election of justices, which was integrated later into the law. These rules foresee that judges are nominated by the legal committee of Parliament and elected by a two-thirds majority of the plenary, but only lawyers of outstanding theoretical knowledge or with professional practice of at least 20 years can be candidates for the election. Additional safeguards for independence included incompatibility rules, immunities, and budgetary autonomy.[6] These three achievements were deemed so significant that they were embodied in the new Constitution on the request of the ORT. Indeed, individual access, annulment powers and appointment procedures aiming at judicial independence proved to be common considerations in subsequent developments in constitutional justice in the region, and the 2008 Constitution of Kosovo also reflects these points in Article 112 et seq. (even though it opts for a constitutional complaint instead of an *actio popularis*).

The Hungarian Constitution was eventually amended on 23 October 1989, and soon after the Parliament adopted the Act on the Constitutional Court (ACC). The Constitutional Court as a completely new institution in the constitutional history of Hungary commenced its function in January 1990. With the new text, practically a new Constitution came into force, which introduced an essentially new legal and political system, different from the earlier quality of the state, with the determination that "the Republic of Hungary is an independent, democratic state under the rule of law."[7] The Constitution set up the CC with the aim to carry out the revision of constitutionality of laws and to annul unconstitutional laws. Some years later this led to the statement that "the Constitutional Court could be the symbol of how paradox was the transformation of the political system, namely a revolution under the control of the Constitutional Court".[8] Certainly the most unexpected new feature of the democratic constitutional system in Hungary was the outstanding importance of the CC, and today, it is considered to have become

6 Act on the Constitutional Court 1989, Articles 10, 12, 13 and 14.
7 Constitution of the Republic of Hungary (in force until 31 December 2011), Article 2.
8 Constitutional Court decision 11/1992, in: László Sólyom/Georg. Brunner (eds.), Constitutional Judiciary in a New Democracy: The Hungarian Constitutional Court, 2000, 221.

a true safeguard of human rights and an institutional guarantee of the separation of powers. Already during the first years of its operation, the Court proved its powerful role in the new political system when it delivered a series of very important decisions pertaining to such significant issues as capital punishment, the interpretation of human dignity, equal protection, tax issues, the compensation acts, presidential powers, abortion, and the lifting of the statute of limitations for political crimes.[9]

In its decisions, the Hungarian CC took a rather active position in both reshaping the legal system and balancing the conflicts of the political powers. This gave the CC a political character, but in turn led to the judicialization of political power, i.e. the development that political conflicts were solved by the judiciary and according to legal rationality. In this context, the cohesive force and the integrity of the constitutional system depended largely on judicial review and its social acceptance. This acceptance hinged also on the perceived role of the CC – whether its primary task is to ensure the abstract constitutional order (and to correct the legal system) or to remedy individual injuries affecting fundamental human rights. The function of adjudicating disputes between political powers, characteristic of the European constitutional courts, is evident in the jurisdiction of deciding conflicts between state organs, the constitutional control of bills before enactment, and the protection of the rights of local self-governments. Other provisions on individual access complement the competencies of the CC, to which we now turn.

2. Competences and types of proceedings

The regulation of judicial review in the 1989 Act on the Constitutional Court followed the European model with a mixture of competences taken from various examples of other constitutional courts. Among the proceedings, the one that became most prominent during the transition period is the posterior constitutional review of legislation initiated by individuals (*actio popularis*). Anyone can submit such requests without need to show personal injury, which has led to a great number of cases. Another specificity of Hungarian constitutional justice is the procedure for legislative omission: the CC may proceed *ex officio* in cases when the legislative organ has created an unconstitutional situation by omitting to carry out its legislative duty. This process, however, may not only be initiated by the CC but also by any person. In the case of declaration of such omission, the

9 See for more *Sólyom/Brunner* (note 8).

legislative body must perform the order of the CC concerning the preparation of the required legislation.

While these two are abstract procedures, concrete cases came to the CC in two ways. Firstly, ordinary judges can suspend the proceedings and initiate the procedure before the CC when they consider a legal norm applicable in the case as unconstitutional. Secondly, anyone may turn to the CC with a constitutional complaint after having unsuccessfully tried all other means to gain legal remedy, when they consider their rights have been violated by the application of an unconstitutional legal provision. Such constitutional complaints also represent posterior norm control, since the CC only reviews the constitutionality of the statutes applied by ordinary courts and not the question of whether the given decision of a court or an administrative authority has violated a constitutional right of the claimant. The CC can provide as the sole remedy to such injuries the prohibition of further application of the statute found to be unconstitutional in the case of the claimant. Owing to these limitations, the claims related to constitutional rights make up only a mere 2% of the total number of claims. As regards claims related to constitutional rights, the power of the CC was not as wide as that of other European constitutional courts that are authorized to review individual decisions of the courts or authorities. This situation as just described changes with the new legal framework for the CC enacted in 2011, which we will address below.

3. The relationship with the ordinary judiciary

The competences and procedures of the CC also define its relationship to the ordinary judiciary, especially to the Supreme Court. This has been a sensitive issue in Hungary as well as other states, so it seems worthwhile to briefly reflect on this issue. There are four main interfaces between the two organs: Firstly, concrete norm control (or otherwise: preliminary ruling procedure) initiated by ordinary judges.[10] Until 2007 the number of these petitions did not exceed 30 initiatives annually, but in the two subsequent years their number rose extensively. The rising number of referrals were related to one specific topic, namely illegal parking. Hundreds of cases were submitted to the Constitutional Court by the ordinary judges related to this topic. The second interface is constitutional review of normative decisions of the Supreme Court, which are issued to secure

10 Art. 38 AC: "Upon noting the unconstitutionality of a law … applicable in the judgement of a case, the judge hearing the case shall suspend the case in the court and submit a petition initiating the proceedings of the Constitutional Court".

the unity of judicial statutory interpretation. The normative decisions of the Supreme Court are aimed at securing the uniformity of interpretation, and are not connected to any specific case. This competence of the Constitutional Court – after years of hesitation – was pronounced by the Court itself in 2005 when the Constitutional Court annulled such a normative decision of the Supreme Court, and this was reaffirmed the next year.[11] The cause of the hesitation was the lack of such an explicit competence, and the debated character of the so-called normative decisions. Under the new Act on the Constitutional Court the question is settled as it enlists as a competence of the Constitutional Court.[12]

The third interface is the constitutional complaint. Here things are somewhat different from other jurisdictions such as Germany or Kosovo, as the Hungarian CC can only exceptionally review judicial decisions, and only when the underlying legal provision is declared unconstitutional. The Court could give remedy against a judicial decision if the underlying statute was unconstitutional. Actually, if ordinary court decisions violated due process but the underlying statute was constitutional, the Constitutional Court could not review the decisions. Cases for the violation of Article 6 ECHR guarantees went directly to Strasbourg. This "limited" constitutional complaint remains valid even in the new constitution but the above-mentioned "real" constitutional complaint will be introduced. Finally, certain competences of the Constitutional Court are essentially that of an administrative court, e.g. the review of local government decrees where the standard of the review is not the constitution but the respective statutes. The local government decrees were challenged by regional administrative agencies and the case was, in first and last instance, decided by the Constitutional Court. This competence was established by the Act on Local Governments.[13] The new constitution transfers this competence to the ordinary courts: under Article 25 ordinary courts shall annul the local government decrees that contradict other laws.

In practice, the relation of the CC to the ordinary courts in general, and to the Supreme Court in particular might easily be loaded with tensions, as has been discussed in the other contributions to this book. In the Hungarian case, there were two main conflicts: the efforts of the CC to avail itself of the competence to review judicial decisions was until lately successfully rejected by the legislature based on the objections of the Supreme Court. On the other hand, the review of the above-mentioned "normative decisions" deeply offended the Supreme Court, which sharply criticized the CC. Yet the tensions between the two courts in

11 Constitutional Court of Hungary, decision 42/2005. (XI.14), and decision 70/2006. (XII.13.) respectively. Available on the homepage of the Constitutional Court: http://www.mkab.hu/index.php?id=decisions.

12 Act No. 151 of 2011 on the Constitutional Court, Art. 37.

13 Act LXV of 1990.

Hungary never led to open conflict; the relation was rather polite.[14] As regards my personal experience, after my election as president of the Constitutional Court, the Supreme Court invited me to its plenary session to deliver a speech. My presentation underlined the necessity of cooperation of the two bodies, not only in the interest of the two institutions, but more importantly in the interest of the ultimate beneficiary of the two courts' activities: the individual citizens.

III. The rise of individual access and the transformation of constitutional justice

The tensions between constitutional courts and ordinary courts occur in the context of a wider trend, affecting most transition states and all countries studied in this book: that is, the tendency to give citizens individual access to constitutional justice. This trend puts citizens in a much more active constitutional role and impacts significantly on the relationship between constitutional courts and ordinary courts, and also more generally on their organization and functioning, as well as their relation to the political branches of government. For example, recent tendencies in constitutional adjudication can rightly be described as the path from the review of constitutionality of laws to the review of the application of laws. This means a shift from the review of the legislator to the review of the judiciary, a basic change in the history of constitutional courts in recent decades. We will discuss the forms and consequences of individual access, notably in light of the recommendations of the European Commission for Democracy through Law (Venice Commission).

1. The history and function of individual access

If we look at the history of the individual access, we see that the past 60 years have brought about a fundamental shift in the importance of constitutional protection of human rights all over Europe and beyond. The respect for human rights is now considered essential in any democratic society. From this basic principle it follows that the mechanisms allowing the individual to directly or

14 See for more on the relationship, *Gábor Halmai*, Who is the Main Protector of Fundamental Rights in Hungary? The Role of the Constitutional Court and the Ordinary Courts, in: Jiri Priban/Pauline Roberts/James Young (eds.), Systems of Justice in Transition, 2003, 50-75.

indirectly invoke these rights become increasingly important. Looking into the European experience, we find that more than 40 countries have introduced direct individual complaints. This includes Hungary, but also all countries discussed in this volume – Albania, Kosovo, Serbia –, and many others.

The trend to individual access, which is also evidenced in this book, indicates a shift from an objective philosophy of constitutional justice to a more subjective one, which is reflected in the competences of the respective constitutional courts. The constitutional court may be designed so as to only protect the objective constitutional order, which emphasizes the protection of the institutional system of the country but may also include the protection of fundamental rights in the sense that these are a part of the objective institutional constitutional order. The other philosophy is at work when constitution-makers draft a specific guarantee of subjective fundamental rights conferred to the individual by the constitution, which can be enforced in the respective constitutional court. The primary function of such an individual constitutional complaint is to protect the individual's subjective rights guaranteed by the constitution, but at the same time such a legal remedy operates to safeguard the constitution as a part of the objective legal order. In this way the two diverging philosophies are in fact interlinked. Still, individual access to constitutional review can take different forms, namely in an indirect way or in a direct way, or through a constitutional complaint.

2. Indirect access

Indirect access means that the individual question reaches the constitutional court for adjudication through a referral by an intermediary body. This intermediary can be an ordinary court or, notably, an ombudsperson institution. Indirect access to constitutional courts through the ordinary courts can be termed preliminary ruling procedure, to use the language regarding the European Court of Justice of the European Union. More than two-thirds of the Venice Commission member states dispose of this preliminary ruling procedure, or in other words, concrete norm control.[15] When an ordinary court has doubts whether a normative act applicable in the concrete case violates the constitution, it formulates a preliminary question to the constitutional court. The strength of this procedure is that ordinary courts are capable of formulating a valid request. Ordinary courts serve as the first filter in this sense and can contribute to reducing the number of abusive or repetitive requests. At least this is what we expect from the ordinary

15 Venice Commission, Study on Individual Access to Constitutional Justice, CDL-AD(2010)039rev, para. 56; see also table 1.1.20.

courts. From my personal practice I have learned that these expectations are not always fulfilled. Another advantage is that preliminary ruling procedures are complementary to the abstract consideration of the legislative provision, as they allow for review related to concrete situations in which a provision is applied or should be applied.The shortcoming of this procedure is that its effectiveness depends heavily on the capacity and willingness of ordinary judges to identify potentially unconstitutional normative acts and to submit preliminary questions to the constitutional court. This depends on the legal culture of the given country, the opinion of the ordinary judiciary on the constitutional court and on constitutional court procedures. It is well-known that the relations of the constitutional court with ordinary courts are not always the best, and the contributions to this volume evidence different degrees of cooperation and conflict between the different courts in the respective countries. The tensions between the two bodies might be among the reasons why ordinary judges do not use the referral tool frequently even if it is available by constitutional regulation. For example, in its first 15 years the Hungarian CC did not receive more than 20 preliminary questions of ordinary courts per year. In the last years, this has changed and the court received hundreds of preliminary petitions coming from ordinary judges.

One way of addressing the remaining shortcomings is that in many states the parties in the trial before the ordinary court may at least suggest that a preliminary question should be submitted to the constitutional court, without precluding the judge's discretion to accept or reject such a suggestion. Albania, Belgium, Bulgaria, Germany, Hungary, Spain, Lithuania might be mentioned in this respect.[16] A reform proposal here would be to strengthen the role of the parties in the ordinary proceedings and give them a procedural remedy, a sort of "exception of unconstitutionality". This remedy may be lodged with an ordinary judge who is then obliged to re-consider whether he wants to submit a referral to the constitutional court, and to motivate an eventual denial or referral on the basis only of a certain number of reasons.

Given the weaknesses of the court referral procedure, many states have opted for an additional way of indirect access to the constitutional court, represented by an ombudsperson empowered to submit cases to the constitutional justices. This institution is welcomed by the Venice Commission, and 48% – basically half of the Venice Commission's member states – dispose of an ombudsman institution, appointed either by national parliaments or by the executive. These ombudspersons are independent and impartial. In many states they are conceived as human rights protectors trying to find viable solutions when human rights are violated. The capacity of an ombudsman to initiate review proceedings gives the individu-

16 *Ibid.*, para. 57.

als the possibility to accede to the constitutional court, if only in an indirect way, in a situation where the individuals sometimes otherwise would not have any access to the constitutional court. In this sense the ombudsperson opens a new way of access for the citizens to the constitutional court. The Venice Commission states that the mandate of an ombudsperson, or in other countries of the so-called human rights defender, should include the possibility of applying to the constitutional court of the country for an abstract judgment on questions concerning the constitutionality of laws and regulations or general administrative acts which raise issues affecting human rights and freedoms.[17] The ombudsperson should be able to do this of his/her own volition or be motivated by a particular complaint made to the institution by the citizens.

3. Direct access for abstract review of legislation

Direct access means that individuals can petition the constitutional court without the intervention of a third party and initiate constitutional review of legislation. 55% of the Venice Commission's member states dispose some forms of direct access.[18] They diverge in their substance and their procedure, but can be classified in three groups. The first main group is when direct access concerns the abstract review of constitutionality, i.e. review not related to a specific case or a specific individual violation of someone's rights. The most obvious way of allowing citizens to access the constitutional court directly is the so-called *actio popularis*. *Actio popularis* means that citizens may challenge the constitutionality of statutes and other legal provisions before the constitutional court without having to show an injury to their own rights. This is a very widespread way of approaching the court, namely in Hungary but also in Macedonia and in Georgia. This access might lead to very far-reaching effects. For example, in Hungary capital punishment was abolished by the Constitutional Court on such an abstract petition for review of the death penalty provisions of the criminal court.[19] To limit such direct access, some countries thus link abstract review to legal interest of the individual complainant, who must show him/herself to somehow be personally affected by the legislation. The second way to directly approach the court in an abstract way is what we call an individual "suggestion". An individual suggestion is a variant of abstract review initiated by the individual that leaves more

17 *Ibid.*, para. 64.
18 *Ibid.*, Table 1.1.21.
19 Capital punishment case: decision No. 23/1990. (X.31.) Constitutional Court decision 11/1992, in: László Sólyom/Georg Brunner (eds), Constitutional Judiciary in a New Democracy: The Hungarian Constitutional Court, Ann Arbor, 2000, 118.

discretion to the constitutional court because the individual cannot insist on the opening of the procedure but leaves it to the discretion of the constitutional court. A third type of access exists in Greece, which is in a middle position between the merely abstract *actio popularis* and a normative constitutional complaint, because the individual petitioner does not need to show a violation of his own individual rights.[20]

4. Direct access related to a concrete case: individual constitutional complaint

The individual constitutional complaint might be raised either as a normative constitutional complaint (in this case the violation of fundamental rights is due to an individual – judicial or administrative – act based on a normative act) or as a complaint against any individual act by the public authority. In the case of the so-called normative constitutional complaint the individual is given the right to complain against the violation of his subjective fundamental rights by an individual act on the grounds that this individual act is based on an unconstitutional normative act. The initiative for review is related to a concrete case, but it is different from the first type in that here the petitioner has to prove that there is a certain likelihood that the statute will be applied in his case and this statute is unconstitutional. That is what he suggests to the constitutional court. This type of normative constitutional complaint, in my own view, is the limited form of constitutional complaint, compared to the German or Spanish type, where the full constitutional complaint is linked to the abstract review of a statute and it is necessary that an unconstitutional statute should underlie the case and not a procedural or other violation of fundamental rights.[21]

The second case is the full constitutional complaint, and the Venice Commission is in favour of it not only because it provides for comprehensive protection of constitutional rights, but also because of the subsidiary nature of the relief provided by the European Court of Human Rights (ECtHR) and the desirability to settle human rights issues on the national level.[22] According to the opinions of the Venice Commission[23], the constitutional complaint has the following characteristics: First, it is a legal remedy of subsidiary character after the exhaustion of

20 See in more detail on the differences Venice Commission, Study on Individual Access to Constitutional Justice (note 15), paras. 74-76.

21 *Ibid.*, para. 77.

22 *Ibid.*, para. 79.

23 See also Venice Commission, Opinion on the draft constitutional amendments with regard to the constitutional court of Turkey, CDL-AD(2004)024.

other legal remedies; secondly, it can be invoked on account of violation of basic rights and liberties; third, it can be invoked against violation either from a law or a statute or an administrative act or a judicial decision or even in the case of an omission of public authorities; the fourth element is that it can be invoked by any person who pretends to be the victim of the violation of basic rights and liberties. The constitutional complaint exists in different variants.

The first is the full constitutional complaint, the constitutional complaint in its genuine sense which now exists in 14 countries. Here an individual may complain against any act by the public authorities which directly and currently violates his fundamental rights. This may include the possibility for individuals to also challenge a general act if it is directly applied in his or her individual case by the judiciary or by administrative agencies. This possibility exists for example in Germany, Spain, Czech Republic, Slovenia, Serbia, and to a certain extent in Slovakia and other countries[24]. In the full constitutional complaint the constitutional court will usually not decide on the merits of the case, but only on the constitutionality problem.

There are other solutions which are not so widespread, for instance the special constitutional petition in Ukraine or other solutions elsewhere in Europe. In any event, with the growing valuation of human rights protection we can observe a clear tendency to a constitutional review of individual or administrative acts and decisions of the judiciary upon application by the individual. This has increased the caseload of the constitutional court, a development that has been exacerbated by another trend in judicial review identified by the Venice Commission, namely, that constitutions increasingly provide for the protection not only of fundamental rights enlisted in the constitution, but also those in international treaties such as the ECHR, with Kosovo being a case in point. More and more countries now allow for a constitutional complaint procedure even in cases where rights enlisted in international treaties are violated, which increases the norms that may justify a complaint and also gives access to more case law, namely that of the ECtHR.

5. The practical consequences of direct access

This growing importance of individual access raises the question of how constitutional courts experience their increasing competence in practice. Elsewhere I called the constitutional complaint a mixed blessing because on the one hand, it

24 Venice Commission, Study on Individual Access to Constitutional Justice (note 15), para. 80.

has a very important role in the protection of individual rights, but on the other hand it causes practical problems for constitutional courts. One major downside in practice is certainly the overburdening, in particular, of those courts which apply the full constitutional complaint. As we know, about 97% of the cases before the German Constitutional Court are constitutional complaints.[25] Another example is the Constitutional Court of Slovenia, which has 4000 constitutional complaints a year and has asked the legislature to limit the possibility to file constitutional complaints.[26] This flood of constitutional complaints in individual cases does give constitutional courts the possibility to remedy more violations of human rights, but it might also hamper the effective functioning of the court, which may not be able to fulfill its function at all.

These pros and cons seem to lead to a paradoxical double tendency in the world. On the one hand countries and constitutional courts that do not have the right to adjudicate individual constitutional complaints seriously consider introducing this method of individual access. On the other hand, countries and constitutional courts which do have that competence seriously consider limiting this possibility. The Venice Commission addressed the importance of individual constitutional complaints in its opinions and in principle welcomed initiatives to introduce the constitutional complaint procedure. For example, in the case of Moldova and Turkey it declared that "the possibility of individual complaint would definitely serve better and more effective protection of fundamental rights".[27] In sum, the rise of direct access accounts for much of the aforementioned shift from constitutional review of legislation to the review of the application of the law.

25 See the statistics on the homepage of the Bundesverfassungsgericht, http://www.bverfg.de/ en/organization.html.

26 *Ciril Ribičič*, Strengthening Constitutional Democracy, http://www.venice.coe.int/WCCJ/Papers/SLO_Ribicic_E.pdf.

27 Venice Commission, Opinion on the draft constitutional amendments with regard to the constitutional court of Turkey (note 23).

IV. Conclusion: Law and politics in constitutional justice

Increased direct access of citizens to constitutional justice has certainly increased the importance, and probably also the power, of constitutional courts. This increase in relevance, and often power, has not only affected the relationship to other courts, but has also impacted upon the position of constitutional justice vis-à-vis the political branches of government. So far, this book has refrained from focussing too intensely on the much discussed question of the relationship between law and politics. However, if this was necessary to state at all, recent developments in Hungary have illustrated the truism that constitutional justice does not operate in a political vacuum, but has a multifaceted, and sometimes precarious, relationship with politics – in particular if it plays such a prominent role as was the case in Hungary. After 20 years, the transition process and constitutionalism in Hungary have reached an important point of change, embodied in the new Constitution enacted in 2011 and entered into force on 1 January 2012. The reforms have been controversial, and much of this has concerned the changes to constitutional justice. It may thus be apt to conclude this book with a few remarks on these reforms and on the political implications of and reactions to constitutional justice in transition, thus situating the events in the age-old debate on the relationship between law and politics.

1. The 2011 constitutional reform in Hungary

After 20 years of experience, dramatic and radical changes in the competences of the CC were made in 2010 and during the drafting of the new constitution in 2011. After the 2010 elections, the new two-thirds parliamentary majority, which is large enough to amend the constitution, announced a proposal to limit the subject matter jurisdiction of the CC. The original plan was to exclude some laws from the constitutional supervision of the CC, such as budgetary, pension and tax laws in general. One month later, the Parliament adopted the constitutional amendment on the limitation of the competences of the CC. According to the new wording, budgetary and tax laws are only subject to constitutional review if the petition refers exclusively to the violation of the right to life and human dignity, the right to the protection of personal data, the right to freedom of thought, conscience and religion or the right connected to Hungarian citizenship. Hence, the Hungarian CC had to suffer limitations of its powers for the first time during its 20-year existence. The new constitution – called Fundamental Law – adopted in April 2011 upheld this limitation and otherwise radically changed the organization and the competences of the Constitutional Court. Furthermore, the new system brought important changes regarding the types of procedures before the

CC. On the one hand, the old *actio popularis* was abolished. On the other hand, the reform introduced a procedure for an individual constitutional complaint against individual acts of public authority.

The changes also concerned the composition of the Court and the nomination of judges. The new Article 24 does not regulate the mandate, organisation and functioning of the Constitutional Court in detail, leaving it to a cardinal law to define more precisely the scope of its competences and related rules and procedures. As far as the composition of the Court is concerned, the new Constitution increases the number of its members from 11 to 15 and prolongs their term of office from 9 to 12 years. In addition, it transfers the election of its president from the Court to Parliament (by two-thirds majority) and prolongs his/her mandate to the entire duration of the mandate. Changes also concern the nomination of judges, which are elected by the Parliament. One of the first amendments to the constitution changed this nomination process. Previously, the parliamentary Nomination Committee comprised one representative of each parliamentary party who all had the same vote. In contrast, under the new constitutional text the number of representatives is proportionate to the number of seats held by each political party in the Parliament.

The motivation behind this constitutional amendment was the long-lasting vacancy of seats due to disagreements on the nomination, which were quickly filled by two new judges after the amendment passed. Many were concerned that the judges would be biased in favour of the ruling party, but shortly after their nomination the two newly elected judges expressed the strongest opinion in favour of the annulment of a symbolic law adopted by the new government, thus giving an example of the "duty of ingratitude". A new conflict developed when the Parliament established a 98 % punitive tax on "unashamedly high" severance payments paid out of the state budget. The Parliament openly declared its intention to depart from the practice of the CC (which was set forth in 1990 in Decision 903/B/1990) and together with an act adopted a constitutional amendment to make it possible to impose the tax with retroactive effect starting from 1 January 2010. Regardless of the passing of the constitutional amendment, the CC held that the act on retroactive tax was unconstitutional, violated even the new constitutional provision, and therefore annulled it.[28]

The reactions to the reforms were mixed. In its opinion on the new Hungarian Constitution, the Venice Commission of the Council of Europe acknowledged

28 On the newly adopted constitution of Hungary see *Kriszta Kovács/Gábor Attila Tóth*, Hungary's Constitutional Transformation, European Constitutional Law Review 7(2) (2011), 183-203; *Lóránt Csink/Balázs Schanda/ András Varga* (eds.), The Basic Law of Hungary - A First Commentary, 2012.

that "since 1990, the Constitutional Court has played a vital role in the Hungarian system of checks and balances. Moreover, the Venice Commission is pleased to note that the Court has gained international recognition through its case law."[29] In the Venice Commission's view, the above-mentioned changes in the composition and mode of election of the CC must also be assessed in conjunction with the competences of the Court. On the one hand, the Venice Commission noted with satisfaction that the individual constitutional complaint has been introduced into the constitutional review system. It welcomed the introduction of the "real" constitutional complaint that makes possible the review of the decisions of the ordinary judiciary. On the other hand, in the light of the 2010 curtailment of the Court's powers which were confirmed by the new Constitution, the Commission is concerned that a number of provisions of the new Constitution may undermine further the authority of the CC as a guarantor of constitutionality of the Hungarian legal order.[30]

2. Law and politics – conventional views and new developments

The debate on the virtues and vices of the reforms touches upon the age-old debate on the relationship between law and politics. Of course, the interaction between constitutional courts and politics manifests itself in multiple ways. The political majority may respond to a court decision by accepting it and implementing it in future legislative acts. But the reaction may also be the evasion of the decision, explicitly or implicitly rejecting it. Politicians may respond even more harshly by politically intervening into the composition or competence of the court. Finally, they may also amend the constitution.

Orthodox legal doctrine looked at the relation of politics and law as a strict dichotomy, separating the two realms by a "Chinese wall". Politics is understood as decision-making by choosing among uncertain alternatives. Law in this view is reduced to a coherent system of rules. The best example of this approach, Kelsen's pure theory of law[31], comprehends law as a relatively self-contained system of norms and rules. The commitment to an idea of law as unity, integrity, and system excludes political considerations from law, and especially denies the view that law is an expression of political power. The rise of judicial review, the supervision of laws by the judiciary, essentially challenged this view. Carl

29 Venice Commission, Opinion on the new Constitution of Hungary, CDL-AD(2011)016, para. 91.
30 *Ibid.*, paras. 93, 97.
31 *Hans Kelsen*, Pure Theory of Law, 1963.

Schmitt[32] pointed out during his debate with Kelsen that the defence of the constitution by a constitutional court would mix politics and law; and by the interpretation of vague constitutional notions the judges would act as law-makers.

These doctrinal arguments have been, over time, reflected in judicial practice, where courts developed different approaches to cope with the relation of politics and law, be it to justify restraint or a more "activist" practice. In the traditional view, this relationship is decidedly dependent on the model of constitutional review. The political question doctrine developed in American jurisprudence excludes questions from judicial review which belong to the competence of other branches of power (legislation or executive), or questions lacking a judicially cognizable standard for decision. Thus controversies which revolve around policy and value choices are excluded from judicial review. In contrast, in the European model constitutional courts exercise political competences as they often act on the initiative of political factions and are obliged to proceed in all cases. For instance, the original French approach was considered as a clearly political review, and the *Conseil Constitutionnel* exercised judicial review as part of the legislative process. Yet, independently of which tradition they emanate from, constitutional courts will always have to act prudently, and will have to find reasonable doctrinal arguments for their decisions which do not compromise their neutrality and legitimacy.

The situation in practice has become even more complex with the emergence of the international and supranational courts, such as the ECtHR and the European Court of Justice. These courts themselves arguably operate as constitutional courts in three ways: Namely, towards the lawmakers of their level, by reviewing member state legislation, and, in a sense, also in relation to the national constitutional courts. Most transition countries have experienced the influence of the ECtHR, including Hungary and the other states discussed in this volume. Hungary is, in addition, subject to the jurisdiction of the ECJ in many fields, thus its constitutional court and constitutional politics are involved in a constant dialogue with the ECJ concerning such important issues as the supremacy of community law over national constitutions, or the supremacy and the national protection of fundamental rights. These conflicts led to successful outcomes, especially if we think of the introduction of a charter of fundamental rights into the Treaty of Lisbon, which now also restrains domestic politics, and thus impacts on the old relationship between law and politics anew.

All these developments decry the classic belief and dogma that judges obey only the law. The reality is much more complex. Courts are constrained to take into consideration and pay attention to a much broader context. They cannot dis-

32 *Carl Schmitt*, Der Hüter der Verfassung, 1931, 88.

tract themselves from the processes of the larger political environment in which they have to act, survive, and fulfil their proper task. Public reaction to the court decision must not be a decisive factor; nevertheless it is difficult to completely ignore it. An honest discourse on this topic might lead to a more realistic evaluation of the proper role of constitutional justice and of law and politics in the transition processes of the countries studied in this book, and beyond.

Kolibri 360 GmbH
Ferdinand-Jühlke-Straße 7
99095 Erfurt, Deutschland
produktsicherheit@kolibri360.de